AUSTRIA 1918–1972

By the same author

Truce in the Balkans
Macedonia: Its Place in Balkan Power Politics
Britain in a Divided Europe, 1945–1970
The Cold War

AUSTRIA
1918–1972

Elisabeth Barker

University of Miami Press

Coral Gables, Florida

Published in Great Britain by
The Macmillan Press Ltd, 1973
Published in the United States by
the University of Miami Press, 1973
Library of Congress Catalog Card No.: 73–80034

ISBN 0–87024–262–8

Manufactured in Great Britain

Contents

PART III

Austria Under Occupation, 1945–1955

PART IV

Independent Austria, 1955–1972

List of Plates

The plates are reproduced by permission of the following: Associated Press (7, 8, 10, 11, 13, 14);

Eduard Beranek, Vienna (1, 3); Camera Press (9, 15, 16); Österreichische Nationalbibliothek, Vienna (2, 4, 5, 6); Votava, Vienna (12).

List of Maps

Preface

The theme of this book is the interplay of the internal and external forces determining the course of Austria's history since the break-up of the Habsburg Empire. Its argument is that although the external forces have appeared far more powerful, the Austrians have nevertheless striven stubbornly and ingeniously to manipulate them to their own advantage. Admittedly in the 1930s they seemed hypnotised by Hitler; but so also were almost all Europeans. Internally they have insisted on evolving their own political, economic and social forms. Austro-Marxists were certainly Marxists, but of a particularly Austrian kind; Austro-Fascists were also peculiarly Austrian; the type of democracy which Austria has created since 1945 is far removed from any East European People's Democracy, yet has characteristics which distinguish it from typical West European democracy and which have their roots in past history.

In illustrating the play of external forces on Austria, I have drawn freely on British Foreign Office documents, now available up to 1945 (the period 1939–45 in the Public Record Office only). This seemed illuminating since Britain, even when aloof from the Continent, always wanted to have a finger in every European diplomatic pie. For the period 1945–55, I have been able to draw on the records of the Allied Commission in Vienna; for this I am grateful to the Foreign Office Library and to Mr R. R. Mellor in particular.

Among others whom I should like to thank for valuable help and guidance are Miss I. L. Giachardi, formerly of the

Foreign Office Research Department (for the period 1945–1955); Mr Paul Lendvai, *Financial Times* correspondent in Vienna (for recent developments); and Mr Erich Strauss (for first-hand knowledge of the Austrian Socialists in the 1930s). My thanks also go to the staff of the Library and Press Library of the Royal Institute of International Affairs; to the Bundespressedienst, Vienna (especially Dr Mecznik); to the Österreichische Gesellschaft für Aussenpolitik und Internationale Beziehungen, Vienna; to the Austrian Institute, London. There are others too whom I should like to thank but who would prefer not to be named. None of the above are in any way responsible for any errors or omissions there may be in the book.

I am grateful to Penelope Brown for the interest and persistence with which she pursued the pictures which illustrate the book.

October 1972   E.B.

PART I

The First Austrian Republic and its Fall, 1918–1938

1 Austria's Point of Departure

From the very beginnings of their life as a small central European republic, Austrians have had to practise the arts of rapid adaptation to unforeseen and unfavourable circumstance, ingenious improvisation, precarious balance between conflicting forces, and the extraction of strength from weakness. One of their weaknesses was of a special kind: their own uncertainty whether or not Austrians were Germans, and if they were, what being German meant. Hitler tried to answer this question for them, first by a five-year campaign of political, economic, physical and psychological intimidation, and finally by force. In this crisis the Austrians were betrayed less by their own uncertainty than by the weakness and passivity of the West European Powers. In any case, Hitler's answer was not final and was reversed with his downfall. At this point the Austrians had again to exercise the arts of adaptation, improvisation, balance and exploitation of weakness, in a totally new but equally unfavourable set of circumstances – this time, it seemed, with solid and lasting success.

In a wider context, Austria's problems can be seen as common European problems of the twentieth century: the loss of an 'imperial' or great power role, and the search for a far more modest but still worthwhile role; the loss of one identity and the search for a new identity; the transformation of a predominantly rural society into a modern industrial – or 'post-industrial' – society. In Austria, however, these problems were sometimes presented in a peculiarly sharp and painful form.

*

The Austria which was left over after the wreck of the
Austro-Hungarian Empire of the Habsburgs in 1918 was
like a piece of driftwood cast up on the shore after a great
storm.[1] The Austrian Socialist, Otto Bauer, wrote soon
after: 'German-Austria is not an organism which has followed the laws of historical growth. It is nothing but the
remnant of what remained of the old Empire after the
other nations had broken away from it. It remained as a
loose bundle of divergent Lands . . .'[2] The British diplomat
and historian, Harold Nicolson, wrote of his own feelings
towards Austria at the start of the 1919 peace conference:
'In regard to Austria I had a *"de mortuis"* feeling . . . I did
not regard her as a living entity: I thought of her only as a
pathetic relic.'

This seemed a fair judgement, in terms of Austria's population and economic viability. The Empire had had a
population of over 50 million, and had been formed by ten
nations or 'nationalities': Hungarian, Czech, Slovak,
Ruthene (or Ukrainian), Polish, Rumanian, Croat, Slovene,
Serbian and 'German-Austrian'. It had formed a fairly self-
sufficient economic area centred on the Danube. After the
other nations or 'nationalities' had broken away to form or
join separate states, the remnant, 'German-Austria', had
a population of about 6½ million. It had a concentration of
industry in Vienna and the towns of neighbouring Lower
Austria, but was cut off from its natural source of food in
Hungary and from the coal of the Czech lands and Silesia
and other raw materials. Psychologically, the 'German-
Austrians' had lost their role as a governing elite in a
multinational Empire which, even in decline, had been
one of the historic great powers of Europe.

In itself, Austria was a 'bundle' of hereditary 'Lands',
each with sharply distinct history, traditions and way of
life, which had been acquired in various ways by the
Habsburgs from the Middle Ages onwards. Even if they
were all German-speaking this did not mean that they
loved one another; fierce local loyalties were often stronger

than the bond of a common language. The main link between them had been their varying loyalties to the Habsburg dynasty; and the dynasty had fallen.

To the 'German-Austrians' therefore the collapse of the Empire was a great psychological blow. Few of them, apart from Left-wing Socialists, had seriously expected it, even if they had often talked gloomily about the Empire's impending doom. The last Habsburg, the Emperor Karl, believed up till the last moment that the Empire could be saved by emergency reforms.

Even to the non-Germans of the Empire, the final collapse was a shock, whether pleasurable or painful. Many of them, including the Slavs, fought loyally against Tsarist Russia in the early war years. Otto Bauer wrote later: 'So long as Russian Tsardom remained intact, the existence of the Austro-Hungarian Empire was a historical necessity. Had it been overthrown, the Slav states which would have emerged from it would inevitably have become vassal states of Russia. Its downfall would therefore have established the domination of Tsardom over Europe.'³ Bauer did not foresee that his judgement might eventually prove applicable to post-Tsarist Russia.

The Russian revolutions of 1917, combined with the political action abroad of exiled leaders such as the Czech, Thomas Masaryk, and the South Slavs, Anton Trumbić and František Supilo, changed the mood of the Slavs, turning them against the Empire and towards hopes of full independence. As the Empire's military defeat became more and more certain, those Slav politicians who had believed in the need to preserve the Empire in a new form steadily lost ground.

As for the Western Allies, they did not go to war to break up the Habsburg Empire, even though it was Austro-Hungarian aggression against the small neighbouring state of Serbia which had been the immediate cause of the war. And until the last months of the war, they had still not finally made up their minds whether they wanted to see it destroyed. Some Western politicians believed strongly that it should be preserved, in a new form, as a bulwark against Germany's expansion into south-east Europe. This belief was badly shaken but not finally destroyed when in May 1918 the Austrian Emperor Karl was forced to atone for a clumsy private effort at peace negotiation by concluding an agreement with Germany – the Spa Agreement – apparently establishing permanent German economic domination over Austria-Hungary.

Apart from questions of long-term European policy, the Western Allies had an urgent short-term interest in weakening the enemy by splitting tactics. They could either try to make a separate peace with the lesser enemy power, Austria-Hungary, behind Germany's back, or else split up the Habsburg Empire from within. In effect, they followed both courses as opportunity offered. In the last year of the war they encouraged the anti-Habsburg activities of Masaryk, Trumbić and Supilo, and conducted propaganda aimed at disrupting the Empire. In particular, they paid more and more heed to Masaryk, who perhaps did more than any single individual to ensure the Empire's downfall. A Czech National Council was set up in France with a branch in Russia; a Czechoslovak Legion was formed in Russia from (Austro-Hungarian) prisoners of war, which eventually numbered around 50,000 men.

This Legion turned out to be an important factor in the Empire's destruction. The Bolshevik revolution in the autumn of 1917 allowed the Germans to switch a million men to the West to launch a new powerful offensive. The Western Allies desperately wanted to form a new front in the East. A possible nucleus seemed to be the Czechoslovak Legion, which found itself for some months the only efficient military force in Russia, holding a large and strategically important area astride the Trans-Siberian Railway. The Legion therefore gave much greater political leverage to Masaryk.

Nevertheless, the Western Allies still wanted to keep all

options open. At the beginning of 1918 the British Prime Minister, Lloyd George, was still publicly calling for autonomy, not independence, for the nations of the Habsburg Empire. And when President Wilson defined United States war aims in his Fourteen Points on 8 January, Point Ten read: 'The peoples of Austria-Hungary, whose place among the nations we wish to see safeguarded and assured, should be accorded the freest opportunity of autonomous development.' Desultory contacts between the President and the Emperor Karl followed.

However, the turning of the tide of war, the Spa Agreement, and Masaryk's patient pressure on President Wilson in Washington, all pushed the Western Allies into giving formal recognition to the Czech-Slovak and South Slav claims for full independence. The decisive moves were made first by France, then by Britain, then by the United States, between June and early September 1918.

Yet even then the decision of the Western Allies did not seem to be final. Masaryk was still afraid that the Empire might somehow survive military defeat. Emperor Karl still hoped it could be saved by last-minute reforms. Masaryk later recorded how he heard, in Washington, early in October 1918 that the Emperor was planning a manifesto promising to transform Austria into a federal state. 'He was a drowning man clutching at a straw,' Masaryk commented. 'Nevertheless his idea was dangerous, and it was necessary to forestall the effect which the manifesto might have in quarters that still retained considerable sympathy with Austria.'[4]

So Masaryk set out to forestall and outbid the Emperor. On 14 October the establishment of a Provisional Czechoslovak Government was formally notified to the Allies, who duly accorded it recognition. On 17 October there was published in Vienna Emperor Karl's manifesto to 'my loyal Austrian peoples', declaring that 'in accordance with the will of her peoples, Austria will become a Federal State in which each race within its natural domain shall form its

own national state'. In Washington, Masaryk immediately
countered the manifesto by issuing a Declaration of Independence. And President Wilson sent a letter to the
Emperor on 19 October, saying that he no longer stood by
Point Ten. This was the final death-blow to the Empire,
even if the Emperor still did not recognise it as such. The
Austro-Hungarian army continued to fight on the Italian
front. The armistice between Austria-Hungary and the
Allies was not signed until 2 November.

While in retrospect the break-up of the Empire seemed
inevitable, and to many desirable, there was in fact great
uncertainty and confusion about its fate up till the last
weeks of the war, not only in Vienna and elsewhere in the
Empire, but also in Western capitals.

In October 1918, therefore, the vast majority of 'German-
Austrians' entered their new life in a rump Austria in a
state of shock and bewilderment, unprepared either
psychologically or politically. The victorious Allies, for
their part, seemed to have little idea of what they wanted
to do with the 'remnant' Austria.

One of the problems facing the 'German-Austrians' at the
very start was what to call their country and themselves.
For centuries past, 'Austria' had meant the realm ruled by
the Habsburgs at any one time. So the Netherlands, Spain
and northern Italy had all at times been part of 'Austria',
or at least 'Austrian' possessions. 'Austria' was in fact a
loose, ramshackle empire of formerly independent kingdoms and other historic lands, acquired mostly by
marriage or inheritance. In the early nineteenth century,
the Napoleonic wars and the following period of repres-
sion led to the awakening of national feelings, based on
language, culture and past history, inside 'Austria' as also
in Germany and elsewhere. This was the beginning of
what Austrian Marxists later called the bourgeois national
revolution in Europe – a revolution which depended for

its success on the growth of a strong, nationally conscious middle class, and which finally triumphed in 1918.

For the 'German-Austrians', national awakening brought them up against the fact that many more Germans lived outside the Habsburg Empire than inside it. In earlier centuries, this had been blurred: for nearly 400 years the ruling Habsburg had also been the Holy Roman Emperor, or titular head of the loose cluster of German states which was later to become Germany. In 1806 this arrangement was destroyed by Napoleon; the ruling Habsburg renounced the Crown of the Holy Roman Empire, which vanished. When therefore the 'German-Austrians' were caught up in the general upsurge of national feeling, they awoke, not to a sense of an 'Austrian' identity, but to a feeling of unity with the Germans outside the Habsburg Empire.

Although after the revolutionary year, 1848, Emperor Francis Joseph succeeded in suppressing the newly-aroused national feelings, he could not destroy them. Nor could he prevent the unification of Germany, which was completed by 1871, when Bismarck cut the last remaining links between the Habsburg Empire and the new and powerful German Empire, which thereafter overshadowed 'Austria' and exercised a magnetic attraction on a considerable section of 'German-Austrians'.

The Emperor Francis Joseph, for his part, pursued the simple aim of preserving the dynasty and the Empire, making as many concessions and compromises – and no more – as were necessary to keep his subjects reasonably docile, while playing off the various nations one against another. He had no political ideology to offer them, except loyalty to the throne. Efforts to create a specifically 'Austrian' patriotism seemed curiously artificial.

This was brilliantly shown by the Austrian writer, Robert Musil, in his novel *The Man Without Qualities*. This gives a satirical account, set in the period 1913–14, of a (fictional) Patriotic Campaign to celebrate the

Emperor's forthcoming jubilee. A Council of notable people, including Ministers, generals, bureaucrats and society beauties (together with a German business tycoon out to buy up Austrian oilfields) holds endless meetings to try to find a central 'Idea' as theme of the Campaign. They feel that this must somehow be found in an Austrian 'mission' – a world mission vaguely connected with the idea of peace; 'Universal Austria' could perhaps be the slogan and there could be an 'Austrian Year' or a 'Universal Year'. But all the talk is futile; all that happens is that the German tycoon exploits his new-found contacts to further his industrial interests. Musil also makes the point that the Campaign's promoters expect the 'German-Austrians' to be the most difficult problem – because they feel 'less allegiance to their country than to the German nation'. Yet another obstacle is the fact that 'Austria' is not the Empire's official name: the correct title of its western half is 'the kingdoms and lands represented in the Council of the Imperial Realm' – which, of course, 'naturally means nothing at all'.

When therefore the 'German-Austrians' looked round at the wreckage of October 1918, they had neither a ready-made name for their country, nor a ready-made patriotism towards it. While the Hungarians, Rumanians, Czechs, Slovaks and Croats of the Empire all had stirring national hymns, the 'German-Austrians' had nothing but the official anthem, 'God save our Emperor. . . Closely with the Habsburg throne, Austria's fate remains united'.[5] But the Habsburgs had fallen.

Nor did the 'German-Austrians' know what the boundaries of their new state were to be. Apart from the solid group of hereditary Lands – Upper Austria, Lower Austria, Styria, Carinthia, Tirol, Salzburg and Vorarlberg – where 6½ million of them were living, there were over 3 million 'German-Austrians' in Bohemia and Moravia – the Czech Lands – and around 200,000 more south of the Brenner Pass in South Tirol. The Tirolese, both north and south of the Brenner, regarded themselves as one people not to be divided. But Britain and France, by the secret agreement of 1915 which brought Italy into the war on their side, had promised South Tirol to Italy. There was a smaller number of 'German-Austrians' living in western Hungary close to Lower Austria and Styria. On the other hand, in southern Carinthia there was a considerable minority of Slovenes, living close to the borders of the new Yugoslav state, and a smaller sprinkling of Croats in southern Styria, also exposed to Yugoslav claims. There were therefore unsolved and difficult frontier questions on the north, south and east.

There was also real danger that one or more of the Lands would break away – Tirol and Salzburg to Germany (or an independent Bavaria), Vorarlberg to Switzerland; Styria at one point seemed to be flirting with the idea of some sort of independent existence. There was very little common ground and a great deal of antagonism between the western Lands – rural, traditionalist, strongly Catholic, with strong local loyalties – and Vienna, the imposing imperial city of two million people, a big financial, industrial and cultural centre, sophisticated, cosmopolitan, full of Socialist-minded workers and rich and poor Jews.

Vienna's hunger for food was, in 1918, a special barrier. Under the Habsburg system there had been relatively little contact among the Lands, or between the Lands and Vienna. Vienna's main source of food had been Hungary. But in the course of the war, Hungary had cut off normal food supplies to Vienna and Lower Austria, which then had to make bigger demands on the farmers and peasants of the Lands; they, however, did their best to follow Hungary's example and keep their food to themselves. When the war ended, they saw no reason to change this practice; in any case, because of the disruption of the war years, they were often short themselves. The resulting clash of interest sharpened the traditional antagonism between the western Lands and Vienna, which developed into a deep political division in the years ahead.

Finally, there was the problem of the break-up of the large economic unit formed by the Empire – a unit which had been fairly well balanced and self-sufficing, possessing raw materials needed for its growing industries and food for its growing cities and towns. The 'remnant' Austria had lost this big market and source of supply and found itself shut behind sealed frontiers because of the hostile suspicion of the newly-independent states on the north, east and south. In particular Vienna, the old Empire's financial and trading centre, seemed to have lost its role, a city doomed to wither away.

The 'German-Austrians' therefore found themselves faced with a terrifying array of problems, internal and external, psychological, political and economic. The weapons in their hands were few but important. They had leading men of great intelligence and determination, who were heirs to a wealth of experience in dealing with other peoples and powers, in government, administration and diplomacy. Since the 'German-Austrians' had supplied most of the senior bureaucrats and army officers of the western part of the Empire, they had learnt to grapple with apparently hopeless situations and to tackle apparently insoluble problems. Moreover these men, though conscious of their position as a governing elite, had been taught to regard themselves as loyal servants of a Habsburg master rather than as members of a master race among inferiors. Emperor Francis Joseph, in his later years, was careful to avoid giving the other nationalities the impression that the 'German-Austrians' were specially favoured – in fact, rather the reverse. This experience probably made it easier for them to adapt to the role of a small nation among equals.

What they unfortunately lacked was experience of real parliamentary government. Although Francis Joseph had permitted the establishment of a parliament for the western part of the Empire, he had never granted it real powers. In any case, its proceedings were taken up with manoeuvres and quarrels among the various nations and nationalities, rather than with party politics in the normal sense. After 1918 the 'German-Austrians', though familiar with parliamentary procedure and with party warfare, found it hard to make the parliamentary system work effectively or smoothly. No party trusted the others to stick to the rules. From this mutual mistrust stemmed many of Austria's difficulties in the years ahead.

2 The Austrian Political Parties

In spite of later difficulties and failures, it was the three main political parties of the 'German-Austrians', acting through Parliament, which, when the Empire was collapsing, seized the initiative and laid the foundations of the new state. And these three parties, in one form or another, became the constant political factors in Austrian life, surviving suppression by Hitler and maintaining surprisingly constant relative strengths, in spite of great fluctuations in Austria's fortunes. (See table on p. 15).

In 1918, for special reasons, the dominant party was the Social Democratic Party. It was a party which had intellectually gifted leaders of wide outlook (several of them Jewish) and had already amassed great experience in organising and educating the workers, fighting for their rights and improving their conditions. It was very closely linked with the trade unions which had won the right of free association in 1866, and the right to strike a few years later; this however had been harshly suppressed during the war, when factories were placed under military control. The party's strongholds were first and foremost Vienna itself, the industrial areas of neighbouring Lower Austria and parts of Styria, together with patchy support in Upper Austria. It had no firm hold in the western Lands.

It had remarkable men among its leaders. Its founding father, Dr Victor Adler, a doctor of medicine from a rich middle-class Jewish family, had started his political career in the (Austrian) German nationalist movement in the

Relative Strength of the Three Main Austrian Political Groups, 1918–71
(*Seats in Parliament*)

Election	Social Democrats/ Socialists	Christian Socials/ People's Party	Heimat- block	German Nationalists/ successor parties	Com- munist Party
16.2.1919	72	69	—	26	—
17.10.1920	62	79	—	18	—
21.10.1923	68	82	—	15	—
24.4.1927	71	73	—	12	—
9.11.1930	72	72	8	19	—
25.11.1945	76	85	—	—	4
9.10.1949	67	77	—	16	5
22.2.1953	73	74	—	14	4
13.5.1956	74	82	—	6	3
10.5.1959	78	79	—	8	—
18.11.1962	76	81	—	8	—
6.3.1966	74	85	—	6	—
1.3.1970	81	79	—	5	—
10.10.1971*	93	80	—	10	—

*(total of seats increased)

Figures for 1919–30 are taken from Walter Goldinger, *Geschichte der Republik Österreich*. Other historians give different figures for 1919 and 1920.

Voting Trends 1919–30 (*percentages*)

1919	40.76	35.93	—	20.72
1920	35.88	42.27	—	17.16
1923	39.60	45	—	12.76
1927	42	49	—	6
1930	41	36	6	5

Source: Foreign Office Documents FO/371/26538. Percentages do not add up to 100 because of tiny groups other than those listed.

1880s and was one of the authors of its 'Linz Programme' which had called for social and political reforms and very close ties with Germany.[6] But Adler could not stand the growing anti-semitism of the nationalist movement; he left it and took over the leadership of small, weak socialist groups which, working with Karl Kautsky, he united into the Social Democratic Party in 1889.

The new party's programme – the Hainfeld programme – called for social reforms such as a maximum eight-hour day, no night work, no child labour under fourteen years of age, and social insurance. Considerable progress was made in this field in the following years. Adler believed in working by parliamentary methods; so the grant of the vote to all males over 23, in 1907, was an important step forward, even though the voting strength of the Social Democrats remained small. The long-term aim of the Social Democrats was to come to power through the ballot-box, not revolution.

Another reformist and parliamentarian was the considerably younger Social Democrat, Karl Renner, who was to be twice Austrian Chancellor at a time of great national crisis. Renner was an intellectual who had been librarian in the National Library in Vienna,[7] becoming an active Social Democrat after 1900. Further to the Left was Otto Bauer, a Marxist theoretician and a gifted political writer. He, like his close associate, Julius Deutsch, was a Jewish intellectual. Also to the Left of the main party leadership was Victor Adler's son, Friedrich, a burning pacifist who, unlike the majority of the party, strongly opposed the 1914–18 war and, acting on his convictions, shot dead the war-time Prime Minister, Karl Stürgkh, in a Vienna restaurant. For this he was sentenced to death, reprieved, and, after the collapse of the Empire, became for a short time a much admired leading member of the party's Left wing.

The Social Democratic leaders were not only active inside the Empire; they also carried weight in the international socialist movement. Renner had worked out a scheme for solving the Empire's national problem through a complicated system of cultural autonomy based, not on territorial units, but on community of language – a system which looked unworkable but was designed to fit the intermingling and overlapping of nations and languages within the Empire, especially in Bohemia and Moravia. Otto Bauer took up the plan and pushed it further in his book, *The Nationality Question and Social Democracy*, which appeared in 1907.

The work of Renner and Bauer on the national problem was of great interest to the Russian Marxists, beset by similar problems in their own country; and Stalin, in his *Marxism and the National Question*, of 1913, said to have been written on Lenin's instructions, attacked Renner (under his pseudonym, Springer) and Bauer at considerable length, chiefly for failing to recognise the nations' full right to self-determination, including the right of secession, and for following an 'evolutionary' national policy.

Bauer later moved forward to Stalin's (theoretical) position (which was soon abandoned, in practice, after 1917). Following the general line of the Social Democratic Party, Bauer fought in the Austrian army against Tsarist Russia, was taken prisoner, was released after the 1917 revolution, and came home. He now favoured full self-determination for the nations of the Empire, and formed a group which pressed this programme on the Social Democratic Party. Bauer wrote later: 'The historical significance of the nationality programme of the Left consisted in the fact that it prepared the party for the tasks of the future. At first the programme aroused violent opposition inside the party. . .' But on 3 October 1918 the Social Democratic deputies adopted the Left's programme. 'The differences within the party were by this means overcome. The party regained a unanimous conception of its immediate task.'[8]

On the question of relations with Germany, the Social Democratic Party's policy had never been entirely clear-cut. Bauer, in his book, *The Nationality Question and Social Democracy*, had warned workers against joining in the 'frivolous agitation of pan-German adventurers'; but he added the poetic prophecy: 'Patience, the day will come when a single tent will be stretched over the whole German land.' In practice, this meant that under the Empire, the Social Democrats refused electoral pacts with the (Austrian) German Nationalists; but, especially from 1917 onwards, good Marxists like Bauer thought in terms of a wider European revolution in which socialism would triumph – in Germany as in the Empire. In 1918, when the Empire collapsed and socialism appeared to be triumphing in Germany, it became an article of faith for Bauer and his group that the 'remnant' Austria must join Germany, since that would be the path not only of economic survival but also of strengthening and safeguarding socialism. This article of faith was accepted, though with considerably less enthusiasm and in a more pragmatic spirit, by moderate Social Democrats such as Renner.

(In the party's later history, the German question caused some confusion: all the party strongly opposed the idea of joining Hitler's Germany, but once Hitler had imposed the union by force, the party's Left wing – or at least those in exile – argued that on theoretical grounds it would be a reactionary step to undo the union. However, seven years of occupation by Hitler destroyed this theory, and by 1945 the German question was finally solved for the Social Democrats.)

Associated with Bauer on the party's Left wing was Julius Deutsch. He was a lesser man, but in 1918, having spent the last few months of the war in the War Ministry, as an adviser on labour questions, he acquired the reputation of a military expert, which he used for the party's political purposes in the post-war period. Among the moderates associated with Renner was Karl Seitz, later

Mayor of Vienna and a prominent and respected member
of the party.

It was one of the party's great strengths, both in 1918
and later, that it managed to accommodate opposing views
and factions and sharp personal enmities, and yet to maintain a surprising degree of unity. This unity was possible
because the differences between rival groups were usually
much less deep than they seemed on the surface. On the
one hand, apparently doctrinaire and uncompromising
Marxists such as Bauer were not nearly as revolutionary as
their words might imply. Though he talked about proletarian dictatorship, Bauer was in fact always preaching
patience and the need to wait until the time was ripe. He
was quite firm in declaring that Austrian socialism must
not go the Russian way. He wrote in 1920 that it was
different from Russian Bolshevism on the one side and
English 'industrial democracy' on the other. It could not
use the same methods of struggle or of exercising power as
the Russians.[9] On the other side, moderates such as Renner, who believed deeply in constitutional methods and
the parliamentary system, did not, when out of favour
with the Left, attempt to split the party. Renner quietly
withdrew from the political limelight, waiting until he
could again be of use.

The fact that a Left wing which was outwardly militantly Marxist and revolutionary could be contained within
the party had one very important advantage for Austria.
The Social Democrats could – and repeatedly did – out-
manoeuvre the Communists and spike their guns, so that
in neither of the two danger periods, after the First and
Second World Wars, were the Communists ever able to
make a really serious bid for power: they never gained
the allegiance of more than a small minority of the
workers.

One great source of strength to the Social Democrats at
all periods was their extremely thorough and comprehensive organisation at all levels of party work. Moreover they

offered the workers, and their families, a complete way of life: social centres, lectures, libraries and educational openings, children's parties, country rambles, nesting-boxes in the Vienna woods. In Vienna, there was also the powerful pull of the big new housing blocks built from the early 1920s onwards by the Socialist city administration. The party's hold over its members was therefore strong and enduring.

Above all, the basis of the party's power was a fairly solid, homogeneous and compact social group – the urban working class, not seriously divided by any internal conflict of interests.

All these factors together enabled the Social Democrat Party to play a leading role in two great crises in the history of the 'remnant' Austria.

The other big party, the Christian Social Party (in 1945 re-named the People's Party), did not represent a single clearly-defined social group. It was a combination of different social groups, and their interests were not always the same. Even if it could command more votes than the Social Democrats, it tended to be weakened by this inner diversity.

The founder of the Christian Social Party, like the founder of the Social Democratic Party, had been close to the German nationalist movement. But Karl Lueger broke away from it not, like Victor Adler, because of its anti-semitism – which he shared – but because it was hostile to the Church and to the Habsburgs. Lueger was a lawyer with an attractive and forceful personality, who was active in Vienna city politics, eventually becoming a very popular Mayor; he stood up for the small shopkeepers, artisans and traders who felt themselves threatened by the Jews. In 1885 he was elected to Parliament and sought a wider field of activity; in 1891 he joined in founding the Christian Social Party, which aimed to represent the 'small man' not only in the cities and towns but also in the country; it supported the Empire, the Habsburgs and the Catholic Church; it was anti-semitic but did not approve of the excesses of some of the German nationalists.

In its early years it was regarded as a party of the Left, and as such frowned on by the Emperor and his Ministers, even though it received the approval of the Vatican. At first its power base, like the Social Democrats', was in Vienna, though the efforts of one of its leading members, Leopold Kunschak, to organise Christian Social trade unions had only limited success. Over the years, however, electoral alliances followed by fusion with a clerical party produced a vast change in the party's character: by 1911, a year after Lueger's death, its chief supporters were the peasants, its power base was in the western Lands, and it had lost out in Vienna. As the historian, C. A. Macartney, wrote: 'The Christian Socials had . . . sacrificed almost all their original inspiration for the sake of office . . . They were now essentially a Catholic Conservative Party, resting on the rural electorate of the Alpine Lands.'[10]

In the 'remnant' Austria, the Christian Socials retained their character as a Catholic Conservative party; after the Second World War, as the People's Party, they saw themselves as the counterpart of the Christian Democrats of Italy and West Germany. For votes, they depended on the peasant-farmers, and on the small shopkeepers and office workers of the cities and towns; for financial backing, on the business interests which wanted to keep the Socialists out of power and the workers under control. They also provided a home for monarchists; some of their leading members believed in an eventual Habsburg restoration, though as a matter of faith rather than of practical policy. Even after the Second World War, they showed a special tenderness for the Habsburg family.

Given this variegated support, it was difficult for them to make their political creed at all precise, except in so far as they stood for devotion to the Church and hostility to the Socialists, whom they liked to see as godless revolutionaries. Some of their leaders felt that their strength should be in a specifically Austrian patriotism, as indeed it came to be, during the Second World War and in the years that followed it. But up till 1938, their patriotic appeal was vitiated by the ambivalence of their feelings towards Germany and the nature of Austrian–German relations, which was revealed in such tortured and obscure phrases as Kurt von Schuschnigg used in the face of Hitler's threats.

Ambivalence and mental confusion about the question of union with Germany was to be found even among the German Nationalists – the third of the political groups which, under varying names, played a continuing role in Austria in the half-century after the break-up of the Empire, though a much smaller one than that of the two big parties. This group traced its origins to the Linz Programme of the 1880s (see above, p. 16). This represented the views of the moderates; a more extreme creed was preached by Georg von Schönerer. Most of the German Nationalists did not go beyond a desire to protect the position of the Germans within the Habsburg Empire as its governing elite and its 'cement', and of the German language as the language of government and administration; admiration for the new, vigorous, united Germany of Bismarck; and anti-semitism. Schönerer, however, went further and wanted to break up the Empire and join the German Reich. For the most part, however, it was only young students who followed him to this length. As Macartney wrote: 'Hardly any Austrian of maturer years really wanted to see his country swallowed up in a Germany dominated by upstart, Protestant Prussia, and if his personal inclinations pointed that way strongly, he emigrated (as did Hitler, who admired Schönerer immensely).'[11]

While, therefore, in the last decades of the Empire, the

German Nationalists won considerable power in parliament, they did so on the basis of a policy of defending the rights and interests of the Germans inside the Empire, rather than of breaking away from it. They kept their anti-semitism, some in moderate form, others indulging in pseudo-mystical theories of blood and race which were later popular among Hitler's National Socialists.

After the fall of the Empire, they were much less powerful though they were sometimes an influential balancing factor between the two big parties. Right up till the forced union with Germany in 1938, there seemed to be mental confusion among their leading men – even those closest to Hitler – about what sort of union with Germany they wanted, on what terms and at what price. After Hitler's downfall, their political heirs, under whatever name, for obvious reasons disclaimed all connexions with Hitlerism and were extremely discreet and vague about the kind of links with Germany which they wanted Austria to have. But they provided a home, not only for lesser former Nazis, but also for those Austrians who still believed strongly in their country's 'German-ness'.

The German Nationalists' traditional base was the urban middle class, especially the professional class and the bureaucracy, and they were always strong in the universities. Under the Empire, they regarded themselves as the champions of liberalism and progress, also of freedom from State controls in the economic field. After Hitler's fall, this came to be one of their chief planks. It naturally brought them sympathy from the industrialists and business interests, but, since they were politically weak, not much financial support.

By tradition, they were strongly anti-clerical: 'Away from Rome' was a popular early slogan. They either lacked devotion to the Habsburgs or were positively hostile to them. These things kept them apart from the Christian Socials. So the two 'bourgeois' parties, in spite of their common opposition to the Socialists, never combined in one big conservative party, and temporary alliances between them were always uneasy.

The basic pattern of Austrian political forces from 1918 onwards was therefore the three-party system. The strange distortions and aberrations of the pre-Hitler phase of Austrian sub-fascism and the period of direct rule by Hitler completely failed to destroy it. It survived all assaults intact.

3 The Establishment of the Austrian Republic

In 1918, the creation of the new Austrian Republic was the joint work of the three political parties – Social Democrats, Christian Socials and German Nationalists. As the Socialist, Bauer, wrote: 'The Austrian State was fundamentally the product of a *contrat social*, an agreement to found a State, arrived at between the various classes of the Austrian people, as represented by the political parties. On the basis of a compact between the parties, the whole of the . . . deputies constituted themselves a provisional national assembly and proclaimed the establishment of the Austrian State.'[12]

In October and November, the leaders of the three parties found themselves caught in a whirlpool created by the foundering of an empire. Deeply divided as they were among themselves, they worked together with surprising reasonableness and level-headedness to save their people from being sucked under. The pattern of cooperation in crisis which they set was followed and repeated at many levels throughout the German Lands of the old Empire. Both leaders and ordinary people showed a talent for day-to-day, hour-to-hour improvisation.

The dominant figure during the crucial weeks was the Social Democrat leader, Victor Adler, who suffered from severe heart trouble and died when the first essential tasks had been done, on 11 November. A fellow-socialist wrote of him: 'His incomparable practical sense told him day by day what had become possible and indeed inevitable. His sense of responsibility would not allow us to try to take today at the cost of severe sacrifice what was bound to fall into our lap as ripe fruit tomorrow.'[13] The same sort of 'practical sense' was shown at many levels.

The other notable thing about the crucial weeks was the way in which a multiplicity of overlapping, rival, even mutually hostile political organs existed side by side without direct clash, even with some mutual understanding and toleration. Where civil war seemed inevitable, there was in fact a sort of gradual, piecemeal transition from imperial rule to Socialist-led republic.

There was the Emperor Karl, well-meaning but futile; there was his last government, containing some distinguished and intelligent men, among them the prelate, Ignaz Seipel, who later dominated the Christian Social Party for a decade. There was – until 22 October – the old multinational imperial parliament. But by that time there was also the new Provisional National Assembly summoned by the three German-Austrian parties to prepare for the new State. There were the political parties themselves, each conducting separate private discussions or conferences to take vital decisions on the future. In the Lands, there were demands for self-determination, yet also cooperation between the local leaders of the three political parties.

At yet another level, there was a real revolutionary movement, first and foremost of soldiers returning in bitterness and anger from defeat at the front, but also of factory workers equally embittered by years of military control of industry, and by their memories of the harsh suppression of the big strike movement of January 1918. They knew about the Russian revolution of 1917 and many of them saw it as a shining example. First of all soldiers' councils, then workers' councils, sprang up spontaneously in Vienna and elsewhere.

In the middle of anarchy and chaos, there was a great deal of organised and purposeful activity. When all the old sign-posts were being torn down, a good many people still seemed to know where they were going; and even if they were heading in different directions they seemed prepared to go along together for the time being. Moreover they moved fast.

On 1 October the Emperor's government proposed the transformation of the Empire into a federation. On 3 October, the Social Democrats recognised the right to full self-determination of the nations of the Empire; but they claimed the same right for the 'German-Austrians' who should, they said, be united in a German-Austrian State, which would then freely settle its relations both with the neighbouring nations and with Germany. On 4 October the German Nationalists accepted the principles of the Social Democrats' programme as a basis for discussion. On 8 October the Christian Socials also accepted these principles, but with reservations about their 'religious and dynastic convictions'. Negotiations then started among the three parties; the Social Democrats urged the formation of a new Provisional National Assembly, but the other two were not yet ready.

On 12 October the Emperor called a meeting of party leaders of all the nations at his palace at Schönbrunn. The German Nationalists talked of a constitutional monarchy and self-determination for the nations of the Empire; the Christian Socials advocated a monarchy and a federation. For the Social Democrats, Victor Adler said that the party's aim was a democratic republic, but that the decision should lie with a freely elected Constituent Assembly; 'German-Austria' should be ready to form a federation or league of nations with the neighbouring peoples; failing this, it would be compelled to join Germany as a 'special federal State'. Only the tiny National Socialist Workers' Party – its name was soon to be annexed by Hitler – and another small extremist German Nationalist group rejected the idea of a federation with the nations of the Empire and wanted nothing but union with Germany – the *Anschluss*.[14]

Four days later, on 16 October, the Emperor Karl issued his manifesto offering to transform the Empire into a federation, which President Wilson and Masaryk promptly killed. (See p. 8 above.) By 21 October, the negotiations between the three German-Austrian political parties had led to agreement on the next step: the first meeting was held of a Provisional National Assembly formed by all the German deputies elected to the imperial parliament in 1911. The Social Democrats therefore formed a small minority; they had 37 representatives compared with 65 Christian Socials and 106 German Nationalists and associates. (The political weight of the Social Democrats had, however, been strengthened by their capture of the majority of votes, though not of seats, in the Vienna City Council in 1914.)

The Provisional Assembly decided to set up a Political Council representing all three parties; it declared unanimously that 'the German people in Austria are resolved to determine their future form of State, to form an independent German-Austrian State, and to regulate their relations with other nations by free agreement'. The Social Democrats wanted to come out immediately in favour of a democratic republic, but the other two parties were still not ready. However, Karl Renner set to work on a provisional constitution for a republic.

On the next day the old imperial parliament held its last meeting. The representatives of the non-German nations made it clear that they wanted nothing to do with the Empire, however transformed.

On 25 October, the Provisional Assembly of 'German-Austria' called on the Lands to form their own provisional assemblies and governments on a three-party basis – which, in spite of chaos and separatist tendencies, they were either already doing (as in Salzburg and Styria) or very rapidly did.[15] On 27 October, the Emperor appointed a government, headed by a pacifist professor, which immediately asked for a separate peace. Oddly, this had a shattering effect on many German-Austrians – including some Social Democrats – who felt a sense of loyalty to Germany as an ally. It strengthened the feeling in favour of union with Germany: belief in the possibility of federation with the other nations of the Empire had been badly shaken, if not totally killed, by the last meeting of the old imperial parliament three days before.

On 30 October, as the fronts were crumbling and soldiers were streaming back homewards, a vast mass meeting was held in Vienna, which showed the strongly revolutionary mood of the moment. On 1 November, a Provisional Central Committee of Soldiers was set up, which later moved into the War Ministry.

To the 'bourgeois' leaders, it seemed clear that salvation lay with the Social Democrats who alone might be able to canalise and restrain the revolutionary forces. This, through their strong organisational network, inside the army as well as in the factories, they did with a surprising degree of success, so that the soldiers' councils which had sprung up overnight could, up to a point, gradually be transformed into disciplined bodies tending to maintain some kind of order.

Already on 1 November, a party conference of the Social Democrats issued an appeal for discipline. At the same time it authorised its leaders to join the 'bourgeois' parties in forming the government of the new State. In the resulting coalition government, Social Democrats held key positions: Renner was Chancellor; Victor Adler (soon to be succeeded by Bauer) was Foreign Minister; and there were Social Democratic Secretaries in the Interior and War Ministries. With the Social Democrats firmly entrenched, the tiny Communist Party, formed in 1917, had little chance of capturing control of the revolutionary movement.

So the death of the Habsburg Empire and the establishment of the new Republic came without violence. On 2 November the armistice was signed in Padua – though as a result of confusion 350,000 Austrian troops were taken prisoner by the Italians in the final hours of war. On 11 November Emperor Karl lay down his responsibilities and left Vienna – though not at first Austria – without actually abdicating. Seipel, who had belonged to the Emperor's last government and had wanted to keep him as a means of securing the preservation of a 'greater Austria', was by now ready to accept a republic. On 12 November, the Provisional National Assembly declared German-Austria as a Republic, formed by 'burghers, peasants and workers': 'We are now one people, of one stock and one language, united not by force but by the free decision of all.'

Yet if the Republic was new, the old bureaucracy remained. In particular, Johann Schober, the Vienna Police Chief under the Habsburgs, was asked to continue at his post, and took the oath to the new State.

4 The Two Faces of Austrian Socialism

From the start of the new Republic, the Social Democrats felt themselves to be conducting a struggle on two fronts, both on the Right and on the Left. At the moment of crisis, the 'bourgeois' parties – the Christian Socials and German Nationalists – seemed happy to lay the chief responsibility on the Social Democrats. For one thing, the Social Democrats seemed to stand the best chance of controlling the revolutionary upsurge and checking excesses. (This calculation proved correct.) For another, through their early recognition of the right of self-determination of the other nations of the Empire, they seemed best fitted to undertake any future negotiations with them. (This hope proved vain.) For the same reason, they seemed best fitted to win the sympathies of the victorious allies and ward off vengeance against a defeated enemy: the touching faith of many Austrians in Wilson's peace programme – his Fourteen Points – strengthened this belief. This faith proved ill-founded; but probably the Social Democrats made as good a job of negotiating with the victors as anyone could have done. Finally, the Socialist upsurge in defeated Germany seemed to point the way and set the fashion of the times; and the Austrian Social Democrats had long-standing ties with their German opposite numbers.

Yet at the same time there was both fear and hostility among 'bourgeois' Austrians towards the Social Democrats, and these feelings soon spread to the peasant-farmers when the new government, and still more the soldiers' and workers' councils, started trying to requisition food from the countryside for the starving townspeople.

The Social Democrats therefore believed that they had to deal with two dangers. On the Left there was the danger of a violent 'proletarian' revolution. But much more serious, they believed, was the threat of reaction or 'counter-revolution' on their Right, in particular from the peasant-farmers of the western Lands and from the various armed organisations which were springing up there spontaneously at the moment of defeat and collapse. With this danger in mind, the party conference at the beginning of November 1918 had authorised the party leaders to enter a 'bourgeois' government, so as to 'safeguard the democratic achievements'.

Both dangers – on the Right and on the Left – were very real in the early months of the new Republic. The Social Democrats saw it as their task to maintain a balance of social forces, to prevent civil war, and to prevent invasion or intervention from outside. Otto Bauer summed up the party's role:

Austria is divided into two areas nearly equal in population, . . . the great industrial district of Vienna, Lower Austria and Upper Styria, . . . the great agrarian region which includes all the other provinces. . . It was impossible to govern the great industrial district in opposition to the workers, but it was equally impossible to govern the great agrarian district in opposition to the peasants. . . The economic structure of the country therefore created an equilibrium between the strength of the classes, which could only have been abolished by force in a bloody civil war . . . A double task devolved upon Social Democracy: on the one hand, by taking advantage of the powerful revolutionary agitation among the masses . . . , to capture for the proletariat the strongest and most permanent positions in the State and in the workshop, the barracks and the schools; but on the other hand, to prevent this revolutionary agitation from developing into civil war . . . which would have opened the gates to famine, invasion, and counter-revolution.[16]

This doctrine of a balance of social forces was naturally unattractive to the more revolutionary workers and to intellectuals such as the journalist, Egon Erwin Kisch, who commanded the unit known as the Red Guard, stationed close to the centre of Vienna, and who led the demonstration of 12 November, when the Austrian Republic was being officially proclaimed in front of Parliament, resulting in a clash, probably accidental, some shooting, two dead and many injured.[17] But the Red Guard was soon split up and weakened – mainly through the work of the Social Democrat, Julius Deutsch, now State Secretary at the War Ministry, though the excellent information service and constant warnings of the Vienna Police Chief, Schober, no doubt played their part.

Deutsch, who had spent his months in the imperial War Ministry preparing a secret organisation among troops stationed in Vienna,[18] was building a new republican army, the Volkswehr. This, like the Social Democratic Party itself, was intended to deal with two dangers. On the Left, it was intended to counterbalance the soldiers' councils and eventually take over from them. On the Right, Deutsch was determined to destroy the power structure of the old imperial army. In this he was perhaps correct, since the willingness of the new leaders of Germany to leave the old army hierarchy intact was later to do great harm to the German democratic system. Deutsch, however, went too far in the other direction: believing that the 'bourgeois' forces would inevitably try sooner or later to overthrow the democratic republic and the 'achievements' of the Social Democrats, he built up a Volkswehr under Social Democratic domination. So the 'bourgeois' leaders – ignoring its services in countering and absorbing revolutionary elements – could claim, with justice, that it was purely a Social Democratic party guard.

Moreover, at a time when Austria was threatened with

frontier disputes on all sides, it was very inefficient, at least
in the judgement of outside observers. A not unsympathetic
British historian, C. A. Macartney, wrote of it: 'This force
proved so undisciplined that parts of it could not be
trusted by its own masters; while from the military point
of view it was a tragic farce.'[19] Yet the detailed examination
of contemporary official records carried out by a later
historian, F. L. Carsten, gives a rather more favourable
picture of it as a force which became steadily more disciplined and, at least in some places, a force capable of
maintaining order.[20]

During 1919, the period of the Hungarian Communist
regime of Béla Kun presented new problems. On the one
hand, some of the Austrian Communists and revolutionaries
went off to fight for Béla Kun, which relieved some of the
pressure from the Left inside Austria. On the other hand,
Béla Kun, hoping for substantial help from Austria, supplied money and arms to build up the strength of the
Communists and their supporters. However, the Austrian
Social Democrat leaders firmly withstood demands and
pleas from Hungary and maintained their control of the
situation at home.

The workers' councils never presented such a serious
problem as the soldiers' councils. The Social Democrat
leaders were soon able to turn them into what Bauer called
'extra-parliamentary social organisations', a term which
he used to cover both the trade unions (which trebled their
membership between 1913 and 1919) and the workers' and
soldiers' councils. These, he believed, could all be brought
to collaborate in the whole process of government, and
with individual ministries. The machinery of government,
Bauer said, worked in this way:

All important governmental actions were concerted by
the Social Democratic members of the government
with . . . the directing organs of the party, of the trade
unions, and of the workers' and soldiers' councils. Then

it was the task of the Social Democratic members of the Government to pilot these decisions through the coalition Government and the Parliament. The leaders of the labour organisations had to gain the support of the masses for the policy which they had arranged with the members of the Government.[21]

This use of 'extra-parliamentary social organisations' alongside party and government, and closely interlocking with them, curiously foreshadowed the wider, more complex, and better-balanced use of extra-parliamentary social organisations in the second Austrian republic, after 1945, with its Chambers, interest groups, and its extra-parliamentary but powerful Parity Commission for Wages and Prices (see pp. 223–34 below).

In the 1918–19 period, the Social Democrats could use the extra-parliamentary social organisations partly to hold and secure their position on the Left, partly to add to their political weight in their dealings with their 'bourgeois' coalition partners on the Right. However, within Parliament they soon ceased to be the weakest party and became – briefly – the strongest. In the first general election in the new Republic, held on 16 February 1919, they won 72 seats, against 69 for the Christian Socials and only 26 for the German Nationalists, who were badly handicapped by disunity and who then quitted the coalition. Renner remained Chancellor, and Social Democrat representation in the government was strengthened. Gradually the power of the soldiers' and workers' councils waned, and finally vanished. But the weight of the Social Democrat-dominated trade unions remained as a constant power factor in political life, even after, in 1920, the Social Democrats lost their parliamentary lead and left the government, and after the Volkswehr had been replaced by a new and more orthodox army formed under Christian Social auspices.

In opposition, the Social Democratic leaders still felt that they must carry on a struggle on two fronts. Their former 'bourgeois' collaborators now saw them as revolutionaries, and therefore as a threat to law, order, the orthodox political freedoms and private property. But sections of their own supporters, and those further to the Left, saw them as half-hearted reformists (for Communists, a term of abuse) who did not dare to seize power even when it was within their grasp. The leaders wished to see themselves as revolutionaries, but in a very special sense: the social revolution was to be achieved by non-violent means, by democratic political processes.

In a wider context, they wanted to mark themselves off clearly from the Russian Bolsheviks on the one side, and yet to show that they were more genuinely revolutionary than the West European Labour movement and the German Majority Socialists. In the hope of taking up a stand midway between the Moscow-dominated Third International and the West European Second International, they made the brief experiment of what became known as the 'Two-and-a-half International', in which they were joined by the British Independent Labour Party and the German Minority Socialists. But in 1923, through British mediation, they re-joined the Second International, and developed close and enduring links with the British Labour Party.[22]

Having renounced violence the Social Democrat leaders saw the republican constitution and parliament as their most important achievement and their most valuable weapon in the political struggle. They believed that the growing industrialisation of Austria would in the end make the class of industrial workers more numerous than the other social classes. Irresistible economic and social forces would therefore give them a permanent parliamentary majority.

This was where 'proletarian dictatorship' came in. This, according to Bauer, was to be used, not in order to seize power, but only as a defensive weapon, *after* power had been achieved by parliamentary means, against attack from the class enemy, who would almost inevitably use force, or 'counter-revolutionary methods', to try to destroy the legitimate and constitutional power of the workers. In such circumstances, 'proletarian dictatorship' would be legitimate and necessary. This doctrine of Bauer's, later enshrined in the party's Linz Programme of 1927, was enough to convince the 'bourgeois' that the Social Democrats were really planning to seize power by force; or rather, perhaps, it gave the 'bourgeois' party leaders a very valuable propaganda weapon against 'Austro-Marxism', which could be depicted as a dangerous and savage beast, rather than the fairly domesticated and civilised animal it really was.

Inside the leadership of the Social Democratic Party, the main quarrel was over tactics rather than policy. Renner, a man with a strong historical sense and a natural parliamentarian, believed in using the republican constitution and parliament in a positive way, by entering coalition governments, even when the party was weaker than its chief opponent, the Christian Social Party, and by influencing the government's actions from inside. After all, Renner had produced the original draft of the republican constitution and wanted to make it work in practice.

Bauer, the theorist and prophet, took a more doctrinaire and rigid view. He held that in a parliament dominated by 'bourgeois' parties, the Social Democrats should not enter the government but should exercise a negative parliamentary control over its actions, blocking all moves which might undermine the republican constitution and parliament.

The split between Bauer and Renner on tactics which grew up at the beginning of the 1920s and lasted into the 1930s did not seriously disrupt the party. Renner's ideas were too sophisticated and smacked too much of compromise with the 'bourgeois' to appeal to the masses of the Social Democratic Party, so he withdrew from the foreground, though he continued to defend his view – for instance, at the Linz party conference in 1927, when Karl Seitz tried to mediate between him and Bauer.

Bauer emerged as undisputed party leader, with an extraordinary hold over the rank and file. He had an impressive personality, and a gift for beautifully simple exposition and for inspiring faith in the 'revolution' as a certain, if distant, goal. His personal authority survived even the civil war and the suppression of the party in 1934, his own flight into exile, and the party split which followed.

Yet Renner outlived Bauer, and his ideas outlived Bauer's ideas. They became a formative influence in post-Hitler Austria, with its twenty-one-year period of coalition government – a political device which won for the Austrians the real national independence, political stability and economic prosperity which had eluded them between the two world wars.

5 The New Austria and the Outside World

The Social Democrat leaders, in the period 1918–20, found themselves not only taking the lead in ordering the affairs of the new Republic, or at least those of Vienna and the industrial south-east, leaving the western Lands to go very much their own way. They also had to face the victorious Allied Powers and their immediate neighbours. Of these, the new states, Czechoslovakia and Yugoslavia, were now counted as lesser allied powers. Hungary, like Austria itself, was usually reckoned an ex-enemy; internally, during this period, it veered from progressive liberalism to 'Red' Communism and then back to 'White' reaction. Germany was the great ex-enemy power; internally, it was still a battleground for rival political forces ranging from 'Red' to 'White'.

In the face of the outside world, Austria was particularly helpless: the townspeople were near starvation, and even in the countryside there was food shortage because of the disruption of war. And there was no coal.

However, the Austrian leaders succeeded in using differences among the allies and their own grave weakness so as to bring their country through the peace conference and the following period of unrest without suffering dismemberment or total economic disaster.

The pattern of Austria's future external relations – a pattern which recurred, with variations, in its later history – soon became clear. France, led by the implacable Clemenceau, was above all determined to weaken

Germany and therefore to prevent the union of Germany and Austria. The British and Americans did not attach such great importance to banning the *Anschluss*. The British, at least, were embarrassed by such an obvious violation of the right of national self-determination as propounded by Wilson and endorsed by themselves; this was a feeling which, nearly twenty years later, they used as an excuse for their own passivity when Hitler imposed the *Anschluss* by force. Britain and America were, however, very much afraid of Austria's becoming 'Bolshevist', that is, Communist. Italy was determined to get South Tirol, at whatever cost; but once that was settled, it was eager to back Austria against Yugoslavia – Italy's new rival in the Adriatic – and to prevent the Yugoslavs from acquiring territory at Austria's expense. The Italians took up a similar attitude towards Hungary; they seemed to be feeling their way towards a special protective relationship with both Austria and Hungary as a counterweight to France's special relationship with Yugoslavia and Czechoslovakia.

The Yugoslavs were obsessed by their territorial claims on the Austrian Lands of Carinthia and Styria, though not otherwise especially hostile. The Czechs regarded the new Austria with a good deal of suspicion and a sense of moral superiority, but showed some interest in encouraging those political elements in Austria which were anti-Habsburg. Both Czechs and Yugoslavs, short-sightedly, were much more obsessed by fear of a Habsburg restoration than by fear of the *Anschluss*; they were afraid that some of their own people still had nostalgic yearnings for the old Empire.

Relations between Hungary and Austria tended to be largely a matter of the political colour of the government in power in each country at any given time. But the Austrian claim to German-speaking 'West Hungary' was inevitably a special barrier in the early years.

The differing or conflicting fears and hopes of the bigger

and smaller allies could be used by the Austrian leaders to
secure tolerable frontiers for the new Republic, to free it
from at least part of the burden of war guilt which was
laid so heavily on Germany, and to obtain food, coal and
credits from the Allies. This they did. The chief responsibility lay with the Chancellor, Renner, who from July
1919 on was also Foreign Minister. He personally led the
interparty delegation to the Paris Peace Conference, kept
things calm during the frustrating and humiliating months
of waiting to receive the draft treaty, and, after obtaining
some concessions, signed it and thereafter got it through
the Parliament in Vienna.

The question of Austria's war guilt, as successor to the
Habsburg Empire, was discussed by the victorious Allies
on a fairly futile level. France argued that Austria must be
regarded as the direct legitimate heir of the old Empire.
The British regarded it as a new State; the French then
recalled that President Wilson had said that Austria should
be regarded as a new *and* enemy State.[23] Eventually all
agreed on a covering letter to the treaty which named the
Austrian Republic as direct successor. Thus, although the
British economist and reparations expert, Maynard Keynes,
had threatened to resign over the issue,[24] reparations
clauses were included in the treaty which were totally
unrealistic. Winston Churchill later called them 'this pure
nonsense' which 'of course could never be applied'.[25]
Already during the peace conference, the British Foreign
Secretary, Arthur Balfour, suggested that the Reparations
Committee should think first of making Austria a paying
concern before trying to get money out of it.[26] And, in
practice, 'the Reparations Commission, under Sir William
Goode, early transformed itself from a machine for getting
money out of Austria into one for putting it in'.[27]

Then there was a tussle over Austria's name, which
merged into the problem of banning the *Anschluss*. On
29 May a letter had been sent by the Peace Conference
authorities to Renner, saying that the Allies had decided

to recognise the new State under the name of 'Republic of Austria'. The Austrian peace delegation, however, continued to use the name 'German-Austria' in all communications addressed to the Conference. Balfour remarked tolerantly that if the people of Austria chose to call themselves citizens of German-Austria, it did not seem possible to compel them to do otherwise.[28] However, 'Republic of Austria' was the term used in the treaty which Renner signed, and came to be accepted by the Austrians themselves.

Over the ban on the *Anschluss*, the French set out to use both stick and carrot, mainly the stick. Clemenceau remarked that Austria was being allowed to have an army of 30,000 men, although half that number would have sufficed, in order to 'conciliate her and detach her from German influence'. But soon after the French Foreign Minister, André Tardieu, proposed that Austria should undertake a very far-reaching commitment 'not to tolerate on her territory any act whether of propaganda or of any other sort by Austrian subjects or by foreign subjects with a purpose subversive of Austria as an independent State'. If there should be any conflict of interpretation of this undertaking between Austria and one of the Allies, the 'discrepancy' was to be referred to the League of Nations or the International Court of Justice. Italy and Britain opposed this suggestion, as interference in Austria's internal affairs. Balfour said it would mean imposing domestic legislation on Austria and 'maintaining police authority over private, as well as public, speech', which would be 'very repugnant to all that constituted an independent State'. The only way to prevent Austria from gravitating towards Germany, Balfour added, was to make terms such that she would be content to live apart.[29]

By this time Renner had reconciled himself to the inevitability of an anti-*Anschluss* clause in the peace treaty. He had also met Otto Bauer – at that point still Foreign Minister – at Feldkirch, had agreed with him on the need of a change of tactics, so as to win over France and get better economic treatment. Since Bauer himself had been a sharp critic of French 'imperialism' and strong advocate of the *Anschluss*, he resigned his post as Foreign Minister, devoting himself from then on to the leadership of the Social Democratic party.[30] This move favourably impressed the French, who thought Renner reasonable. As Bauer himself remarked of his party rival, his 'uniformly skilful conduct' at the peace conference had 'considerably strengthened his position in Austria, and also gained sympathy for him in France'.[31]

As a result, the final treaty, signed at St Germain on 10 September 1919, contained some economic concessions and an improvement in the frontier with Yugoslavia. It also contained a much modified anti-*Anschluss* undertaking, in Article 88: 'the independence of Austria is inalienable otherwise than with the consent of the Council of the League of Nations. Consequently Austria undertakes, in the absence of the consent of the said Council, to abstain from any act which might directly or indirectly or by any means whatever compromise her independence. . .'

This had its counterpart in Article 80 of the Versailles Treaty with Germany: 'Germany acknowledges and will respect strictly the independence of Austria . . .; she agrees that this independence shall be inalienable except with the consent of the Council of the League of Nations.'

These two clauses, it might have been thought, gave France as much security as practicable. But there was a clause in the new German constitution which said that 'German Austria, after its junction with the German Reich, receives the right to participation in the Reichsrat [Upper House] . . . Till then the representatives of German Austria have a consultative voice.' The French were determined to get this clause annulled. Clemenceau, to win his point, threatened to resign: if, he said, Britain and America refused to support France at this juncture, 'the weight of enforcing the peace treaty would be thrown on his country, and a position would result which would be quite intolerable to him'.[32] Balfour was luke-warm but Clemenceau got his way and the Germans produced the required disavowal of the offending clause.

This, of course, was by no means the end of the matter for the Germans. But no later French leader ever had Clemenceau's unbreakable toughness.

The 'save Austria from Bolshevism' argument was particularly impressive during the peace conference because during the summer of 1919, Hungary, on Austria's eastern border, was under Béla Kun's Communist regime (established in March), while in April the Communist, Kurt Eisner, set up a short-lived workers' republic in Bavaria, on Austria's western border. The Austrian leaders understood how nervous the Allies were about Austria's fate, and how this might serve Austria's interests. Bauer pointed out that the Allies' decision to award the German-speaking section of Hungary to Austria, without a plebiscite, was taken 'in the weeks when the Austrian working class was repelling the onslaught of the Bolshevist forces mobilised by Hungary'. The Allies, he thought, 'desired to strengthen our position against Bolshevism'.[33]

The Americans were particularly sensitive about 'Bolshevism'. In July, Balfour said that a 'somewhat over-eager' invitation was being extended to Austria to join the League of Nations. The American representative replied that it was desirable to encourage the Austrians, by reason of the threat of Bolshevist Hungary at their very doors.[34] When Herbert Hoover, the American who had undertaken the gigantic task of emergency relief in Europe, appeared at the Peace Conference in July, he spoke of the desperate food situation in Austria; the Austrian authorities had gone so far as to offer the national art galleries as pledge of payment for food. It was only Allied help, Hoover said, that had hitherto kept Austria from Bolshevism. The Italians argued that if it were left to the Communist Hungarians to send food, this might turn Austria Bolshevist.[85] It seems clear that Austria might have come still closer to real famine, and might have had to accept even tougher economic clauses in the treaty, if it had not been for the threat of 'Bolshevism'. As it was, in a covering note to the treaty, the Allies did at least promise short- and long-term credits to Austria.[86]

Over frontiers, Austria – given its extremely weak position as 'direct successor' of the Habsburg Empire, and therefore a guilty party – did reasonably well. The biggest loss, in terms of population, was that of three million or more German-Austrians of Bohemia and Moravia. The new Czechoslovak leaders were immovable in their demand for the 'historic frontiers' of these lands. But the loss had been expected in Austria from a fairly early stage: most of the three million lived on the northern borders of Bohemia or scattered in the interior. On purely geographic grounds, it would have been almost impossible to draw a frontier bringing them into the new Austria.

The loss which Austrians felt most bitterly was that Italy should be given South Tirol and its 200,000 German-Austrians, pushing its frontier up to the Brenner Pass. This naturally aroused particularly strong feeling in (Austrian) Tirol, driving the Tirolese into the idea of forming a separate state or uniting with Germany. But France and Britain had given their promise to Italy in 1915 and Italy would not yield.

In return for this gain, the Italians devoted plenty of energy to helping the Austrians resist Yugoslav claims, which were based on the existence of a considerable Slovene minority in southern Carinthia and a smaller number of Croats in Styria, and much smaller Czechoslovak claims on northern Austria and the Bratislava area, which were based on strategic, not linguistic arguments.

The Italians also gave Austria what might be called tactical support. On 12 July Clemenceau produced in the peace conference a bitter complaint from the Yugoslavs that the Italian military authorities were supplying the Austrians with information about Yugoslav troop movements on the borders of southern Carinthia.[37]

In the end, Austria got a satisfactory frontier with Yugoslavia – in Styria, without a plebiscite; in Carinthia, after a plebiscite which was, surprisingly, bloodless, in spite of the activities of armed bands of a Yugoslav patriotic organisation, the Sokols, and of equally armed bands of workers and students from Vienna; the presence of fifty-eight Inter-Allied officers as observers apparently kept the peace.[38] The results showed that many of the Slovenes of Carinthia had voted to remain in Austria. This wounded the pride of the Yugoslavs, and during and after the Second World War Marshal Tito revived the old claims – again without success.

Austria's one gain, territorially, was the award of German-speaking Western Hungary. But there were long delays in putting this award into effect; the Hungarians resisted it and the Allies were unwilling to intervene actively. The matter then became entangled in Austrian and Hungarian internal politics. However, the final outcome was satisfactory to Austria – and also reasonably fair.

The separatist tendencies of some of the western Lands –Tirol, Salzburg and Vorarlberg – were discouraged by the Allies. They had no desire to see Tirol and Salzburg gravitate into the arms of Germany (although some months later, in 1920, the French and the Vatican were believed by Renner to be encouraging the creation of an independent, Catholic South German State embracing Salzburg and perhaps other western Lands too).[39] Vorarlberg's movement to join Switzerland was squashed during the Peace Conference by Clemenceau, who did not want to see the balance between the German-speaking and French-speaking Swiss upset.[40] Tardieu added that the Conference was trying to meet the Austrians as far as possible, and they would be 'greatly offended' by any move to deprive them of Vorarlberg.

Overall, therefore, Renner could feel that he had done a good job at the Peace Conference, using the right tactics to obtain the least harsh terms possible. He clearly impressed the Allied delegations and knew how to handle them; at one point, he issued a private warning that if he did not get what he wanted, he would very probably not be authorised by the Austrian parliament to sign the peace treaty: he would then be forced to resign and a change of government would result.[41] The warning was effective; at this stage the Allies preferred Renner to any alternative. Renner's diplomacy – a mixture of civilised reasonableness, toughness within realistic limits, and what might be called strength through weakness – set a pattern which succeeded well at later phases of Austria's history, more particularly in the post-Hitler period.

6 Foreign Loans and Internal Politics

Once the Allies had concluded the Treaty of St Germain, they quickly lost interest and left Austria to grapple with almost overwhelming short-term economic problems and the long-term problem of adapting the remnant of an empire to the scale and requirements of a small and weak state. In particular, there was the burden of a top-heavy bureaucracy and of a great capital city which had lost its imperial role.

There were endless delays and difficulties over the promised Allied credits; and the more desperate the situation became, the less willing were foreign governments or banks to lend money to Austria. Caught in this vicious circle, Renner's leadership of the coalition government became more and more discredited.

The slowness of the Allies to give aid stemmed from the rigidly orthodox and unimaginative economic and financial doctrines of the period. These involved a belief that money should be lent only to those who were credit-worthy, which usually meant, in practice, that those who most needed the money could not get it. There was, however, in Britain a popular desire to help Austria. In February 1920 the British Foreign Secretary, Lord Curzon, urged the Council of Ambassadors in Paris – representing the victorious Allies – to take action: 'it seems essential that a comprehensive scheme for the economic reconstruction of Austria should be worked out to meet the situation which will shortly arise . . . In view of the strong feeling on this sub-

ject in Parliament and the country, I should be glad to . . .
receive concrete proposals with as little delay as possible . . .'[42] Yet nine months later the Austrian Section of the
Reparations Commission was still calling for 'remedial
action of the most urgent and drastic character'; there was
a danger of 'the dissolution of all social and economic life
in Austria', and to 'the continued existence of the country
as a political entity'.[43]

This was perhaps an exaggeration, designed to compel
the Allies to switch over from the practice of the piecemeal
grant of small short-term credits to a comprehensive long-
term policy of financing Austria's economic reconstruction.
With the help of these small credits, the Social Democratic
leaders had followed a policy of full employment and
getting the economy moving again as quickly as possible.
During 1919 the factories had got to work again, and the
number of unemployed, which had been as high as 185,000,
dropped to as little as 14,000. In November 1920 the
British High Commissioner in Austria, Mr F. O. Lindley,
reported that there was more food and more in the shops
than a year earlier; the workers had 'freed themselves from
the Bolshevik virus' and were anxious to work.[44]

By this time, however, the Allies were disinclined to give
credit to a government led by Social Democrats, whom
they regarded with distrust and disapproval because of
their unorthodox social, economic and financial policies.
The Renner government had raised wages and provided
an unemployment benefit which was high by contemporary
standards; they had introduced the eight-hour day, holi-
days with pay, collective contracts and works' councils in
the factories; the power of the trade unions had grown
greatly; they kept the price of bread and rationed food-
stuffs artificially low. But this large-scale social expenditure
was achieved by allowing a runaway inflation (which hit
the salaried or pensioned middle class especially hard),
and – worst of all, in Allied eyes – by running up a record
budget deficit. The Austrian Section of the Reparations

Commission reported in November 1920 that this 'relatively enormous deficit' totalled over one and a half times the total revenue; the value of the Austrian currency had fallen over 100 per cent during the past four months.[45]

The Social Democratic leaders had yet another economic doctrine which caused trouble. They believed that Austria should rely as little as possible on aid from foreign capitalists; instead, economic recovery and reconstruction should be financed as far as possible from domestic resources. By this they meant a tax on wealth. This was inevitably very unpopular and was regarded as a revolutionary move.

From 1918 to 1920 the Social Democrats were of course only partners in a coalition government. But they were regarded as the dominant partners. The Christian Socials played a relatively negative role, leaving the Social Democrats to bear the blame not only for unpopular economic policies but also for the many hardships and failures of the time, and giving them little credit for their services in warding off the danger of any real revolution.

The coalition could not continue on this basis. In March 1920, the Christian Socials, at a party meeting, voted for continuing the coalition. But some of their leading men, including Seipel, were beginning to plan for its end.[46] Many Social Democrats were also becoming impatient, feeling that their party was getting all the kicks and none of the ha'pence. On 10 June a sudden, unimportant flare-up in Parliament provided a pretext for a break.

One Austrian historian has described this as one of the most fateful days in the history of the Republic.[47] Renner would have liked to continue the coalition, but Bauer, on the one side, and Seipel, on the other, were against it. A purely temporary expedient was found in a *Proporzkabinett* or Proportional Cabinet – a curious invention, by which each party selected its own members of the government and accepted no responsibility for the representatives of other parties.

In October 1920 new elections were held. The Social

Democrats lost their leading position, winning only 62 seats. The Christian Socials moved into the lead, winning 79 seats; the German Nationalists lost ground, but, since the Christian Socials lacked an absolute majority, could still play an important and sometimes destructive role as a balancing factor.

The Communists won only 20,000 votes, although Lenin was said to have instructed all Communists to take part in the election.[48]

The Social Democrats now finally left the government. The German Nationalists did not wish to commit themselves. The Christian Socials could not govern alone. So yet another expedient was considered: a government headed by the Vienna Police Chief, Schober, well-liked by the Christian Socials, yet still respected by the Social Democrats.

The idea of a 'neutral' government appealed to the British and the Americans who decided to back it. The French, who had consistently supported the Christian Socials,[49] were probably less keen. Until then, the British had followed a policy of strict non-intervention in Austrian internal affairs; in June 1920, when the coalition broke down, Mr Lindley had devised a splendidly impartial formula, which was approved by the Foreign Office. This was that the attitude of the British would not be influenced by the complexion of any Austrian government provided that it was legally constituted, that it loyally carried out the peace treaty, and that it had nothing to do with the Habsburgs. Soon after this formula had been enunciated, however, the British began to feel that the Social Democrats were going too far; they were particularly shocked at a boycott on 'White' Hungary imposed by Social Democrat-dominated railway and postal employees. The Americans also turned against the Social Democrats. An American representative, in December, reproved Otto Bauer for a verbal attack on Schober, and told him that Austria could hope for no financial help either from the American government or from American individuals 'unless these methods were dropped.'[50]

The American Ambassador consequently proposed that the Allies should give 'moral support' to a Schober government, if formed. The British High Commissioner – arguing that the Social Democrats' attempt to form a new Socialist International ruled out a renewal of the coalition – also recommended support for a 'neutral' government.[51] On 31 December 1920, after due thought, the British Foreign Secretary, Lord Curzon, told Lindley that he could inform Schober that in the opinion of His Majesty's Government a 'neutral' government would be 'the surest means of maintaining internal order and restoring Austria's credit and prosperity'.[52]

This first attempt by outside Powers to intervene in Austria's internal affairs did not succeed. The Austrian political parties were determined to have their say. Schober's chances of becoming Chancellor were blocked by the small but vigorous group of German Nationalists, who regarded him as a Habsburg bureaucrat of the old school, and therefore unacceptable. An interim government of Christian Socials and officials was left to struggle helplessly with a constantly worsening financial situation, made still more difficult by a renewed wave of agitation for an *Anschluss*, promoted and financed from Germany. This made the Western Allies even more reluctant to lend Austria money.

In June 1921, Schober at last became Chancellor, and the British and Americans got the 'neutral' government they wanted. Britain gave Schober backing by granting a £2 million credit in February 1922. But the Schober experiment did not last. Schober's conclusion of a treaty with Czechoslovakia enraged the German Nationalists. The Christian Socials did not want him to be able to claim success in restoring Austria's economy.

In May 1922, Schober was manoeuvred out of office, and succeeded by the strong man of the Christian Socials, Dr

Seipel, who thereafter dominated Austrian politics for the rest of the 1920s.

In Seipel – a prelate, a Jesuit, a powerful and cogent speaker who made a big impression in the League of Nations – the Western Allies at last felt that they had found a man whom they could regard as politically, and even more financially, reliable.

Seipel also knew how to exploit Austria's weakness to advantage, as also differences among the Allies. He proclaimed openly that the country was on the verge of economic collapse – thereby causing the currency to fall still more swiftly and stimulating rumours that the country was about to disintegrate. Then, by a sudden and somewhat mysterious round of visits to Berlin, Prague and Rome, in August 1922, he played on the fears of all concerned – fears of an *Anschluss*; fears that Austria was about to become a protectorate of Italy (which Czechoslovakia and Yugoslavia would have very much disliked); fears that Austria might draw closer to Czechoslovakia and Yugoslavia (which would have frustrated Italy's plans). The result was that Czechoslovakia strongly championed a loan to Austria and the other Allies, including Italy, followed suit: their national interests and aspirations might conflict, but in the last resort they had a common, if negative, interest in keeping Austria intact and in some sense independent.

Through a League of Nations Committee, agreement was reached on a £30 million loan to Austria, guaranteed by Britain, France, Italy and Czechoslovakia. These four governments promised to respect Austria's political independence, territorial integrity and sovereignty. Austria for its part reaffirmed Article 88 of the peace treaty and promised to abstain from any negotiations or agreement calculated directly or indirectly to compromise Austria's independence, and 'to refrain from granting to any State a special régime or exclusive advantages calculated to threaten this independence'.

This agreement, signed on 4 October 1922, became known as the Geneva Protocol. Financially, with the aid of Seipel's Recovery Programme, it succeeded rapidly in stabilising the currency and balancing the budget – though only at the cost of high unemployment and alternating periods of deceptive boom and more real economic stagnation.

Politically, the price which Austria had to pay was a reaffirmation, in stronger terms, of its peace treaty pledge not to unite with Germany. It was a price which many Austrians would have thought cheap, if solid and lasting economic prosperity had resulted. Unfortunately – mainly for reasons beyond Austria's control – it did not. The Western Allies seemed to have failed to provide Austria with a satisfactory basis for economic existence. It was then natural that Austrians should again be drawn, as if by a powerful magnetic force, to the belief that their economic problems could only be solved through union with Germany.

7 Class War and Private Armies

During the decade which followed the Geneva Protocol of 1922, bitter strife, verging on class warfare, grew up between the two big political parties, and private political armies mushroomed. Otto Bauer interpreted the 1922 Protocol as Western capitalism's move to replace the 'bourgeoisie' in power in Austria. There was some truth in this. But it may have been more significant that the Geneva Protocol coincided in time with Mussolini's March on Rome and coming to power in Italy. In the next year, Hitler won European attention by his abortive Munich coup, and from then on pursued his self-imposed role as prophet of the German people in its widest sense. Both Mussolini and Hitler used private armies as instruments for acquiring power and suppressing opponents. Moreover in Britain and France – the supposed watch-dogs of Austria's independence – there were influential admirers of Mussolini and Hitler. The European atmosphere of the decade was therefore one in which class warfare and private armies seemed quite respectable.

The bitter, dogmatic antagonism between the Christian Socials and Social Democrats also stemmed from the leading personalities on the two sides, each lacking the tolerance, pragmatism and willingness for compromise usually thought to be typically Austrian.

On the one side, Seipel dominated the Christian Socials, either as Chancellor or as the power behind lesser Chancellors such as Ramek, Streeruwitz, Schober and Vaugoin. A diabetic with an iron will, Seipel believed passionately in the historical role of the Catholic Church and saw the

Social Democrats as the Church's enemies. As Renner remarked, 'he took the utterances of the party's left-wingers as the literal expression of its general policies, regardless of the way in which the party behaved in action'.[53] He therefore saw it as his mission to clean up 'the revolutionary garbage'.

Seipel was also a man who liked to act in an authoritarian and secret way, often failing to consult his own party supporters, let alone the opposition Social Democrats. He was a complex character. One of his much younger admirers, Josef Klaus, later Chancellor, wrote of Seipel's sphinx-like sayings, adding that from behind his eagle's head there sometimes looked out a cunning fox, and that within his political archangel's form, Mephistopheles had his hidden place.[54]

Seipel was therefore a man who did not seek compromise, but the conquest of his enemies. Renner believed him to be moved by unforgiving hatred.[55] To achieve victory over the Social Democrats he placed most reliance on the backing of the big industrialists and financiers, also embracing the pro-Habsburg legitimists and the old aristocracy, and welcoming the German Nationalists as allies; that is, he aimed to bring all elements into a 'bourgeois bloc'. His respect for parliamentary democracy as enshrined in the 1920 republican constitution was limited. Renner claimed that for a long time Seipel avoided using the world 'republic'.[56]

On the other side, Otto Bauer thought and spoke in terms of Marxist theory, and liked to feel that he had led one revolution – the Austrian 'revolution' of 1918. But he had to admit that in the 1920s the task of the working class was 'limited to defending the achievements of this revolution' and endeavouring to restore the balance of power between the classes 'which had been upset by the Geneva Protocol'.[57] Yet, perhaps just because this aim was so non-revolutionary, Bauer was anxious to avoid the charge of willingness to work inside the capitalist system or of compromising with 'bourgeois' parties. He therefore clung tightly to the purity of an opposition role, and so found himself in the rather illogical position of arguing that a parliamentary democracy could best be defended by refusing to share the responsibility of power.

It may be that simply because both Seipel and Bauer had taken up such rigid political postures, there was a certain understanding between them. Seipel once remarked that he could get on well with Bauer in private encounters, but had no contact with Renner. Renner, to whom he made this remark, replied: 'The explanation is simple. Both of you . . . are filled with the idea of class war. And there is doubtless truth in it. But you both exaggerate the idea, and that does not do for me.'[58]

The atmosphere of class war thickened rapidly. Seipel's Recovery Programme, following the Geneva Protocol, demanded sacrifices all round, but these soon fell heavily on the workers, who were all the more bitter because in 1919 and 1920 they had experienced a real improvement in living standards. They felt they were being robbed of their gains.

The middle classes and the country people, on their side, increasingly resented the workers' determination to preserve and extend their 'achievements', and took fright at all the talk of class war – all the more because the Christian Social leaders deliberately lumped the Social Democrats and the (virtually non-existent) Communists together as though there were no difference between them.

In particular, the middle class and the western Lands resented 'Red Vienna', a striking and successful experiment in Socialist municipal administration, admired outside Austria, which the 'bourgeois' government could not check. This was because under the 1920 constitution, Vienna had become a Land, on a level with the existing seven 'hereditary Lands' of the Habsburg era; and as a result of Christian Social pressure and against Social Democratic wishes, the Lands had been given wide financial powers. When the Social Democrats found

themselves out of power in Parliament but in control of
Vienna, they knew how to exploit the situation.

The Vienna city government, and in particular the
financial councillor, Dr Hugo Breitner, put through an
ambitious programme of re-housing workers' families in
big new blocks of flats, and building schools and a wide
range of social amenities. Since three-tenths of Austria's
population and a very much greater proportion of the
country's wealth were concentrated in Vienna, heavy taxes
imposed on the well-off people of the city could finance
this programme.

All this seemed a Socialist provocation to the bulk of the
middle class – as also to the Catholic Church. The Christian
Social government could not stop 'Red Vienna' from
building a crematorium, regarded by the Church as an
offence: it was reduced to trying, ineffectively, to prevent
the cremation of the first corpse.[59]

There were other reasons for middle-class fear of the
Social Democrats. One was the great efficiency and com-
prehensiveness of the party's organisation, ensuring a
surprising degree of loyalty and discipline among members; there was nothing comparable in the 'bourgeois'
parties. More important still, in parliamentary elections,
the Social Democrats showed no signs of losing ground:
from a low point of 35 per cent of the votes in 1920 they
rose to 39 per cent in 1923 and 42 per cent in 1927, with a
very small drop to 41 per cent in 1930. They therefore
appeared to their opponents as a very large, compact
minority which, given social trends, might well eventually
achieve an absolute majority – or, as the Social Democrats
themselves put it in their Linz Programme of 1927,
'conquer State power by means of the universal franchise'.

In these circumstances it was not surprising that party
strife, with its overtones of class war, was not kept inside
the parliamentary framework but was also waged by other
means.

The private armies owed their origins, not to the party

struggle, but to the chaotic situation in the Lands, especially along the southern frontier, after the collapse of the Habsburg Empire. As Austrian soldiers made their way home from the front, many kept their weapons or sold them privately; in any case there had always been many guns in private hands, especially in Tirol. In the months after the collapse, armed bands sprang up spontaneously, to keep order, protect property and above all to guard the threatened frontiers, especially in Carinthia and Styria. In the early days, Social Democrats sometimes belonged to the armed bands; but soon the 'Home Defence' groups – the Heimwehr or Heimatschutz – became predominantly conservative and anti-socialist.

Throughout 1920, the Allied Powers were trying to get successive Austrian governments to disarm the private formations and collect the arms. In January 1920 the British High Commissioner reported: 'what makes the situation particularly precarious is the fact that . . . there are . . . large depots of arms insecurely guarded as well as many arms in the hands of workmen and peasants . . .'[60] In February the Conference of Ambassadors in Paris endorsed the British view that it was 'urgently necessary to proceed to the disarmament of the civil population of Austria and to the seizure of secret stores of arms'.[61]

In July 1920, the British High Commissioner was approached by 'a certain Baron Hausner', who said he was preparing an organisation, 'to be armed at the proper time', on behalf of the Christian Socials. The High Commissioner warned the Baron of the danger of civil war: 'the organisation of forces by private enterprise was a dangerous undertaking and might lead to a disaster'.[62] It seems likely that the Baron was hoping to get arms with the help of the Right-wing Hungarian government of Admiral Horthy: according to Hungarian documents, Seipel had a secret talk with the Hungarian Minister in Vienna in March 1920 and told him that when the Christian Socials came to power they would need support, and asked for financial aid in arming the Heimwehr for this purpose.[63]

Seipel's reason for such a move must have been the existence of the Volkswehr – the army created by the Social Democrats and dominated by them. Soon after, however, the Volkswehr was replaced, as the official Austrian army, by the Bundeswehr, or Federal Army. Many of its officers were sympathetic to the Heimwehr, who could in some places help themselves to arms from army depots.[64] By 1923 there were Heimwehr groups in Upper and Lower Austria and Burgenland as well as Tirol, Carinthia and Styria.

As a counter-move, in April 1923 the Social Democrats' private army, the Republican Schutzbund, or Defence League, was officially established. It got arms from the Arsenal in Vienna, which was for a long time under Social Democratic control. Arms were often kept in the Workers' Centres – the Arbeiterheime.[65] Its chief organisers were Julius Deutsch and a professional soldier from the Habsburg era, Theodor Körner.

After Seipel became Chancellor, he must soon have realised that he did not need the arms of the Heimwehr to defend him against the Social Democrats. But he did nothing to curb the Heimwehr. So, with two rival private armies – Heimwehr and Republican Schutzbund – conducting rival marches, direct clashes seemed inevitable. In January 1927, a clash occurred in Schattendorf, in Burgenland: two workers were killed. When in the following July the news broke in Vienna that the men accused of the killing had been acquitted, there was enormous indignation among the workers, and a great spontaneous demonstration took place outside the Palace of Justice, which was set on fire. The Republican Schutzbund could not be mobilised in time to keep control of the demonstrators, as it often did. The Social Democratic Burgomaster of Vienna, Dr Seitz, appearing on a fire-engine, tried personally to appeal for restraint, as did other leading Social Democrats, without success. Mounted police intervened, shots were fired, and in the resulting rioting many were killed. Of the eighty-four dead, four were policemen; there were five hundred injured. The memory of this day left a wound which was slow to heal.

While the fighting was still going on, the Social Democrat leaders demanded Seipel's resignation, which, naturally enough, he refused. They were then faced with demands from militants that the Schutzbund should be issued with arms and put into action. But the Social Democrat leaders, apparently fearing that the resulting civil war would lead to the occupation of Austria by foreign powers,[66] decided against this course. Instead, to canalise the workers' feelings, they called a one-day general strike, to be followed by a transport strike of indefinite duration. Seipel stood firm and the strike petered out.

During the crisis, the government had mobilised the Heimwehr in the Lands. In Styria, and also elsewhere, the Heimwehr forced workers to call off the strike; it also set about forming workers' groups to act as strike-breakers. The Industrialists' Association was said to have given 50,000 schillings to help equip the Styrian groups.[67] In 1928 the Heimwehr group in Vienna gave as its first aim, on its enlistment forms, 'the protection of national industry' – a clear enough indication of where its money came from. In addition, German heavy industry, decreasingly, and Italy, increasingly, supplied money and arms to the Heimwehr.

The dream of a 'march on Vienna' – to match Mussolini's 'March on Rome' in 1922 – became a Heimwehr slogan, and in 1929 was coupled with proclamations of a fight to the finish against the Social Democrats. However, Schober, from his stronghold as Police President, declared that the government forces would be capable of defeating any attempt to seize power; the Heimwehr then said that its proposed 'march on Vienna' was meant only in a spiritual sense.[68]

Around this time the power of Seipel was beginning to wane, and the Christian Socials made no very serious effort to check Heimwehr excesses. In May 1930, at Korneuburg, the Heimwehr leaders went a step further and proclaimed that they accepted the principles of Fascism and rejected Western democracy and the existing form of the Austrian state; they declared that they aimed to seize power and bound themselves by an oath. Confusion followed inside the Heimwehr itself and among the 'bourgeois' parties, some of whose members also belonged to the Heimwehr. In the event, the Heimwehr did not attempt a coup and the government did not take action against it, but, instead, instituted a more intensive search for the arms of the Social Democratic Schutzbund.

About this time the Heimwehr claimed to have 400,000 armed men. The true figure was certainly far lower, and many of its members were peasants who would not operate away from home. There were probably not more than 30,000 who could count as a fighting force. This was around the same size as the Schutzbund's fighting force – the kernel of its very much larger total membership.[69]

The greatest weakness of the Heimwehr was that it had far too many leaders each wanting to be cock of his own particular dung-hill. Even Prince Starhemberg, who became the national leader, never fully established his authority, and in the 1930s was at loggerheads with the Vienna leader, Major Fey. Moreover, the organisation's political colour varied greatly from Land to Land; some local leaders were close to the Nazis, others to the Italians. It thus never became a really serious political force. When it tried to fight in the 1930 elections, Starhemberg's 'Heimatblock' won only 6 per cent of the votes, even though by that time Starhemberg had been brought into the government as Minister of the Interior.

While from 1930 onwards the Heimwehr was, on its own showing, a fascist-type movement, it lacked the 'dynamic' leader, strict discipline, organisational unity, demagogic appeal – and, usually, the ruthlessness and savagery – of a truly fascist organisation. Hatred of the Social Democrats was the only drive which united its members – and even that not very effectively.

The Heimwehr's real function, up till 1932, was to serve the Christian Socials and their 'bourgeois' allies as a deterrent, a threat and an instrument of pressure against the Social Democrats. It was the extra-parliamentary factor which could be used to counter the solid and growing parliamentary strength of the Social Democrats, which could not be matched by the increasingly fragmented 'bourgeois block' created by Seipel. The Christian Socials, who had won 49 per cent of the votes in the 1927 election, dropped back to 36 per cent in 1930; the Social Democrats, with 72 seats, formed the strongest solid block in Parliament, even though they could not form a government.

Seipel never, it seems, thought seriously of disarming the Heimwehr. Nor did the Western democracies ever seriously press him to do so. Renner wrote that Otto Bauer and Julius Deutsch made genuine proposals for disarmament of both the Heimwehr and the Schutzbund, but that Seipel saw these as signs of weakness.[70] In 1928 Seipel called an interparty conference on disarmament; the Social Democrats proposed disarmament without conditions, but Seipel said that the parties must first bring about 'conditions such as to make disarmament possible'. Until he could be sure that no one need any longer fear the Social Democrats, there could, he said, be no peace or disarmament in Austria. The only outcome was a yet more vigorous search for the Schutzbund's arms.

At the beginning of the 1930s, the rise of Hitler and the accompanying upsurge of Nazi activity cast a lengthening shadow over the little Austrian struggle of the classes and their private armies. But at first neither side seemed to see how great was the danger to them both.

8 The Austrian–German Customs Union and the Western Veto, 1931

During 1931, Austria was the centre of a minor European crisis. Again, as in 1922, the West European Powers intervened; again, the root cause was Austria's economic weakness.

From 1929 on, the world economic crisis hit Europe and resulted in a general rush to raise barriers to international trade. Austria, heavily dependent on foreign trade, was particularly hard hit. The League of Nations' efforts to lower barriers through a world economic conference were not successful. Then, in May 1930, the French Foreign Minister, Aristide Briand, launched his daring plan for a European federation, inspired politically by the ideas of the singular Austrian, Count Richard Coudenhove-Kalergi, a dedicated, life-long champion of European unity, who had launched his Pan-European Union in 1924, had won Briand's support, and had persuaded him to preside at its first congress in Vienna two years later.[71] The Briand plan of 1930 was, however, also intended to solve Europe's economic problems. Britain was lukewarm, for imperial and other reasons; Germany and Italy wanted first priority given to disarmament. But the League set up a special committee to study the Briand plan.

These wider factors combined with local factors in Germany and Austria to spark off the crisis. In the German election of September 1930, Hitler's National Socialists had an unexpected success and emerged as the second strongest party. In the Austrian election of November 1930 the Christian Socials suffered an unexpected reverse; this resulted in disarray inside the Christian Social party and a weak government which Seipel refused to join. Both the German and Austrian governments therefore felt the need for some success in foreign policy. In Germany the Chancellor, Heinrich Brüning, felt it particularly keenly. The outstanding Foreign Minister, Gustav Stresemann, who had worked for conciliation with the West, had died, and had been succeeded by a lesser man, Julius Curtius. His Foreign Ministry advisers believed that of all the possible moves which could provide Brüning with the success he wanted, the establishment of closer ties with Austria would be the least likely to come up against insuperable opposition from the West.[72] It would of course also enable Brüning to steal some of the Nazis' thunder.

On the Austrian side, a plan for a special economic relationship with Germany had been worked out as early as 1926 by Richard Riedel, then Minister in Berlin, together with some Austrian industrialists. In September 1930 it was taken up in secret talks between the Austrian Foreign Minister, Schober, and Curtius, who believed that they could disarm opposition by setting it in the framework of Briand's project for a European federation. In March 1931 Curtius visited Vienna and the two Foreign Ministers agreed on a joint recommendation to the two governments. But, because of differing views over timing and a disastrous leak in the leading Vienna newspaper, the *Neue Freie Presse*, they failed to make the essential preliminary soundings with the Western Powers and Italy.

France, extremely sensitive about anything that smacked of the *Anschluss*, reacted immediately to the leak, proposing a *démarche* in Vienna by the governments which had signed the 1922 Geneva Protocol, France, Britain, Italy and Czechoslovakia.[73] Briand was particularly angered by the Austrian-German move because his European project and his policy of reconciliation with Germany were already highly unpopular with the more nationalist-minded French politicians.

The British reacted cautiously, anxious to avoid unpleasantness. When the Austrian Minister called at the Foreign Office to present documents on the projected Austrian-German agreement, on 21 March, he was mildly warned against presenting Britain with a *fait accompli.*

The documents, although they sought to present the plan as a purely economic regional arrangement which would in no way infringe the full political independence of both parties, did make it clear that import and export duties between the two countries were to be abolished, along with all 'import, export or transit prohibitions'. On the face of it, this seemed in fairly clear contradiction to the 1922 Geneva Protocol. Briand told the German Ambassador in Paris that the proposed agreement constituted a real customs union, foreshadowing the *Anschluss*; it would alienate Austria's independence in the economic field. Briand added that his own proposal on European federal union had been meant to apply in the framework of Europe as a whole. Moreover, he added, the secrecy of the Austrian-German negotiations showed their tendentious character.[74]

The German Ambassador in London, Freiherr von Neurath (later Hitler's Foreign Minister) met with rather softer reproaches: the interested parties should have been consulted sooner; 'in many quarters', the plan had been interpreted as a prelude to the *Anschluss*, 'a subject which it was well known could not be touched'. To this von Neurath replied that he hoped there would be no question of an *Anschluss*: '90 per cent of the German political world was against it, and the only result would be that more Socialists and Catholics would be elected to the Reichstag, and these were already as strongly represented as the average German desired'.[75]

Throughout, the British let it be seen that they objected

to the plan much less strongly than the French, but that they intended to back the French, and in particular Briand himself. The Labour Foreign Secretary, Arthur Henderson, instructed the British representatives in Berlin and Vienna to make it clear to the government concerned that 'the position of M. Briand has become one of great difficulty, and the influence which he has only at great trouble been able to exercise for many years past in controlling more extreme tendencies among his own countrymen will be unquestionably affected'. Henderson therefore proposed that the League of Nations Council, under whose auspices the 1922 Geneva Protocol had been negotiated, should be given the opportunity to examine the plan before the two governments went any further.[76]

At this point, Austria and Germany split. In Vienna, Schober was in a hurry to retreat: he told the British Minister that his hand had been forced by the Germans who had insisted on early publication. As for the plan itself, he attributed it to the German side; he said that 'no Austrian government could have resisted the German offer'. In Berlin, Brüning took a tough line; he told the British Ambassador on 25 March that the agreement was 'entirely within the framework of the Geneva Protocol'; there was no reason why the League Council should take it up; and the negotiations must 'naturally' take their course. The Ambassador reported that Brüning's language was that of 'suppressed bitterness'.[77] In Vienna, Schober told the British Minister that the Germans had wanted him to make an equally strong response, but he had refused.

Briand seemed ready to believe that the Austrians were innocent and the Germans the responsible party, and Arthur Henderson was willing to agree with him about the 'clumsiness of the German action'.[78] But from the British Ambassador in Berlin came pleas that Brüning should not be unduly embarrassed, and warnings against impairing his prestige: 'this is the first time that Germany has asserted herself in an important matter'.[79] But the British thought it more important to back up Briand, so that his policy of conciliation should not be wrecked. On 30 March Henderson told the House of Commons that he intended to raise the proposed Austrian-German agreement at the next League Council meeting; he earnestly hoped that the Austrians and Germans would do nothing before then to 'prejudice the friendly atmosphere'.[80]

The Austrians were in no position to defy the Western Powers, since they were hoping to negotiate further loans, though they did not want to offend the Germans. Schober was quite ready to agree with the British Minister that 'the main thing was to save the face of the German Chancellor and of the French Minister of Foreign Affairs'.[81] By 8 April he had given a promise to the French Minister not to begin negotiations with Germany before the League Council met. In view of the Austrian attitude, there was little that the German government could do, except try to avoid a public climb-down. Mussolini stood somewhat apart, but on 4 May the Italian Ambassador in London said his government was most anxious to cooperate with the British in the matter.

The League Council met and on 18 May, on Henderson's proposal, asked the International Court of Justice to give a ruling on the compatibility of the proposed Austrian-German agreement with the 1922 Geneva Protocol. Briand and the Italian Foreign Minister supported the proposal. The danger remained, however, that the Court might rule in favour of the agreement, and in this case the French would refuse to accept the ruling as final. The French Ambassador in London said his government was determined to oppose the plan, which it saw as a preface to the Anschluss and calculated to disturb European peace.[82]

However, this danger was quickly removed. At the beginning of June, the news broke that the Creditanstalt, the prominent Vienna bank which financed the Savings Bank and much of Austrian industry, had crashed. This was bound to have serious repercussions not only in Austria but in the neighbouring states which had formerly belonged to the Habsburg Empire, and beyond. The Governor of the Bank of England was reported to have said: 'South-East Europe has gone up in flames'.[83]

This event wrecked the proposed Austrian-German customs union once and for all. In order to save the currency, Austria urgently needed foreign credits, in the first place from France. The French, however, set conditions, in particular, the renunciation of the customs union plan.[84] The Bank of England provided a short-term credit of £2 million, to tide things over; the Austrian Social Democrats could claim some responsibility for this, since they were on good terms with the British Labour government of Ramsay MacDonald. But the good will of the League, and above all of France, were needed for long-term financial aid.

So the French got their way. On 3 September – *before* the International Court had spoken – Austria and Germany publicly announced that in view of 'economic developments' throughout Europe, they had decided not to pursue the customs union plan. Two days later the Court declared its opinion that the plan was incompatible with the 1922 Protocol. The votes had been 8 to 7; the British member of the Court voted with the minority.

This was the last time when the West European Powers intervened effectively in Austrian-German relations. In July 1932, in what became known as the Lausanne Protocol, Britain, France, Italy and Belgium guaranteed a large loan to Austria, to enable it to restore the national finances and settle the Creditanstalt affair; in return, Austria reaffirmed the 1922 Geneva Protocol banning the *Anschluss*.[85] But once Hitler came to power, the diplomatic and financial pressures which had been decisive in 1922 and 1931 no longer worked.

The crisis of the summer of 1931 also produced a belated effort – the last – to restore a Christian Social–Social Democrat coalition in Austria. In the turmoil which followed the Creditanstalt crash, the ailing Seipel – who had already lost much of his power – made a move to form a coalition in which Otto Bauer would be Vice-Chancellor and other Social Democrats would be included. The Social Democrats, Renner among them, gave an evasively negative answer: they were not against a coalition in principle, but wanted assurances of good behaviour by the 'bourgeois parties'; failing such assurances, conditions for their entry into the government did not exist. The main stumbling-block for the Social Democrats was Seipel's apparent intention to give government posts to the Heimwehr's parliamentary group, the Heimatblock, which had only eight seats in parliament against the Social Democrats' seventy-two.

The abortive negotiations of June 1931 marked the end of the Seipel era, and also the Social Democrats' last chance, in the First Republic, to share the responsibility of power.

9 Dollfuss: Fascist or Austrian Patriot?

The man who signed the Lausanne Protocol for Austria was Dr Engelbert Dollfuss. He had entered the government in March 1931 as Minister of Agriculture, and as its youngest member, aged 38. Of Lower Austrian farming stock, he studied economics in Berlin, made his name as an agricultural expert, and became secretary of the Lower Austrian Peasant-farmers' Federation. He had little experience of parliamentary politics. It is not clear why he was chosen as Chancellor in May 1932, in succession to Karl Buresch, who had failed to clear up the mess created by the customs union fiasco, the the Creditanstalt crash, and the unending feuding and trouble-making of the Heimwehr.

Perhaps Dollfuss, although a Christian Social, seemed a new kind of man, right for the times. Renner remarked that at this point the older politicians, who had experienced parliamentary life under the Habsburgs, and who believed in the merits of the parliamentary system and were skilled in its inevitable compromises and make-shifts, were leaving the centre of the stage; their place was being taken by younger men who had served at the front in the 1914–18 war, and who believed in action, authority and discipline and were impatient with party politics.[86]

Dollfuss fitted into this category. He had volunteered for war service, was at first rejected (possibly because he had the physical stature of a young boy), thereafter accepted, and had an honourable war record, becoming a

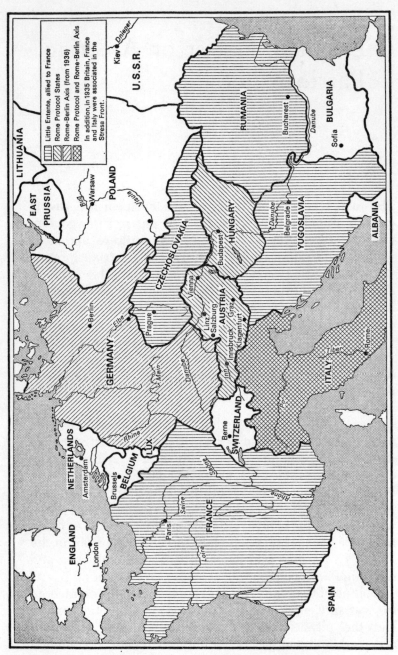

Map 1   Europe in 1934–8

first lieutenant. He was a devout Catholic who, after a brief connexion in 1920–1 with the Social Democrats, had naturally gravitated to the Christian Socials. He was obviously extremely ambitious. He liked to think in very simple clear-cut terms; Renner's word was 'simplistic'. Temperamentally, he was optimistic. He could exercise a boyish charm. He had considerable physical and moral courage.

This he certainly needed. Already in 1932, Hitler was casting a long shadow over Austria, where the National Socialists, after their failure in the 1930 national election, scored a success in the Vienna city elections in April 1932, winning fifteen seats – only four less than the Christian Socials, who lost badly. (The Social Democrats, gaining one seat, continued to dominate Vienna with 66 out of 100 seats.) This made it obvious to Dollfuss that he could not hope to govern with only the Christian Socials and their more reputable allies for support. So he turned to the Heimwehr. Its leaders were willing to back him, but only in the hope that this would be a first step towards setting up a Heimwehr State. Dollfuss, however, had no intention of letting the Heimwehr take over; he intended to keep power in his own hands.

First, however, he had to deal with the old political parties and with parliament. After forming a coalition government in which the Heimwehr were given three posts, Dollfuss had a majority in parliament of only one. There was a long parliamentary struggle over the Lausanne Protocol; partly because the Social Democrats did not want to press him too hard, Dollfuss survived this and later challenges. But on 4 March 1933, Otto Bauer offered Dollfuss an unexpected chance to get rid of parliament, which he promptly seized. In a debate affecting railway-men's interests, and in order to deprive Dollfuss of his majority of one, Bauer instructed Renner[87] to resign his position as Speaker so as to become free to vote against the government. But Bauer's plan misfired: Renner's move was rapidly followed by the two deputy Speakers, a Christian Social and a German Nationalist, and parliament was left without a Speaker. Dollfuss thereupon declared parliament incapable of functioning and prevented it from reassembling by barring access to the parliament building. He was now free to move towards an authoritarian, Christian, corporative system in which he hoped to have untrammelled power.

On the day after the parliamentary debacle in Austria, Hitler won sufficient seats in the German parliament to consolidate his absolute power. This was inevitably a signal for an outburst of Nazi agitation and violence in Austria, with virtually open German backing.

Yet Dollfuss, with his inborn optimism, thought he could fight a two-front political battle at home and ride two horses in his foreign policy. He set out to curb and ultimately suppress the Social Democrats on one side, and to keep the Austrian Nazis at bay on the other. On 31 March 1933 he dissolved the Social Democrats' Republican Schutzbund and instituted systematic seizure of its weapons. In July, following mounting Nazi terror acts backed by a propaganda barrage from Munich radio, he banned the Nazi Party. Both these moves were less drastic than they sounded; both organisations continued to exist 'illegally' without very much difficulty, though the Schutzbund was both weakened and infuriated by the arms searches.

By this two-front war at home, Dollfuss turned his back on those Austrians who might have given him the most reliable support against the Nazis – the Social Democrats. Loyal to Bauer's line, they had been pro-*Anschluss* in principle until 1933; but now Hitler was savagely oppressing the German Social Democrats, and union with Nazi Germany was out of the question for them. From time to time, therefore, even as late as December 1933, they sought contacts with Dollfuss with the aim of striking a bargain with him. Dollfuss kept the Social Democrats dangling but never seriously tried to negotiate with them.

His attitude towards the Nazis, and to Hitler, was more complex. Like his successor, Kurt von Schuschnigg, he had been a member of the C.V. – the Cartellverband, a German Catholic students' organisation which operated in the German Reich, Austria, and the Sudeten areas of Czechoslovakia, and which sought to inspire not only devout Catholicism but also a fervent, high-minded sort of German patriotism. (It also had a reputation for placing its members in important and influential positions.) Dollfuss therefore had a feeling of devotion to 'Germany' in the abstract. But he was determined not to let the Nazis come to power in Austria, and liked to believe that at some point Hitler might be brought to see reason and to tell the Austrian Nazis to behave themselves.

In the short term however – even though he wanted to keep open the option of coming to terms with Hitler – he was determined to stand up to him, and to oppose his intervention in Austrian affairs. He expelled Hitler's Reich Commissioner for Justice and Nazi propagandist, Hans Frank, from Austria in May 1933, and so provoked Hitler into imposing a tax of 1000 German Marks on every German wishing to visit Austria, which hit the Austrian tourist trade very badly.

Dollfuss was not quite so optimistic as to think he could make Hitler see reason single-handed. From the moment of his first meeting with Mussolini in Rome in April 1933, he believed he had found his natural ally and protector. According to the account given to the British Minister in Vienna, Mussolini 'showed himself most sympathetic and promised cordial support'; he did not conceal that he 'strongly deplored' the trend of events in Germany, but he hoped gradually to induce Germany to be more reasonable. Mussolini said he was whole-heartedly against the *Anschluss* and wanted Austria to remain independent.[88]

Mussolini must also have urged Dollfuss to move

towards creating a fascist-type regime. On his return home, Dollfuss took the first step to meet Italian wishes, in so far as they chimed with his own. On 21 May, he set up his authoritarian, patriotic, Catholic movement, the Fatherland Front (V.F.) at a big ceremony at Schönbrunn, the former imperial palace. Starhemberg publicly associated the Heimwehr with the new Front, but the exact relationship between the two remained obscure.

Dolfuss also set out to create a specifically 'Austrian' ideology, to drive out National Socialism on the one side and Social Democracy on the other.

Austria has a European mission [he said in May 1933]. Lying in the heart of the Continent, Austria is the predestined intermediary between the all-German culture, of which for centuries the Austrian people were the oldest and most distinguished bearers, and the other nations . . . Austria, this small but honourable German Danubian and Alpine land in the heart of Europe, has for centuries taken a creative part in world events . . . Vienna was for more than half a thousand years the symbolic city of the Germans, of the all-German Emperor . . . We will be true to the inheritance of our forefathers. . . .[89]

This nostalgic appeal to Austrian pride, like the Fatherland Front itself, had, at a time of tension and economic distress, only a strictly limited impact.

The Western democracies, Britain and France, were amicably disposed towards Dollfuss but, like him, were inclined to look to Mussolini to check Hitler over Austria. Renner later harshly condemned the idea of making Mussolini Europe's gendarme. At the time it seemed reasonable to hope that Austria would at least be a bone of contention between the two dictators, and that the *Anschluss* would be the one thing that Mussolini would not swallow.

In Britain, Dollfuss appealed to sentimental and sporting

instincts; he and his country were both so small, and he was standing up to the big bully, Hitler. However, his harshness towards the Social Democrats was an embarrassment. Britain still had the former Labour leader, Ramsay MacDonald, as Prime Minister, even if the government was predominantly Conservative. In the Spring of 1933, the British Minister in Vienna offered polite advice that Dollfuss should not let himself be persuaded by the Heimwehr to take 'too extreme measures against the Socialist Municipality' [Vienna].[90]

In June 1933 Dollfuss visited London. He was welcomed by the government and the press, and thanked the Foreign Secretary, Sir John Simon, for the kindness and encouragement he had received.[91] However, an 'Agreement of Understanding and Cooperation' between Britain, France, Germany and Italy had just been concluded and this made Britain reluctant to make any firm move to restrain Hitler over Austria. Dollfuss drew his own conclusions. He went to Italy for a second meeting with Mussolini.

A forthright exposition of Dollfuss's views at this time was given to the British Foreign Office by the League of Nations representative in Austria, Rost van Tonningen (later a leading Dutch Nazi) who had clearly been briefed by Dollfuss himself. Dollfuss could not accept British advice that he should reach a working arrangement with the Social Democrats: his whole strength was based on the peasants, who expected him to 'defend their interests against those of the Socialist population of Vienna, from whom they had suffered grievous wrongs during the last 15 years'. In Dollfuss's view the Austrian Socialists were near-Communists, very different from the British Labour Party; an arrangement with an 'extremist' like Otto Bauer would be 'an extremely difficult and dangerous procedure'. Also, it would be 'very unpalatable' for any Austrian government to burn its bridges with Germany: in spite of the present bitter quarrel, 'every Austrian considers it essential that neighbourly relations should be re-established

at some time. . .' And the only common platform on which
the German Nazis and Dollfuss might one day agree was
a common front against Socialism.

As for the Western democracies, Rost van Tonningen
said, Dollfuss felt that Britain, though sympathetic, was
far away. France was 'unreliable and too flagrantly anti-
German'. Dollfuss therefore felt compelled to rely almost
entirely on Italy; and Mussolini might stop supporting him
if he came to terms with the Austrian Social Democrats.[92]

In this Dollfuss was right. Mussolini was quite determined that the Social Democrats should be suppressed. In
a letter to Dollfuss on 1 July, Mussolini urged him to carry
through at once a programme of basic internal reforms 'in
the decisive Fascist sense'. The Social Democrats, Mussolini admitted, were not a danger to the regime, but if
Dollfuss did not use the anti-Marxist weapon, he would
allow the Nazis to come as saviours from Bolshevism. So
he must strike a blow at the Social Democrats in their
stronghold, Vienna, and extend the purge to all the
country.[93]

Mussolini also had a special reason for bearing a grudge
against the Austrian Social Democrats. In January 1933
Austrian railwaymen had revealed, through the Social
Democratic Party newspaper, that arms from Italy were
being sent to an Austrian arms factory at Hirtenberg for
reconditioning, mainly for the Heimwehr. It later emerged
that the deal had been arranged between Mussolini and
Starhemberg. The revelation caused a big stir in the Little
Entente countries – Czechoslovakia, Yugoslavia and
Rumania – especially since some of the arms were supposed to be going on to Hungary; this had led the Western
Powers to make representations in Vienna, on the grounds
that the Austrian peace treaty was being violated. The
affair had placed Mussolini in a rather embarrassing and
undignified position, though the Western Powers had
smoothed it over quickly.

Dollfuss gave the appearance of being ready to do what

Mussolini wanted. In a letter to Mussolini of 22 July, he spoke of removing 'the rubbish accumulated under the Republic', adding: 'we are determined . . . to drive the Marxists from the positions of power which they hold as soon as the situation permits.'[94]

It was easier for Mussolini to tell Dollfuss what to do to the Social Democrats than it was to tell him how to deal with Hitler. By midsummer 1933, inflammatory broadcasts from Munich were being reinforced by leaflet-dropping over Austria by aircraft from Germany and there was an alarming rise in terrorist acts inside Austria. By July, the Austrian Nazis assumed that Dollfuss was sufficiently softened up and asked for two seats in the government. Dollfuss refused, thereby infuriating them.[95] In the following month, reports of a planned *putsch* by Austrian Nazis, to be backed up by an incursion from Germany, caused agitation in European capitals. The British thought that they, the French and the Italians should jointly make representations in Berlin to stop Hitler – always within the framework of the four-power 'Understanding'.

The French were willing, but Mussolini was determined to act separately, relying on his 'special position' in relation to Hitler because of the 'affinities' between Fascism and National Socialism. Mussolini also argued that the Germans were 'not in a normal state of mind but far from it', and joint representations would make them 'quite intractable'.[96] He therefore made a 'strong private and confidential representation' at the end of July. In response, the German government said that it would *try* to prevent incursions into Austria by aircraft and to check radio propaganda by tightening censorship. British and French representations then seemed superfluous.

The Germans obviously did not *try* very hard. In August the British Foreign Office began to think that further action might be needed, and put forward a suggestion that Britain might eventually have to raise the Austrian problem in the League of Nations, which 'could and presumably would lead at least to the application of economic pressure' on Germany.[97] The British Cabinet discussed the suggestion on 5 September and took fright: 'no definite decisions were taken; the general view was that, if it were decided that we must take some initiative, we should not be drawn in the direction of referring the question to the League'. It therefore remained British policy to rely on Mussolini to guarantee Hitler's good behaviour.[98]

When Mussolini met Dollfuss for the third time at Riccione in late August, he again urged that Austria should be turned into a fully Fascist state. There shoud be a new constitution and a single national front; the Heimwehr leaders should be in the government which should be markedly dictatorial; there should be a government commissioner for Vienna (that is, the Social Democrats should be evicted). Dollfuss, according to his own account of the meeting, evaded any undertaking about greater power for the Heimwehr; he did not record Mussolini's pressure for action against the Social Democrats nor his own response.[99]

So far as the move towards Fascism was concerned, Dollfuss was willing to go a long way to meet Mussolini. Already on 21 August, the British Legation in Vienna commented: 'Dollfuss must be considered as Fascist linked for the time being with Italy . . . Austria would appear to have avoided Nazi domination by accepting Fascism.'[100] Great celebrations were being held in Vienna to celebrate the 250th anniversary of the defeat of the Turks at the city's gates. Dollfuss deliberately used these to try to arouse Austrian patriotic feeling. On 11 September – a date previously agreed with Mussolini – Dollfuss made a speech at the Trabrennplatz in Vienna to give a public launching to his new Fatherland Front, the infant V.F. He attacked materialism, 'godless Marxism', and 'so-called democracy'. The era of Marxist misrule and party rule was over; there was to be a 'social, Christian, German State of Austria, on a corporative basis, under strong authoritarian leadership'. The Fatherland Front was to be a great patriotic movement, vanquishing the 'party State'. 'Austria, awake!' Dollfuss proclaimed. Later he rode on horseback in uniform at the head of armed formations marching along the Ring Road, to the sound of military music.

To the Heimwehr, it probably seemed that Dollfuss was getting too much of the limelight, even though he had paid tribute to Starhemberg as descendant of the man who had defended Vienna 250 years earlier. At a Heimwehr demonstration outside the Vienna Town Hall – the seat of the Social Democratic city government – Starhemberg proclaimed that it would soon be conquered and that the head of the Jew Breitner (whose name was linked with the big city housing programme) would soon roll in the dust. Dollfuss placated the Heimwehr while trying to keep control in his own hands: he re-formed the government on 21 September, getting rid of some of his old political allies and giving more power to Heimwehr, but taking five cabinet posts for himself. He was also skilled in exploiting differences among the Heimwehr leaders, especially between Starhemberg, the national leader, and Major Fey, the Vienna leader. Starhemberg, who had long been in contact with Mussolini, was by now firmly anti-Nazi; Fey's attitude to the Nazis was less clear.

Dollfuss still hoped to keep the sympathy of the Western democracies. Two weeks after the Trabrennplatz speech he saw Sir John Simon in Geneva during the League Assembly. Simon told Dollfuss that he must not forget that British public opinion was profoundly attached to democratic and parliamentary ideas; already Lloyd George had been saying that the Austrian regime was developing into a dictatorship. Dollfuss countered by saying that he had to concentrate all available forces in his fight against the Nazis.[101]

Dollfus let it be known that he was willing to negotiate with Hitler, but only on the basis of Austria's independence and German non-interference in Austria's internal affairs. The British approved this attitude. At the end of

October Dollfuss told the British Minister in Vienna that Berlin seemed more disposed to an 'accommodation' with Austria. Early in January, he seemed on the verge of negotiating with an agent of Hitler's, but he was dissuaded, possibly by Starhemberg.

Instead, Dollfuss sent a note to the German government on 18 January saying that he might have to raise Germany's conduct in the League of Nations, mentioning the heightened Nazi agitation, the concentration of large bodies of Austrian Nazis in Germany near the frontier, the supply of explosives and the anti-Austrian broadcast and press campaign.[102] Dollfuss may perhaps have hoped that this move would persuade Hitler to negotiate with him in preference to a major dispute in the League. But the Western Powers were thrown into confusion. The British remained nervously aloof, the French were favourable to action in the League, the Italians blew first hot then cold.

What Mussolini really wanted was to bring Dollfuss to the boil over action against the Social Democrats. It was perhaps remarkable that Dollfuss had managed to hold out against him so long. He had held him at bay by lesser moves against the Social Democrats: after the Schutzbund had been banned, there had been ceaseless searches for its weapons; distribution of the Social Democrat Party newspaper, the *Arbeiter Zeitung*, had been banned; works' councils in State concerns had been abolished. The party had been reduced to impotence and inner turmoil, with the Schutzbund pressing for a fight, but the leaders hoping against hope for a political deal with Dollfuss. Yet as 1934 opened the Social Democrats still had a legal right to exist.

Mussolini could not tolerate this. On 18 January his Foreign Under-Secretary, Fulvio Suvich, arrived in Vienna to put pressure on Dollfuss. To the British Minister, Suvich remarked that Mussolini intended to go to the uttermost limit of his capacity to defend Austrian independence; but the Austrian political system was out of date and must be 'renovated'. Questioned later by the British Ambassador in Rome about the meaning of 'renovation', Suvich said it meant the suppression of the Socialist municipality of Vienna. Dollfuss, he said, must 'move to the Right'; and he hoped that such movement would not be discouraged from outside.[103]

The Italians therefore gave advance notice to the British of what was coming and warned them not to interfere. At the same time they had to make sure that the British and French would not withdraw their support from Dollfuss because of action against the Social Democrats. This was important because there was a very real danger that Hitler might exploit civil war as a pretext for intervention in Austria, and Italy might need help in stopping him. So at the beginning of February the Italians started pressing Britain and France to agree to issue 'analogous' declarations of support for Austrian independence. The British were unenthusiastic, even more so when the civil war actually started. That night the Foreign Secretary sent a telegram to Rome: 'I trust the Italian government realise that if Dollfuss establishes a Fascist or quasi-Fascist regime in Austria . . . there is bound to be, both here and probably also in France, a very marked cooling in the unanimity of support hitherto given to Austria by the press and public opinion, and further attempts by His Majesty's Government to assist Dr Dollfuss may be rendered increasingly difficult.'

By that time it was too late for warnings. Following the Suvich visit to Vienna, the final plans for suppressing the Social Democrats had been drawn up – probably by Fey, who was in charge of the security forces. At the end of January, Dollfuss received a harshly negative reply from the German government to his note saying that he might go to the League: all hope of negotiation with Hitler seemed ruled out – and with it, all hope of using the question of suppressing the Social Democrats as a bargaining counter with Hitler.

At this point Dollfuss seems to have yielded to Mussolini and to the Heimwehr who were pressing for action. In Vienna, the local Schutzbund leaders throughout the city were arrested on 9 February. On Sunday 11 February Dollfuss was at a meeting where the final decision was taken to move against the Social Democrats on the following Wednesday. On the same day Fey said publicly: 'this week we're going to do the job thoroughly'. Starhemberg, in an interview in a Budapest newspaper, said: 'this week we shall conquer, with or without the government'.

By this time, the Social Democrat leaders had had to face the hard fact that there was no chance of reaching an understanding with Dollfuss. On 18 January Dollfuss had publicly called on 'honest workers' leaders' to help build a new Austria and defend Austrian independence. Ten days later the Social Democratic leaders had said they were willing to cooperate provided that Dollfuss, in his proposed new constitution, maintained the universal franchise and the right of free association for workers. No response came from Dollfuss. On 7 February the Social Democrat leaders took the decision not to give in without a fight – that is, without calling a general strike, which they expected to lead to fighting.[104]

10 The Civil War, February 1934

The civil war started two days before the date set in the Fey plan – but not by the will of the Social Democrat leaders. In Linz, the police were ordered to search Schutzbund headquarters at the Hotel Schiff; the local Schutzbund leaders decided to resist. The party leaders in Vienna tried to restrain them, but their message did not get through. Fighting broke out on Monday 12 February, between the Schutzbund and the police who were later reinforced by the army. News reached Vienna during the morning. At 11.47 a.m. the Vienna trams stopped running, because the electricity workers had gone on strike. This was the agreed signal for a general strike.

But the general strike did not come. Some people in Vienna thought that the stopping of the trams was simply due to a technical failure and went on working as usual. Elsewhere the prearranged signal for the general strike had been a rail stoppage. But the railwaymen – whose numbers had been cut to nearly a half over the past few years, and who were very much afraid of losing their jobs – went on working and failed to give the signal.

In any case the response would probably have been extremely patchy. Ever since the onset of the world economic crisis, unemployment had grown steadily and alarmingly. The annual figure rose from 156,000 in 1928 to 208,200 in 1930, 253,400 in 1931, 310,000 in 1932, and 329,000 in 1933.[105] In 1934, according to the Social Democrat leaders, over one-third of the working force was out of work. The general strike call could hardly be expected to succeed in these circumstances. With the strike fiasco, the leaders' hopes of a 'general uprising' against the government collapsed.

Yet fighting broke out in Vienna in the early afternoon of Monday and went on until Wednesday, even, in isolated instances, until Friday. As in Linz, it was the government forces' attempt to seize the Schutzbund's weapons which sparked it off. The Schutzbund's role was purely defensive – first, to resist the capture of their weapons, and then to defend themselves in workers' centres or the great blocks of workers' flats built by the Social Democratic Vienna city government. The army brought up artillery, including howitzers and trench mortars, to blast holes in the outer walls of the blocks of flats – in particular the Karl-Marx-Hof and the Goethe-Hof. The Schutzbund – many of them unemployed men[106] – often fought bravely. But they lacked their trained local leaders. Moreover the party's political leaders had all been arrested in their offices or homes on Monday morning, except for Bauer and Deutsch. These two tried to help operate a central military command for the Schutzbund, but the area in which it was located was sealed off by the government forces, so they decided they could do nothing and escaped to Czechoslovakia.

At no point therefore was there an overall strategy. The fighting was limited to the outer, predominantly 'proletarian' districts of Vienna: the Schutzbund made no attempt to penetrate the inner districts, still less the 'Inner City' – the seat of the government organs, the big banks and big industrial concerns. Since the waiters did not go on strike and food supplies continued to reach Vienna unhindered, the ordinary 'bourgeois' suffered little except for the noise of distant gun-fire and the darkness imposed by the electricity workers' strike; even so the inefficiency of planned sabotage action made it possible for electricity to be restored before the end of the fighting.[107]

In the Lands, there were isolated pockets of fighting in

industrial areas – Bruck an der Mur, Steyr and elsewhere, but, as in Linz, the Schutzbund were on the defensive, and were isolated. In Leoben, a local leader, Koloman Wallisch, later hanged for his part in the fighting, became for a time a sort of folk hero of the Left in Europe.

The government forces lost 105 dead and over 300 wounded. On a bleak, cold day, an official funeral procession made its way round the Ring Road in Vienna between silent crowds and mourning candles in the windows of public institutions, offices and cafés on the route. The Schutzbund lost 137 dead and almost 400 wounded. The bitterness on both sides was great.

For the Social Democratic Party the February fighting meant, in the short term, a complete defeat, the outlawing of the party, its associated organisations and the 'free' trade unions linked with it. The defeat was freely admitted by the party's exiled leaders. Otto Bauer, in a pamphlet written on 19 February, said that the Austrian workers had been fighting not only against the 'Dollfuss–Fey dictatorship'; their fight had really been a despairing struggle against two great powers – Hitler's Third Reich and Mussolini's Fascist Italy. The enemy had been superior both in leadership and in weapons. But even if the workers had been beaten, they had gone down with honour and fame – unlike the workers of Italy and Germany. Thereby they had restored the self-respect and courage of the Socialists of the world.[108]

Deutsch tried to defend the party leaders against the charge that they had sinned in following a purely defensive policy instead of going over to the offensive, brought by some fellow-Socialists and also by Georgi Dimitrov, the Bulgarian Communist leader of Reichstag Fire trial fame, in the Comintern journal, *Rundschau*, of Basle. Deutsch said that given all the circumstances, nothing else was possible: the Austrians had been forced to wage a revolutionary battle in a non-revolutionary situation.[109]

Inside Austria, the younger and more militant Socialists

accused the party leadership of having become part of the whole 'bourgeois' political and economic system, thereby acquiring a vested interest in maintaining their position inside it and so betraying their followers. It was true that even after the party had gone into opposition in 1920, on Bauer's insistence, its leaders, through parliamentary committees or less formal contacts, had continued to exercise influence and pressure *inside* the system. Even after Dollfuss shut down parliament, the leaders still believed that they could operate as a power factor, negotiate and extract concessions, from *inside* the political Establishment.

By doing this, it could be argued, the party had had the worst of both worlds: it had neither played the parliamentary political game to best advantage, nor had it been truly militant. However, the Bauer line did at least hold the party together up till 1934 and prevent its militants from straying to the Communists.

There was another sense too in which the Social Democratic Party had become part of the 'bourgeois' system, with big vested interests. This was through the property which it had acquired over a period of fifty years in the form of buildings (workers' clubs, libraries and so on), cooperatives, savings banks and similar institutions, together with party and trade union funds. The leaders felt it was their duty to try to safeguard the property of the workers.

Renner was particularly sensitive on this point, as he showed twelve years later, when he tried to defend Andreas Korp, a member of his 1945 government, against charges of having cooperated with the 'Fascist régimes' of Dollfuss, Schuschnigg and ultimately Hitler. Renner pointed out that he himself had been founder or director of all workers' cooperative societies, including the Workers' Bank, which had been built up over half a century and which had very considerable wealth from the workers' savings. After he had been arrested on 12 February 1934, these were all threatened with forced liquidation (which the Workers' Bank immediately suffered). Senior officials of the co-operatives – naturally Social Democrats – asked for Renner's advice. He said they should not leave their posts but should 'protect the assets of the working class from being removed and destroyed'; the Fascist regime could not last. Korp, both then and later, had followed Renner's advice to 'save what you can'.[110]

The Socialist movement in Austria was therefore a big property-owner, with a big stake in law and order, not in revolution or violence. And, like a good property owner, it later insisted on restoration and compensation for the losses of 1934 and later years.

However great the blow to the Social Democrats in 1934, the February fighting gave them two long-term assets of considerable value. One was a heroic legend which was a source of strength when the party was re-born in 1945 and helped them to restore its old prestige and to outpace and overcome the Soviet-backed Communists. The other was a claim – freely exploited – to a sort of moral superiority over the successors to the Christian Socials of whom Dollfuss had been one – that is, over the People's Party, their coalition partners and political rivals from 1945 on.

An attempt to settle the debts of the past, once and for all, was made on the thirtieth anniversary of the February fighting, in 1964. At a ceremony in the Vienna cemetery at the graves of the victims, a wreath was laid in the name of the government, the two party leaders (Pittermann and Gorbach) clasped each other's hand without speaking. Afterwards, the old party quarrels went on as before.[111]

11 Dollfuss: From Civil War to Assassination, 1934

For Dollfuss, the balance sheet of the February civil war was unclear. At home the fight against Red Vienna had undoubtedly been popular in the western Lands and among country people. Even in sophisticated Vienna the middle class had been ready to believe Fey's propaganda about a Red plot for a Bolshevist take-over which he claimed to have uncovered. But the workers – whom Dollfuss would almost certainly have wished to wean from their leaders and win over by gentler means – now hated him as hangman and tyrant, with a more bitter hate than they felt for Hitler. As for the Heimwehr, Dollfuss could still hope to keep the upper hand: fortunately for him, their performance as auxiliaries to the army and the police had been so poor that they had lost rather than gained prestige. The army had done its distasteful job efficiently; Dollfuss could still hope to use it as a power base.

In his relations with Nazi Germany, the civil war did him no good. He had thrown away the chance of using the suppression of the Social Democrats as a future bargaining counter with Hitler. Now that he had done the deed as a sop to Mussolini, Hitler owed him nothing, but could use his action against him. The Austrian Nazis had proclaimed a 'truce' during the fighting, but then the full blast of Nazi propaganda was turned against Dollfuss and his treatment of Austrian workers. Hitler told the French Ambassador that he considered that Dollfuss had behaved with 'criminal stupidity' in firing on Socialist workmen, women and children. His hands were now 'stained with the blood of his own people' and he would very soon fall and be replaced by a National Socialist government.[112]

On the other hand the British and French governments – though they could not muzzle the press – were restrained by fear of German intervention and by Italian persuasion from openly condemning Dollfuss. Privately, on the second day of the fighting, the British Minister asked Dollfuss to bear in mind public opinion and exercise all possible restraint 'once order had been restored'. Vindictive reprisals, he said, were to be deprecated. Dollfuss replied that he had been 'taken by surprise' by the 'trouble', and promised to heed the Minister's words.[113] (The Minister remained uncertain whether or not Dollfuss had been a 'willing party' to the action; he laid the main blame on Fey.)[114]

The Italians took the line that Dollfuss's action would greatly strengthen his position and might perhaps lead to an arrangement between him and Hitler. This at least was the argument which Suvich used on the British Ambassador in Rome.[115] During the fighting, he pressed Britain and France to reaffirm their support for Dollfuss. The British were at first worried: they did not want to give 'implied approval' to Dollfuss's action: their official line was that 'His Majesty's Government have no intention of intervening . . . or pronouncing judgment on these internal events.' The French, however, were keen on a three-power declaration.

On 17 February – five days after the outbreak of the civil war – France, Italy and Britain said formally that they took 'a common view as to the necessity of maintaining Austria's independence and integrity in accordance with the relevant treaties'. Satisfied with this not very stirring statement, Dollfuss dropped the idea of appealing against Germany to the League of Nations, where he would have been exposed to attack for his action against the Social Democrats.

Mussolini was now ready to go ahead with his long-cherished dream of establishing his 'Danubian' position and forming a political-economic bloc comprising Italy, Austria and Hungary, as three Fascist or quasi-Fascist states: Dollfuss had won his spurs in the February fighting. Mussolini also saw that Dollfuss badly needed some form of economic aid to enable him to stand up to Hitler's pressures. Britain and France looked kindly on the Italian project, even though two of France's allies, Czechoslovakia and Yugoslavia, were pathologically suspicious, seeing it as a step towards a Habsburg restoration – which would never have suited Mussolini – and also as an excuse for moving Italian troops into Austria. Both countries at this point took the line that they would on the whole prefer the *Anschluss* (though Eduard Beneš, the Czechoslovak Foreign Minister, said at one point that he could not 'allow' it). Their views carried little weight with the Western Powers.

On 17 March Dollfuss, Mussolini and the Hungarian President Gömbös signed the three Rome Protocols, providing for cooperation and consultation between the three countries, both in the political and in the economic fields. These gave Dollfuss fresh moral support. Their economic value was, however, limited. The German market was far more important for Austria than anything that Italy or Hungary could offer. The Germans understood this. In addition to crippling Austria's tourist trade by Hitler's '1000-Mark barrier', they manipulated their purchases of Austrian timber for political ends and indulged in such gestures of intimidation as a boycott of the Austrian apple crop.[116]

Dollfuss now moved ahead to proclaim his new 'corporative' constitution. A Vorarlberg constitutional lawyer, Dr Otto Ender, had been working on a draft for months, and had been compelled to make it more and more 'authoritarian). On 1 May – the traditional Labour Day, chosen to blot out memories of past Social Democratic power – the new constitution was finally unveiled. Theoretically based on the Papal Encyclical on social problems, *Quadragesimo Anno*, and on medieval German tradition, it placed great power in the hands of the Federal Chancellor, who was to be helped in his 'strong authoritarian leadership' by 'men experienced in public and economic life, conscious and determined Austrians'.[117]

The new element in the system was to be the 'professional corporations', which were to perform 'preparatory' functions in the process of legislation, making recommendations which would not be binding on the Government. There was to be a Federal Council of fifty-nine delegates from the corporations and the Lands which would have no power of initiative and no right to debate Government statements: it could only accept or reject them.[118] The 'corporations' were to fall into seven groups: agriculture and forestry; public service; industry, manufacturing; commerce and transport; banking and insurance; free professions. The intention was to group employers and employees together in the same corporation, but no one could solve the question of where the new trade union organisation, theoretically purged of Social Democratic influence, was to fit into the general scheme.

Much of the constitution was destined to remain a dead letter. But Dollfuss hailed it on 1 May as 'the christening robe of the new Austria' – the new 'Christian, German, federal state on a corporative foundation', as it was described in the preamble of the constitution. The corporations, Dollfuss said, had been for centuries 'the foundation of the social organisation of our German fatherland'. He also pointed out that the proclamation of the new constitution coincided with the conclusion of a Concordat with the Vatican, which established the Catholic character of the Austrian state to an exceptional degree (and which caused a great deal of trouble in the post-1945 Austrian Republic).

Dollfuss tried hard to present the new constitution and the ideology behind it as specifically Austrian and specifically Catholic, not as an imitation of the Italian Fascist model. Mussolini probably did not mind this, so long as the principle of authoritarian leadership was sufficiently stressed.

For Hitler the Dollfuss constitution was a setback: it ruled out the possibility of the Austrian Nazis' capturing power by the same method as he himself had used in Germany – that is, by exploiting the weaknesses of the Parliamentary system so as to set up a party dictatorship.

Hitler therefore – ironically – became the fervent champion of free elections in Austria. When he met Mussolini in Venice in June 1934 – when Nazi bomb outrages in Austria were at a high point – he told him that either elections should be held at once in Austria, or else Nazis should be admitted to the government. Mussolini (according to Suvich) replied that given existing Nazi pressures, to ask Dollfuss to hold elections would be to ask him to sign his own death warrant; Austrian Nazis could only be admitted to the government if they genuinely supported Austrian independence.[119]

By this time, Dollfuss's death warrant had perhaps already been signed, though not by himself. Already in the autumn of 1933 there had been an attack on his life in which he was wounded. On 25 July 1934 about 100 men – Austrian Nazis – attacked and entered the Chancellery in Vienna and captured Dollfuss and Fey. (Since there had been some advance warning of trouble, other Ministers, after an unusually early Cabinet meeting, had already left.) Soon after midday Vienna Radio, which had also been captured, announced that Dollfuss had resigned and that the pro-Nazi Anton Rintelen was to replace him.

Meanwhile the Ministers who were free, headed by Karl von Schuschnigg, had met at the Defence Ministry, in the hope of negotiating Dollfuss's release. They learned that he had been wounded; he had in fact been shot while trying to escape by a private staircase. His captors did not allow him to see a doctor or a priest, and he died at about

6 p.m. The assailants left the Chancellery at 7 p.m. believing that they had been promised safe-conduct to the German frontier. Schuschnigg, however, said that Dollfuss's death had created a new situation, and they were arrested. On 31 July Otto Planetta, who had confessed to shooting Dollfuss, and another were executed; six others were later similarly executed.

Seeing that less than a month earlier Hitler had personally taken part in the murder of his close associate, Ernst Röhm, there was no reason whatever to suppose that he was not involved in Dollfuss's death. There were reports that in Germany, there was rejoicing in the Nazi party that Dollfuss, 'the worst enemy in Europe of National Socialism', had gone.[120] It was beyond doubt that the Austrian Nazis in Bavaria were involved. Their armed formations had moved towards the Austrian frontier in the days and hours before the attempted *putsch* in Vienna. According to a British source, they were turned back by the German Army – the Reichswehr.[121] It was reported that on hearing of the *putsch*, the Reichswehr leaders warned Hitler strongly that international embroilments must be avoided.[122]

In London, Sir John Simon, the Foreign Secretary, felt none of the inhibitions that he had felt about Dollfuss's suppression of the Social Democrats. He told Parliament on 26 July that the government had expressed its 'horror at this cowardly outrage'; he reaffirmed British support for Austria's independence and integrity. *The Times* went so far as to declare that the events of 25 July made National Socialism stink in the nostrils of the world.

Of more practical importance, Mussolini ostentatiously announced that at 4 p.m. on the day of the assassination of Dollfuss, 'in view of possible complications', movements of Italian land and air forces had been ordered towards the Austrian frontier on the Brenner and in Carinthia. These forces were said to be 'sufficient for dealing with any eventuality'. In case this should alarm the peace-loving

British, the Foreign Office was informed by the Italians that these moves were 'purely precautionary'.[123] A few days later Sir John Simon sent Mussolini a personal message: 'it is a very great satisfaction to feel that the correspondence between the Italian and British view is so close'. He trusted that the Italian, French and British governments would continue to co-operate on the basis of their joint declaration of 17 February.

For Hitler, the *putsch* had misfired. It had got him into trouble with the Reichswehr, which he had not yet got under his thumb. It had provoked Mussolini to move troops threateningly, and had solidified the brittle front formed by Italy, France and Britain. Inside Austria it had provoked a wave of sympathy for Dollfus, who was buried beside Seipel in the 'Chancellors' Church' and was revered by some as martyr and hero.[124] This did something to strengthen his Fatherland Front, which until then had for the most part been able to recruit members only from State employees, including railwaymen, who would have lost their jobs if they had failed to join. His successor as Chancellor was neither the Nazi nominee, Rintelen, nor Mussolini's favourite, Starhemberg, but a man much closer to Dollfuss, the devout Catholic lawyer from Tirol, a fellow member of the Cartellverband and a fellow-Christian Social, Kurt von Schuschnigg. Schuschnigg and Starhemberg divided the cabinet posts between them, but Schuschnigg had the upper hand.

12 Schuschnigg's Fight without Weapons

The emergence of Schuschnigg as leader seemed to show that Austrians were still determined not to hand over their country to either of the two dictators. The task of keeping Hitler at bay did not at first seem impossible. Mussolini was still trying to strengthen his influence in the Danube basin and therefore wanted to keep Hitler out of Austria. And he was still to outward appearance stronger than Hitler. Germany was not yet rearmed; Hitler was not yet quite respectable, in terms of European politics. France and Britain were on quite good terms with Italy and, though wary of Hitler, had not yet decided on appeasement. Inside Austria, the army and police had again shown themselves reasonably loyal at the time of Dollfuss's assassination; this event had caused a revulsion of feeling against the Nazis; above all the economic situation was beginning to look more cheerful. Schuschnigg himself was upright and stubborn, even if he was rigid and blinkered and lacked Dollfuss's flexibility and capacity to charm.

Within the next four years, however, many favourable factors changed. Germany rearmed and became stronger than Italy. Hitler established a personal domination over Mussolini. Above all Mussolini, by plunging into his Abyssinian adventure in 1935, found himself at odds with France and Britain and in need of Hitler's backing in Europe. By 1937 he could no longer afford to quarrel with him over Austria. Once Hitler knew that there was no risk of a clash with Italy, and that France and Britain were willing to go a very long way to avoid war, his hands were free to take Austria whenever he wished.

Inside Austria there was a similar shift in the balance of forces between 1934 and 1938. Schuschnigg was temperamentally different from Dollfuss and seemed to lack his fighting instinct and his optimism. According to Starhemberg (who was naturally bellicose) Schuschnigg once said to him: 'I cannot go on working with you, for you believe in force and I hate it . . . Force breeds force.'[125] A very reserved, quiet man – especially after the death of his wife in a car crash in 1935 – he lacked popular appeal and outward warmth.

He also suffered more than Dollfuss had done from the inner paralysis caused by a sense of obligation to the idea of 'German-ness' or *Deutschtum*, which made any policy hostile to Germany – even Hitler's Germany – seem in some way disloyal. Dollfuss's definition of Austria as a 'German, Christian state' obviously meant more to Schuschnigg than it had to Dollfuss himself. Starhemberg said: 'he was, and remained to the end, Pan-German, though not, of course in the Prussian sense of the word. His Pan-Germanism was based on a belief, impossible of realisation, in a greater Germany, modelled on the Holy Roman Empire. It was, as he once said himself, a mystical creed . . . He regarded the fight against the Nazis as a fratricidal war . . .'[126] An English historian, Elizabeth Wiskemann, wrote: 'Like nearly all Austrians of his ex-officer category, he was hypersensitive to any accusation of disloyalty to the Deutschtum of the Austrian State.'[127]

Since Schuschnigg was also at least in theory a monarchist, believing in an eventual, if remote, Habsburg restoration, it was hard for him to follow a single, straight line.

In any case, the steadily increasing external pressures on Austria made it difficult for him to do anything but play for time and hope against hope for an improbable change in the balance of forces in Europe which would somehow rescue Austria from extinction. This meant that he was forced to make one attempt after another to reach a compromise either with pro-Nazi Austrians or with Hitler himself. Nothing could have suited Hitler so well: it convinced first the Austrians themselves and then the rest of Europe that the *Anschluss* was inevitable; it provided Mussolini, the Chamberlain government and others with the easy excuse that since the Austrians themselves seemed to want the *Anschluss*, there was no point in trying to stop Hitler.

Hitler's first act, after disclaiming any connexion with the killing of Dollfuss, was to recall the German Minister in Vienna and replace him by Franz von Papen, the Catholic politician who had paved the way for Hitler's seizure of power in Germany. In Vienna von Papen posed as more Catholic than the most devout Austrian Catholics and a good deal least Hitlerist than Hitler, as a brother officer and comrade-in-arms to former or serving Austrian officers, and as a friend to Starhemberg and the Heimwehr. In his three and a half years in Vienna, he did a great deal first to confuse and then soften up people of all classes, except the workers.

At the beginning, Schuschnigg set out to keep up close ties with Italy. In late August 1934 he paid his first visit to Mussolini, in Florence. A little earlier, Mussolini had told Starhemberg that he had shown his friendship for Austria at the time of Dollfuss's death, adding: 'it was done for Europe. It would mean the end of European civilisation if this country of murderers and pederasts were to overrun Europe.'[128] To Schuschnigg, he said that the Germans would need another four years 'before they counted'; by that time Austria must be domestically consolidated and mobilised, for then 'we must reckon on warlike complications'.[129]

All this was encouraging for Schuschnigg; but there was also a warning note: Mussolini made it clear that he was bent on a campaign against Abyssinia.[130] At this time Schuschnigg can hardly have recognised the full implications for Austria. But in the autumn – without telling Starhemberg, who objected violently when he found out – he started on a policy of 'internal appeasement' inside Austria, trying to win over the German Nationalists and prevent them from lining up with the Nazis. Among those whom he approached were Major-General Edmund Glaise-Horstenau, Dr Artur Seyss-Inquart and Dr Hermann Neubacher. His efforts were futile: all of them later served Hitler.

In the wider European field, the Spring of 1935 seemed surprisingly hopeful. In April, after Hitler broke the Versailles treaty by introducing general military conscription in Germany, Italy, France and Britain joined together to protest against his action, thereby forming what became known as the 'Stresa Front'. It looked at first as if this 'Front' would be strong enough to safeguard Austrian independence.

In October 1935, however, Italy attacked Abyssinia; and a wide breach opened up in the 'Front', with Britain pursuing a policy of sanctions against Italy through the League of Nations, which infuriated Mussolini and tended to unite Italians behind him. The breach was opened still wider by Italian intervention in the Spanish civil war, which started in July 1936. When efforts were made to restore normal relations between Italy and Britain in early 1938, these came too late to help Austria.

Almost immediately after the Italian invasion of Abyssinia, Schuschnigg began to loosen his ties with the Mussolini-backed Heimwehr. In a cabinet reshuffle on 17 October, the leader of the Vienna Heimwehr, Major Fey, lost his post. Starhemberg did not mind; there had never been any love lost between the two men, and there was little in common between the peasant-based Heimwehr of the Lands and Fey's armed bands of urban unemployed. So for the time being Starhemberg remained in the government, and in March 1936 persuaded Mussolini to provide 600,000 Schillings for intensified anti-Nazi

counter-propaganda – in spite of the fact that Mussolini
had just been 'visibly disturbed' by the news that Hitler
had marched into the Rhineland.

Schuschnigg was, however, following a path which led
away from Starhemberg's brutally frank attacks on the
Nazis. Conveniently for Schuschnigg, Starhemberg committed a glaring diplomatic blunder in May, by sending
Mussolini a fulsome public message of congratulation on
the Italian conquest of Addis Ababa. Austria had felt
obliged to vote against sanctions against Italy in the
League of Nations, but there was no point in deliberately
offending the British. On 13 May Schuschnigg removed
Starhemberg from his post as Vice-Chancellor. Hitler's
representative, von Papen, was said to have remarked: 'it's
a pity Starhemberg was so opposed to the idea of reconciliation with Germany. That caused his fall. . .'[131] Some
months later, the Heimwehr was (at least on paper) dis-
banded by the government.

Mussolini seemed very little worried by the sacking of
his protégé. When they met in Rome soon after, Mussolini
said: 'I think you're well out of it. Let Schuschnigg show
what he can do alone.'[132]

Mussolini Yields to Hitler

In 1936, Mussolini was already beginning to loosen his
grip on Austria. In the Spring, at a meeting of the three
Rome Protocol countries (Italy, Austria, Hungary), Mussolini let the Austrians know that in view of the Italian
commitment in Africa, he thought it urgently necessary to
improve relations between Austria and Germany, and that
Schuschnigg should make direct contact with Berlin.[133] So
Schuschnigg took up seriously a proposal which von Papen
had been pressing since the summer of 1935, for a truce in
the press war between Germany and Austria.

A draft agreement between Austria and Germany was
prepared and in June, at Rocca delle Caminate, Schuschnigg showed it to Mussolini, who welcomed it as 'the only

possible solution in the circumstances'.[134] Mussolini re-affirmed his interest in supporting efforts to preserve Austrian independence, but Austria must now stand on her own feet in the world: it would be easier for Italy to help Austria if both Italy and Austria were on good terms with Germany.[135]

The Austrian–German agreement was concluded on 11 July 1936. The German government said it recognised the full sovereignty of Austria, and each government promised not to influence the internal political structure of the other. Next – and this was the key clause – the Austrian government said that 'in general, and particularly with regard to the German Reich, it would maintain a policy based always on the principle that Austria acknowledged herself to be a German state' – though this was not to affect the Rome Protocols with Italy and Hungary. Hitler's 1000-Mark blockade on tourists and other forms of economic discrimination were to end; Austria was to amnesty imprisoned Nazis and include representatives of the 'National Opposition' – that is, pro-Nazis – in the government.

It did not look too bad a bargain, and Austria derived some economic advantage: in 1936–7 Austrian exports to Germany rose considerably; industrial production went up and unemployment fell.[136] But Schuschnigg, writing many years later, said that those Austrians who negotiated the agreement saw it as a necessary evil; no one expected it to stop Hitler from working for the incorporation of Austria. But it might give Austria two years' breathing-space, and during this time the Stresa Front of Italy, France and Britain might be restored.[137] Starhemberg on the other hand attacked it violently: he asked the Italian Minister in Vienna to pass to Mussolini two words: '*Finis Austriae*'.

In London, the July agreement was welcomed by *The Times* which said that Hitler had 'brought off another stroke of policy upon which . . . he was certainly to be congratulated'; the agreement would help to stabilise and pacify Central Europe, and 'pave the way for a permanent settlement between the two main branches of the German race'. The Baldwin government did not want to involve itself in the affair; it was still smarting from a wounding attack by Lloyd George, the former Prime Minister, on its decision to end sanctions against Italy. The British people, Lloyd George had said, would never go to war again for an Austrian quarrel.

In November 1936 there was a further step in Austrian–German reconciliation. Guido Schmidt, whom Schuschnigg had brought into the government as a representative of the 'National Opposition', visited Berlin and concluded a secret agreement about press, cultural and economic exchanges and, while reserving Austria's rights under the Rome Protocols, promised advance consultation with Germany in all other matters. Later that month Germany and Japan signed the Anti-Comintern Pact, to the accompaniment of German declarations which defined Central Europe as Germany's defence area while Italy was allotted the Mediterranean. In other words Austria was excluded from Italy's sphere of interest and placed in Germany's.

Mussolini raised no objection. When he saw Schuschnigg in Venice in April 1937, he said he needed Germany against Britain and the Rome–Berlin Axis had become essential; the question of Austrian independence must be harmonised with it. Amplifying this his Foreign Minister, Galeazzo Ciano, said that Italy was now protecting Austria not militarily but through the Axis.[138]

Mussolini took the final step when he paid his first visit to Germany in September 1937 and was deeply moved by the display of German might laid on by Hitler. One outcome was an understanding that Italy would not be impeded by Germany in the Mediterranean and that Germany's special interest in Austria would not be impaired by Italy.[139] Schuschnigg was not informed. On 6 November Italy joined the Anti-Comintern Pact. By this time Mussolini was saying that if the Austrians wanted the *Anschluss,* he would let things take their course.[140]

At about this time Nazi propaganda was harping on a supposed Austrian plot to restore the Habsburgs – a story designed to kill many birds with one stone. The only substance for it was that as a devoted though platonic lover of the monarchy, Schuschnigg put through two measures, in July 1935 and April 1936, to remove certain legal restrictions on the Habsburg family. He also, at considerable risk, had secret meetings with the exiled Archduke Otto in Switzerland in September 1935, January 1937, and finally in December 1937.[141] Hitler may have known of Schuschnigg's contacts, however secret. That he seriously suspected a pro-Habsburg plot is far less likely. Nevertheless, he saw that the story of a plot would offer considerable advantages as a pretext for armed intervention in Austria.

For one thing, Mussolini was anti-Habsburg. For another thing, Yugoslavia, seriously shaken by Mussolini's intrigues and the disaffection of the Croats (former subjects of the Habsburgs), would be so frightened by the idea of a restoration that the *Anschluss* would seem a much better thing. The Czechoslovak leaders were also afraid of the Habsburgs, although from 1934 onwards they had become almost more afraid of Hitler and had therefore established secret though abortive contacts with Schuschnigg. In any case neither Czechoslovakia nor Yugoslavia could oppose German intervention in Austria to stop a Habsburg plot; and their attitude might influence France and disarm French opposition. Inside Austria, the workers and the German Nationalists – to say nothing of the Nazis themselves – would all be anti-Habsburg.

So when in June 1937 Hitler's War Minister, Field Marshal Blomberg, received instructions to prepare a military plan for operations in Austria, it was given the code-name of 'Operation Otto' and its aim was 'to compel Austria by force of arms to renounce a restoration'. There was to be a march in the direction of Vienna, and all resistance was to be broken, exploiting the internal divisions of the Austrian people.[142]

In the following November Hitler held his meeting with his defence chiefs, including Blomberg, which resulted in the so-called Hossbach Minute. This recorded Hitler as foreseeing military operations against Czechoslovakia and Austria aimed at their incorporation in Germany, which would provide better frontiers and make it possible to raise perhaps twelve new divisions. The Habsburg pretext was not now mentioned.[143] He perhaps thought it had become superfluous.

Hitler had still, however, to fear opposition from some of his defence chiefs. At the beginning of 1938 he therefore got rid of Blomberg and the Commander-in-Chief, General Werner von Fritsch. On 4 February 1938 Hitler himself became Commander-in-Chief of all the armed forces. Von Neurath was replaced as Foreign Minister by the more bellicose Joachim von Ribbentrop, then Ambassador in London. Hitler had cleared the decks for action.

So much was obvious. But no one knew yet whether he was planning to march against Austria, or whether he would be patient enough to bring about the capitulation of Schuschnigg by non-violent means.

The British Yield to Hitler

It was the question of Hitler's methods, rather than his aim in Austria, which had been preoccupying the British government since the previous autumn. The Chamberlain government was trying to perform a complicated acrobatic feat – to work towards reconciliation with Mussolini so that his restraining influence could once again be brought to bear on Hitler, as in 1933–5, and at the same time to throw out feelers towards Hitler himself, by-passing Mussolini. Mussolini, having relinquished his interest in Austria, was in no hurry to reach agreement with Britain, and delayed committing himself until Austria's fate had been sealed. Hitler was chiefly interested in exploring the full extent of Britain's weakness.

This he was given good opportunity to do. The British Ambassador in Berlin, Sir Nevile Henderson, was (according to Anthony Eden, then Foreign Secretary) constantly making excuses for the Nazis, instead of warning them: 'his support of their claims in Austria and Czechoslovakia accelerated events which it was his duty to retard'.[144] The Prime Minister, Nevile Chamberlain, was in sympathy with the Ambassador. Yet even Eden's attitude over Austria was equivocal. His view in 1937 was that Britain's attitude towards Austria should be 'prudent but not disinterested'. He later commented: 'while our military strength was still limited it was the best that we could do'.[145]

In the autumn of 1937, it became known that Lord Halifax was to visit Hitler. As the Editor of *The Times*, Geoffrey Dawson, noted, he was to act as Chamberlain's emissary; his purpose would be to ascertain whether Hitler could be persuaded to pledge himself 'not to attempt forceful solutions in order to obtain his objectives'.[146] Eden did not like the idea. Oliver Harvey, then Eden's principal private secretary, recorded in his diary: 'A.E. very annoyed at the indecent haste with which the P.M. and Halifax are pressing on with it. . . A.E. is opposed to the visit anyway, as having seen Halifax's notes for the proposed talks he finds them very feeble. . .' But Eden gave way.[147]

When the meeting took place, Halifax, according to the record of the German interpreter, Dr Schmidt, spoke of 'possible alterations in the European order which might be destined to come about with the passage of time'; one was Austria; 'England was interested to see that any alterations should come through the course of peaceful evolution and that methods should be avoided which might cause far-reaching disturbance.' As Eden commented, Halifax's 'peaceful evolution' probably meant something quite different to Hitler.[148]

Hitler must now have concluded, correctly, that he had nothing to fear from Britain over the *Anschluss*. As for France, the Foreign Minister, Yvon Delbos, made firm statements but seemed more worried about Czechoslovakia, to which France was bound by treaty, than about Austria. The Chamberlain government shyed away from any proposal for joint British–French warnings to Hitler; there was none of the feeling of solidarity with France which Arthur Henderson had shown in the 1931 Customs Union affair. Delbos's efforts at firmness were frustrated. In any case, the French government was insecure.

As 1938 opened, Chamberlain was full of hope, believing that if Britain offered Germany colonies in Africa (preferably non-British), Hitler would then behave better in Europe; according to Eden, he was 'so impatient to make progress' that he would not be put off by Germany's behaviour to Austria.[149] At the same time he pushed Eden into preliminary talks intended to lead to negotiations for ending the quarrel between Britain and Italy over Abyssinia and Spain and rebuilding the Stresa Front.

Eden disliked the idea; he had become convinced, from secret information, that Mussolini had made a deal with Hitler over Austria. He drew the conclusion: 'If it had been possible to save Austria by a discussion in Rome, I would have been ready to do so, but it was not. Mussolini had no power to hold Addis Ababa and Cadiz as well as Austria.'[150] Chamberlain, however, asserted to the Cabinet on 19 February that Mussolini did not want Hitler to take Austria and was trying to persuade him to adopt an attitude of moderation.[151] The resulting deadlock in the Cabinet ended in Eden's resignation at the moment of greatest crisis for Austria. Chamberlain, optimistic to the last, remained in undisputed control of British foreign policy. Halifax succeeded Eden.

Just a week earlier, Schuschnigg had gone to the meeting with Hitler in Berchtesgaden which sealed Austria's fate. He had been persuaded to go by von Papen, who assured him that the 1936 July Agreement would remain intact. In the event, while Schuschnigg – a chain-smoker forbidden by Hitler to smoke – talked nervously about the importance of the Austrian contribution to German culture, rather unfortunately quoting the German-born Beethoven as a case in point, Hitler stormed and raged, accusing Schuschnigg of disloyalty and betrayal, and threatened German military intervention – a threat made more realistic by a parade of top-ranking generals. Austria, he said, had nothing to hope for from Italy: 'I am in the clear with Mussolini.' England, he went on, 'won't raise a finger for Austria'. The French had failed to move when he marched into the Rhineland; 'now it's too late for France'.[152]

In the end, Schuschnigg signed a ten-point agreement which constituted a blatant intervention in Austria's affairs: in particular all police powers were to be placed in the hands of Hitler's nominee, Seyss-Inquart. Schuschnigg left Berchtesgaden still uncertain whether this agreement, dangerous as it was, might not still give Austria another two years' grace, or whether it was merely the preliminary to German military action. He had, however, been particularly struck by a remark of Hitler's, shortly before he left: 'it would be completely irresponsible and unjustifiable before history if an instrument like the German Wehrmacht were not used'. This clearly showed Hitler's mood, if not his firm decision.

Mussolini sent a special message to Vienna saying he thought the agreement 'entirely right'; for Austria the point was to gain time until the international situation changed. The message led Schuschnigg to believe that the British–Italian talks were likely to succeed quickly, which would create an entirely new situation for Austria.[153] On 21 February the French Foreign Minister, Delbos, said that France could not disinterest herself in the fate of Austria. Encouraged, Schuschnigg made a firm speech on 24 February to show that he would not yield beyond a certain point: 'we knew that we could go, and did go, up to that boundary line beyond which appear, clearly and unequivocally, the words: "Thus far and no farther".[154]

In line with these words, Schuschnigg decided a few days later – on 4 March – that a decisive step must be taken to stop the explosion of Nazi activity triggered off by the Berchtesgaden agreement, which seemed to be leading to armed insurrection. This step – announced on 9 March – was the holding of a plebiscite on the question whether Austrians wanted a 'free, German, independent, social Christian and united Austria, and peace, work and equal rights for all who confess their allegiance to the people and the fatherland'.

This decision, intended to 'put an end to Germany's double game', as Schuschnigg wrote later, did exactly that, but not in the way Schuschnigg had hoped. Hitler could now scrap the irritatingly slow 'evolutionary' method and use the pretext provided by Schuschnigg's plebiscite plan to order the German Wehrmacht to march. This he had probably always itched to do; it was for this that he had purged the German defence chiefs.

There was also the danger, for Hitler, that Schuschnigg might gain great strength from the plebiscite. The pro-Nazi Austrian Minister without Portfolio, Glaise-Horstenau, reported that Hitler 'raged like a madman for an hour and declared that holding the plebiscite represented a defeat for him and he would not allow it'.[155] Sir Nevile Henderson reported apologetically from Berlin: 'I am afraid it will be difficult for Herr Hitler not to yield this time to extremist advice.'[156]

The Social Democratic 'Yes'

Schuschnigg's chance of winning a political success in the plebiscite seemed reasonably good. It was true that Nazi propaganda, terror and bribery, helped by the strain of passivity and fatalism which was one element in the complex Austrian character, had undermined the middle class and the peasant-farmers of the Western Lands, including the old Christian Social party. The German Nationalists, though some of them grumbled about Hitler's ungentlemanly and uncivilised methods, were also an easy prey. But at this particular moment there was a widespread and genuine revulsion of feeling against Hitler's overbearing bullying and his violence and deceit, which produced a flare-up of Austrian patriotism such as Dollfuss, and, until then, Schuschnigg, had been unable to kindle.

The most important single element, however, was the 40 per cent which had voted Social Democrat in 1930 – the industrial workers of Vienna and Lower Austria, Styria and Upper Austria. All of them were now bitterly hostile to the Schuschnigg regime, which they regarded as totally Fascist. It was true that it was repressive; there were widespread arrests, interrogations and imprisonment with or without trial; the concentration camp at Wöllersdorf was usually overflowing. But, as the Social Democrats themselves admitted, terms of imprisonment were usually a matter of a few months rather than longer periods. The confiscation of the party's property was a bad blow; but various groups within the party and the now illegal 'free' trade unions continued to lead a sort of shadow existence without suffering more than petty persecution; their regular meeting places in one or other Vienna café were widely known. The exiled leaders in the Czechoslovak town of Brno – Bauer, Deutsch and others – kept up regular contacts with Vienna, financing such 'illegal' activities as they approved from party funds smuggled out of the country before February 1934.

The February fighting had inevitably produced splits in the party; some joined the Nazis, others the Communists, but most moved back into the Social Democratic fold fairly soon. More serious was the split between those, like Renner, who wanted to keep open the option of working within the existing system, and the militants who wanted a clean break with the past and the supposed shilly-shallying of the old leaders. The militants formed a strictly conspiratorial underground organisation, taking the name of Revolutionary Socialists (R.S.), yet acknowledging the authority of Otto Bauer; they eventually came under the leadership of a young worker from Carinthia, Josef Buttinger. They were uncompromisingly hostile to Schuschnigg and 'Austro-Fascism' and they saw no hope except in full-scale revolution – if possible, a European revolution. But they kept the Communists at arm's length, even when in 1935 the Seventh Comintern Congress proclaimed the united front policy.

After the 1936 July Agreement there were serious disagreements between the R.S., led by Buttinger, who became known as the Pessimists, thinking that Austria was inevitably doomed and that the workers could do nothing to prevent this doom, and Otto Bauer who – from exile – persisted in a more optimistic view. In practical terms, the arguments tended to centre round the editorial control of the party newspaper, the *Arbeiter Zeitung*, which continued to circulate illegally in Vienna and elsewhere. Compromise was inevitable; the exiled Bauer controlled the money while Buttinger controlled the underground organisation inside Austria.

As the climax of the Austrian crisis loomed up, Social Democrats of all colours began to see that they would soon be faced with crucial decisions. At the end of November 1937 there was a new wave of arrests of leading party members; nevertheless at the turn of the year Renner tried to bring about negotiations with the Schuschnigg regime through the trade union network.[157] This produced nothing. The Berchtesgaden Agreement, as Buttinger noted, ended the previously prevailing political apathy among the workers.[158] On 1 March Otto Bauer wrote in the *Arbeiter Zeitung* that the workers must utilise the coming crises and take a hand in them, to save the country from Hitler fascism; the Austrian people should make up their minds to fight.[159]

There were moves for talks between Schuschnigg and

the trade union leaders, whether legal or 'illegal'. In early March Schuschnigg authorised the opening of negotiations about the workers' demands for freedom of political activity and free elections in the trade unions. Efforts were then made to bring about unity between all the sections of the workers' movement. By the time that Schuschnigg announced his plebiscite plan, a fairly representative negotiating body had been formed.

The plebiscite announcement created a new situation. It was very difficult for the R.S. leaders, in particular, to vote for Schuschnigg, even if the rest were willing. However on 10 March, after long heart-searchings by Buttinger, the R.S. Central Committee declared that the workers must not help Hitler by voting 'No'; 'the Austrian worker has no alternative: his Yes vote is not cast for Schuschnigg and the authoritarian régime, but against Hitler'.[160]

It therefore seemed that, by whatever devious theoretical routes they had reached this goal, the workers were prepared to join with their class enemies in a last-minute effort to defend Austria against Hitler. Schuschnigg therefore had a good chance of winning a sizeable majority in the plebiscite. This Hitler was determined to prevent.

Hitler Marches: the British Stand Aside

On 11 March the storm broke: first came Hitler's demand that Schuschnigg should cancel the plebiscite; then, when this was conceded, his ultimatum to Schuschnigg to resign and make way for a government under Hitler's man, Seyss-Inquart; and finally, in spite of Schuschnigg's surrender, the march of the German Army into Austria.

Throughout the day there was unusual activity in the British Foreign Office. On the day before Lord Halifax, now Foreign Secretary, had delivered a vague and carefully-hedged warning about Austria to the retiring German Ambassador, Ribbentrop, who had already been appointed Foreign Minister. Halifax told him that the last thing the British wanted to see was a war in Europe, but if once war should start in Central Europe, it was quite impossible to say where it might not end. In context, these words clearly did *not* mean that Britain had the slightest thought of going to war for Austrian independence.

On 11 March, Halifax followed this up by instructing the Ambassador in Berlin (who was sharply critical of Schuschnigg's plebiscite plan) to make sure that the warning got through to Hitler quickly. When it eventually reached Hitler, it is unlikely that he took any notice of it. Nor, it seems, did Halifax expect him to: he remarked to Foreign Office officials: 'the only thing they understand is force, a warning will be useless unless accompanied by a threat to use force which we cannot do'.[161]

By coincidence, Ribbentrop was lunching on 11 March at No. 10 Downing Street. After the meal news came of Hitler's ultimatum to Schuschnigg. Chamberlain and Halifax took Ribbentrop into another room and 'spoke sharply to him'. Ribbentrop professed ignorance of the facts and said that anyway Britain should welcome 'a peaceful solution'. When Halifax called on Ribbentrop later in the day, Ribbentrop said cheerfully that 'this was much the best thing that could have happened'. It would render Anglo-German relations more easy of solution.[162]

Before yielding to Hitler, Schuschnigg asked for the British government's advice on whether he should resign. The reply sent by Halifax, received in Vienna during the afternoon, was that 'we have spoken strongly to von Ribbentrop on effect that would be produced by such direct interference in Austrian affairs. . .' But, Halifax added, 'His Majesty's Government cannot take responsibility of advising the Chancellor to take any course of action which might expose his country to dangers against which H.M.G. are unable to guarantee protection'.

Both Britain and France – which had no government at that moment – tried to sound out Mussolini, without success. Schuschnigg also tried to contact Mussolini. The only answer he got was: 'under the circumstances the Italian government is not in a position to give advice'.[163]

Schuschnigg, totally isolated, gave way and resigned. In the early evening he broadcast a final message: 'the President asks me to tell the people of Austria that we have yielded to force'. Since he was not prepared, even 'in this terrible situation', to shed blood, he had ordered the troops not to resist. 'So I take leave . . . with a German word of farewell from the depths of my heart, "God protect Austria".'

The German Army – over 100,000 men – marched in unopposed, to be greeted with seemingly near-hysterical joy by large crowds. Hitler himself was particularly moved by his own reception in Linz. The German secret police also moved in, even more rapidly, and there was a wave of arrests of government leaders, Christian Socials, Social Democrats, Jews and others. A later Austrian estimate of the total figure was 70,000.[164]

Hitler then announced his own plebiscite, to be held in early April. Renner, hoping to save arrested Social Democrats, publicly advised Austrians to vote Yes. So also did the Austrian Bishops led by Cardinal Innitzer, hoping to save the Church from Nazi interference. Starhemberg, in Switzerland on holiday, gave the same advice; a secret ballot, he said, was an impossibility, so that to vote No was suicide.[165]

Only the exiled Otto Habsburg promptly protested against Hitler's plebiscite, in a statement from Paris. But this had as little impact on events as had his letter to Schuschnigg of 17 February urging that Austria should turn to the Western Powers and stand firm against Hitler, and that Schuschnigg should hand over to him the office of Chancellor. Schuschnigg, monarchist as he was, had rejected this idea without reservation, and had replied: 'in no circumstances can it be reasonable . . . to lead the country into a struggle which is hopeless from the outset'.

It was perhaps in this spirit, rather than from any deep or

enduring enthusiasm for union with Germany, that over 90 per cent of Austrians voted Yes to Hitler on 10 April 1938.

At the moment of crisis, none of the Powers which had once opposed the *Anschluss* so strongly, and which had undertaken to safeguard Austria's independence, made any serious effort to stop Hitler. Once Mussolini had decided to yield to Hitler over Austria, Britain was the only country which could conceivably have stopped the *Anschluss*. The French would not act without Britain and the British brushed aside French suggestions for joint political action. Not only was Britain unready to fight Hitler, but Chamberlain, pursuing the mirage of a gentlemanly understanding with him, was unwilling even to try diplomatic pressure or what Eden had once called 'the guessing position',[166] that is, to keep Hitler guessing about whether or not Britain might actually use force.

Moreover, very few people in governing circles in Britain – or, probably, outside them – would have been willing to fight for Austria in any circumstances. Oliver Harvey noted in his diary on 15 February 1938: 'A.E. [Eden] determined not to get into the false position of giving the Austrians advice and then being saddled with the responsibility if they accept advice and the situation gets worse. We cannot fight for Austria and we must be careful not to raise false hopes in Vienna ...'[167] Oliver Harvey himself started a comment in his diary a few days later: 'granted, as I always have, that nobody would fight for Austria ...'[168] When Halifax saw the Labour leader, Clement Attlee, on the day after Hitler's invasion of Austria, he found him 'very sensible and intelligent'. Chamberlain could therefore make a virtually unchallenged statement in the House of Commons. He twice denied rumours that the government had given 'consent if not encouragement to the idea of the absorption of Austria by Germany'. 'However,' he went on, 'the government had

recognised Germany's "special interest" in the development of its relations with Austria.' 'But,' he added, 'it had
always been made plain that H.M.G. would strongly dis-
approve of the application of violent methods.'

The same mild criticism of Hitler's methods, not of the
Anschluss itself, was made by *The Times*, after Halifax
had dropped a word in the Editor's willing ear.[169] 'No
country, least of all our own, can afford to be lulled into
false security while these methods prevail on the neighbouring continent', *The Times* wrote on 14 March.[170]
Three weeks later, with almost unseemly haste, Chamberlain gave formal recognition to the *Anschluss* by shutting
down the British Legation in Vienna and replacing it with
a Consulate-General. This was eight days before Hitler's
plebiscite.

The roots of the curious British indifference to the
Anschluss went much further back than Chamberlain's
appeasement policy or Britain's reluctance to rearm. Oliver
Harvey summed up a prevalent official view in his diary
on 16 February, in his comment on the Berchtesgaden
Agreement: 'my instinct is not to take this too tragically:
the prohibition of the *Anschluss* has been wrong from the
start; it was a flagrant violation the principle of self-
determination and perhaps the weakest point in our post-
war policy'. There had always, he believed, been an
Austrian majority in favour of *Anschluss*: '*Anschluss* is
probably inevitable, and to stop it from outside is impossible and indefensible.'[171]

So the British let Austria vanish from the map of Europe
with little more than a nostalgic sigh and raised eyebrows
over Hitler's uncivilised manners. Eden commented later:
'this deed only imposed a temporary check on the optimism
of the appeasers'.[172] The British Chiefs of Staff, asked to
assess the new military situation following the *Anschluss*,
told Chamberlain that Czechoslovakia was now indefensible and that in any case Britain was not in a position to
wage war.[173]

2. Dr Ignaz Seipel, Christian Social leader in the 1920s

1. Otto Bauer, Social Democrat leader in the 1920s and 1930s

3. Burning of the Ministry of Justice, 1927

4. Dollfuss observing shelling of Socialist-held tenements, February 1934

6. Schuschnigg and Prince Starhemberg after Dollfuss's death

5. Dollfuss addressing the Fatherland Front, 1934

8. Occupation: Four-Power patrol of Vienna's Inner City

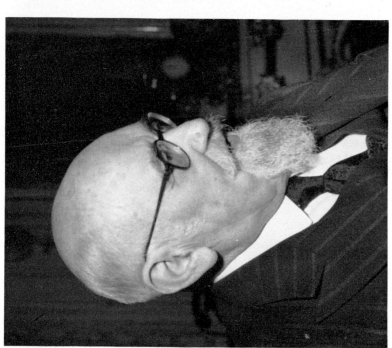

7. Karl Renner, 1947

It was perhaps not surprising if Austrians felt that the Western Powers had first forced independence upon them when they did not want it, and then left them in the lurch when they were trying to defend it. It was also remarkable that, given the powerful pressures exerted on them by Hitler and the ambivalence of their own feelings towards Germany, the Austrians should have managed to resist Hitler for five years.

PART II

Austrians without a State,
1938–1945

13 Austrians under Hitler

Within three months of the *Anschluss* Hitler had not only incorporated Austria administratively and juridically within the German State and in the Nazi power structure; he had also set out to remove all sense of an Austrian identity or an Austrian 'mission'. By doing this, he produced exactly the opposite result. Karl Renner wrote: 'In just three months Austria was liquidated as a State and a nation, but therewith the people's sympathies for the German Reich were also extinguished – apart from a few ideologists and academics remote from the real world and certain non-political writers and artists who wanted their dealy bread and did not look to see who provided it. . . Three months were enough to heal the hearts of real Austrians and to enable them to see clearly . . .'[174]

In the early months, Hitler's rearmament programme gave an impulse to certain sections of Austrian industry; but his campaign against Czechoslovakia in the autumn caused widespread criticism and there seemed to be general sympathy for the Czechs. This was shown by Gestapo reports of the period.[175]

From then on the Austrian economy was subjected to the demands of Hitler's preparations for war. The industrial workers – the vast majority of them politically educated by the Social Democratic Party, a small minority by the Communist Party – had already been psychologically inured to threats and bribes by the period of 'Austro-Fascism', and were mostly impervious to Nazi propaganda. They joined the DAF – the Nazi German Labour Front – but in a totally negative spirit. By January 1939 the deputy

mayor of Vienna was warning those who sought to undermine the state: 'when the time comes, these subversives
will experience the whole weight of National Socialist
justice'. Gestapo reports showed that up to the outbreak
of the Second World War in September 1939, there were a
good many cases of minor sabotage in factories. But go-
slow, work-to-rule and absenteeism were the usual weapons
of the workers, and, in the closing phase of the war, did
real damage.

Nazi rule brought about something which had only
rarely happened under 'Austro-Fascism' – fairly free and
frequent contacts between Socialists, whether Social
Democrats or the post-1934 R.S., and Communists. Yet the
methods of underground resistance employed were very
different. The Communists, following the Moscow line,
were prepared to take great risks for relatively small
results in the way of distribution of propaganda material,
putting up propaganda stickers and painting slogans.
Because of the highly centralised and rigid structure of
the Party, designed to make sure that directives from the
top were thoroughly and correctly disseminated, the
breakdown of one party member under police interrogation could lead to many other arrests. Communist leaders
sent in from Moscow and elsewhere were often casualties,
in the early days. Moreover R.S. members working with
the Communists might also suffer, but this did not stop
cooperation.

The R.S., for their part, had always prided themselves
on a highly efficient conspiratorial organisation designed
to minimise the danger from breakdowns or betrayals. This
meant a much looser and more informal system than the
Communists', mainly in the form of groups of like-minded
people or 'friendship circles' who could trust one another
and exchange information (for instance, news derived
from foreign broadcasts); there was little contact between
such groups. The chief R.S. leaders, including Buttinger,
had, by prior agreement, fled abroad at the time of the

Anschluss. The law court records of the Hitler period show that a majority of offenders were Left Wing and that among them the Communists predominated 'quite out of proportion to their following in the country'.[176]

Opposition was by no means limited to Socialists and Communists. The anti-Catholic campaign which the Nazis launched very soon after the *Anschluss*, in spite of the Bishops' public support for it, was even more violent than the campaign conducted in the German Reich; the attack by Nazis on the Cardinal Archbishop's Palace in Vienna in October 1938 was publicly criticised in the West; in Austria it inevitably produced strong reactions among Catholics. There is plenty of evidence that priests, nuns and other members of the Church became strongly anti-Hitler and sometimes took part in active resistance, but were not normally as harshly treated as the Communists or Socialists.

The leader of one 'Austrian Freedom Movement', Karl Roman Scholz, was a priest and a poet who welcomed members of any political party on the basis of the principle 'freedom of faith'. He and his allies were hoping to plan sabotage and military action and wanted to contact the Western Allies through Budapest.[177] But he was betrayed to the Gestapo, arrested in 1940, and executed on 10 May 1944.[178] The leader of another 'Austrian Freedom Movement', Dr Lederer, planned to recruit ex-army officers and restore an independent Austria. He too was executed.[179]

Resistance in Carinthia and Styria was a special case, because of the existence of the Slovene minority and the contacts which were developed, during the war, with the Slovene partisans on the other side of the frontier, under the command of Marshal Tito. It appears that the 'Anti-Fascist Freedom Movement for Austria' which originally grew up there was basically monarchist but had useful contacts in the armed forces and with the Left and was prepared to cooperate with the Slovene partisans. Thirty-one members were arrested by the Gestapo in 1943, and two at least were executed.[180]

It is not clear exactly what connexion this movement had with the predominantly Communist movement to which both members of the Slovene minority and Austrians of various political shades belonged in the latter part of the war, and which came to be closely linked with Tito's Slovene partisans. What is certain is that the Soviet Union was hoping that a 'Freedom Front' would grow up not only in Carinthia and Styria but throughout Austria, and that by radio propaganda and other means its growth could be promoted from outside the country. Radio broadcasts from the Soviet Union to Austria tried to build up the myth – and if possible the reality – of such a united, all-party (but Communist-led) movement. An article in the Soviet review *War and the Working Class* of November 1943 declared that there had been a 'Freedom Conference' in the mountains in Austria in 1942 at which forty delegates from all walks of life adopted the slogan 'Austria for the Austrians'; it added that between October 1942 and April 1943, over 150 executions of resisters had been publicly announced. The Soviet review, however, went on to say that 'the real underground, nation-wide sabotage against the enslavers, which the Austrian Freedom Front proclaimed, is still lacking . . . the freedom movement in Austria lags far behind the freedom movement in other European countries . . .'

Broadcasts from the Soviet Union continued to provide backing for an Austrian Freedom Front (or ÖFF), but there is no evidence that the ÖFF ever spread beyond Carinthia and Styria. The contacts established between the ÖFF and Tito's partisans (of which Moscow was clearly informed) did, however, produce some results. On 7 October 1944 Radio Free Yugoslavia (based in the Soviet Union) announced these contacts, and a month later broadcast appeals were made to all Austrians in Styria and Carinthia to join Tito's 'Liberation Army': all Austrians who came over would be provided with arms and formed into special Austrian units under their own commanders and with their own red-white-red shoulder flash. At the end of November the formation of the first Austrian battalion was announced: its members were said to be wearing Yugoslav uniform with a red-white-red shoulder flash. Soon after, a second Austrian battalion was said to have been formed. The Austrian Communist, Franz Honner, was sent from the Soviet Union to take up a post as commander (under Tito's Slovene H.Q.). Bruno Kreisky (later Chancellor) who was then in exile in Stockholm told a British official that having spent eighteen months in prison with Honner, he had a high regard for him (though not for other Communists), and wished to contact him.[181] In April a 'memorandum' from the ÖFF reached the Foreign Office in London, claiming that it had been formed in 1938, was composed of patriots of all political parties, and had organised strikes and sabotage and killed German officials. The memorandum was, however, signed by the 'provisional Committee of the ÖFF for Styria and Carinthia'.

It is therefore clear that the ÖFF existed in practice only in these two Lands and never had any real existence elsewhere in Austria, in spite of all the efforts of Soviet propaganda and of Tito's Slovene H.Q. What is interesting is that in these two Lands, non-Communist Austrians were ready to join the predominantly Communist and Slovene ÖFF.

One form of resistance which came near to being of far greater importance than the ÖFF – in practical terms – was the role which Austrians played in the anti-Hitler plot of 20 July 1944, of which the Germans, Carl Friedrich Goerdeler and Colonel Claus Stauffenberg, were the prime movers. The plot failed, but this was not the fault of the Austrians concerned. In Vienna, when the signal came from Stauffenberg in Berlin, the plot was carried out most efficiently, with the prompt arrest of leading Nazi Party and Gestapo officials and the seizure of key buildings. This meant that, when the failure of the plot became known in Vienna, there was harsh retribution on the

Austrians immediately involved – death for Major Robert Bernardis who was Stauffenberg's right-hand man in Berlin and for Colonel Marogna-Redwitz in Vienna, imprisonment for other Austrian officers, concentration camp for those named as the conspirators' political representatives – the Social Democrat, Karl Seitz, the Christian Social Lower Austrian peasant leader, Josef Reither, and later Leopold Figl, who subsequently became People's Party Chancellor from 1945 on.[182] A young officer who had been deeply involved in Vienna, Captain Karl Szokoll, very fortunately avoided arrest and survived to play an important part in the last days of Nazi rule.

From the autumn of 1944 onwards it was clear to leading Austrians that it would only be a matter of months before the Russian armies arrived on the Austrian frontier, from the East. When forces of the Western Allies would arrive was very much less certain. But whatever the timing of these military developments, the need for Austrians to prepare politically for the moment of 'liberation' was obvious. In Vienna a resistance group known as O 5 grew up, and established contacts with the Western Allies in Switzerland. On 18 December, in the flat in Vienna of a Christian Social politician, Wilhelm Spitz, a 'Provisional Austrian National Committee' was set up, but, like O 5, at first lacked any Socialist representative. It was not until February that this difficulty was overcome, after contact had been established by round-about means with the Social Democrat, Adolf Schärf. By this time a young envoy of the group, Fritz Molden, had met the U.S. intelligence chief, Allan Dulles, in Switzerland, and, through the French, had visited the Soviet Embassy in liberated Paris. The Russians received him with interest but made no commitments.[183]

During April 1945, Washington and London were exchanging views on the Provisional Austrian Committee. The British Embassy in Washington – presumably voicing the American view – sent London a favourable estimate.

This was that the committee was becoming 'fairly well organised', and comprised all important Austrian political elements from Right to Left, including Christian Socials, Social Democrats, monarchists and Communists; its supporters were said 'to number perhaps 40,000, nearly half of whom are in Vienna'. It was reported to have infiltrated the Gestapo and to be practically in control of the telegraph system. The committee had asked to send a representative to Moscow and wanted a Soviet liaison officer to be sent to Austria.[184]

The British Foreign Office view was sceptical. It had, it said, also received reports about the committee but was 'inclined, in the absence of more concrete evidence, heavily to discount them'. One official wrote, in a minute of 24 April: 'the facts are that we have no indication of any serious organised resistance in Austria. . . . It is doubtful whether these unfortunate people ever get much beyond talking . . .'[185]

Both Americans and British clearly suffered from lack of information about what was going on in Austria. The Americans filled in the gap with optimism, the British with scepticism. It was, however, undoubtedly true that the Austrians were unfortunate. As the Russian army advanced into Austria from Hungary, the young Austrian officer, Szokoll, who had been deeply involved in the Vienna end of the 20 July plot, determined that contact must be established between the O 5 organisation and the Soviet Command, with the special aim of saving Vienna from destruction. He found the right man for the job in Sergeant-Major Ferdinand Käs, who made his way through the German lines near the Semmering Pass and handed over to the Russians the German plans for the defence of Vienna: it was agreed that action by the conspirators in Vienna should be co-ordinated with Soviet military encirclement of the city. The Russians played their part, but the plans of the conspirators were betrayed (by an Austrian) and the Nazis publicly hanged three Austrian army officers.

Nevertheless, the fighting in Vienna was mercifully brief, even if St Stephen's Cathedral suffered severe damage. The O 5 organisation did some useful work in keeping disorder and destruction to the minimum, cooperating with the Russians after their entry, and making preparations for a new Austrian administration.

If Austrian resistance was relatively small-scale compared with certain of the occupied countries of Europe, it has to be remembered that the difficulties were peculiarly great. At the time of the *Anschluss* the Nazis had seized all the police records of the Schuschnigg regime; thereafter Austria had been totally incorporated into the German Reich; many potential resistance leaders had been arrested before the war started; the work of the German security organs was made easy by the simple fact that Austrians spoke German; the risk of betrayal was heightened by the fact that a good many Austrians, especially in the armed forces, felt a genuine conflict of loyalties.

For their efforts at resistance, the Austrians certainly suffered. According to figures given by the Austrian authorities, which may not be final, 2700 Austrians were condemned and executed as active resisters; nearly 9700 were killed in Gestapo prisons; 6420 died in prison in German-occupied countries.

The other side of the picture is the prominent role played by a number of Austrians in Hitler's service in peculiarly unpleasant tasks – for instance, Seyss-Inquart's role as Hitler's representative in occupied Holland, Otto Skorzeny's work in the S.S., or Ernst Kaltenbrunner's role in the S.D. (security service). But it is ludicrous to attempt to strike any sort of moral balance sheet. What is certain is that the Austrians killed or imprisoned for resistance pale into insignificance compared with the total of Austrian Jews who died in concentration camps and ghettos: this, according to impartial sources, was 65,459. One historian commented: 'the loss to Austria's cultural and economic life is visible on all sides; but far more worrying is the

thought that a crime of such magnitude could be perpetrated against so little opposition'.[186]

If within a few months of the *Anschluss* most Austrians
had turned against Hitler, there was still the question of
what they wanted for the future, after Hitler's defeat. The
Socialists had their long-standing commitment to the
principle of union with Germany – a democratic Germany.
Renner had for short-term reasons endorsed Hitler's
Anschluss in April 1938; Otto Bauer, from exile, had said
in June that the restoration of Austrian independence
would be reactionary; the aim must be an 'all-German
revolution'.[187] The R.S. leaders in exile, and some R.S.
members in Austria, had close links with certain German
Social Democrats and took the attitude that Austrians
should not once again allow independence to be forced
upon them by the capitalist powers.

Yet during the period 1938–42 the general mood inside
Austria changed from active or passive acceptance of the
Anschluss to determination to break away from Germany
and regain independence. The Communists had almost
immediately taken up this position, presumably on instructions from Moscow. In November 1938, the Party Central
Committee passed a resolution on 'the struggle for the
liberation of Austria from foreign rule'.[188] In May 1939
the Communists were circulating a pamphlet calling for
unity in the struggle for 'a free Austria'. In the autumn of
1942 the battle of Stalingrad led – according to the German security organs – to a growth of *Preussenhass* (hatred
of the Prussians).[189] By the summer of 1943 most people,
of whatever party, seemed to have reached the same point:
they wanted an independent Austria.

Adolf Schärf, the Social Democrat who later became
President, recounted how he became conscious of his
changed attitude in a flash of self-discovery. This was
when he was approached in great secrecy in the early

summer of 1943 by a representative of the Goerdeler anti-Hitler conspiracy, who was seeking support among Austrian politicians. The visitor, after explaining the aims of the conspiracy, said that if Austria joined in, it could then be confidently expected that the *Anschluss* would be upheld in the eventual peace treaty. Schärf, to his own surprise, found himself interrupting his visitor and saying: 'The *Anschluss* is dead. Love of the German Reich has been driven out of the Austrians . . . I can see the days, before my eyes, when the Reich Germans will be driven out of Austria as the Jews have been.' Schärf had the feeling that it was not he himself who was speaking, but that another man was speaking through him. But he then found that his friends, including Seitz, the former Social Democrat mayor of Vienna, and Renner had reached the same conclusion.[190]

Less surprisingly, the Christian Social, Lois Weinberger, when approached by Goerdeler, gave very much the same answer: 'we certainly want to do all we can to help you . . . but above all, let us be what we were for so long – Austrians . . .'[191]

After the failure of the 20 July plot, Gestapo interrogation of prisoners in Berlin confirmed the attitude of the Austrians involved.[192]

Monarchists were naturally in favour of an independent Austria. Finally, even within the old Austrian Nazi movement, there was great discontent with the way in which Reich Germans dominated the stage and held all the best posts: this was very far from what they had hoped.

The swing of feeling against union with Germany must inevitably have been strengthened by the growing belief that Hitler would lose the war, and that Austria would do well to break away from Germany. But it is clear that there were also much deeper roots, in a feeling that Austria had a special way of life and identity, a special inheritance and achievement, which had been brutally violated by Hitler, but which must be rescued and preserved for the future.

14 The Allied Powers and the Austrians, 1939–1945

Even if the Austrians knew by 1943 what they wanted, they were in no position to decide their own future. This, once again, was decided for them by outside forces, the Allied Powers. The Allied governments, moreover, were very little influenced by developments inside Austria, about which they lacked information, or by exiled Austrian leaders abroad who, after Otto Bauer's death in 1938, were men without political weight and were quite unable to unite in a single representative body. The Allied Powers therefore settled Austria's future in the light of their own interests, or what one or the other conceived to be the interest of European peace. It was a fortunate coincidence that this time the wishes of the big Powers were in harmony with the wishes of the Austrians.

The Allies fighting Hitler – in the first place France and Britain, later the Soviet Union and the United States – had to deal with three aspects of the Austrian question. First there were the Austrians in exile: could they or should they form a representative body which could be of use to the Allied war effort? Next, there was Austria's political future: this came up both in the short-term context of stimulating Austrian resistance to Hitler and in the long-term context of planning for post-war Europe. There was also the wider question of Austria's place in relation to the other countries of the Danube basin; and this touched sensitive spots in the troubled relationship between the Western Powers and the Soviet Union.

The Austrian exiles

It may perhaps in the long run have been fortunate that the Austrians in exile were too divided themselves ever to form a single united body which might have gained recognition from one or more of the Allied Powers. If any such body had been formed in the West, the Russians would have regarded it with great suspicion and the question of its return to post-war Austria might well have caused bitter dispute between the West and Moscow. Even if an Austrian representative body had succeeded, as the Czechoslovak President Beneš did, in concluding a wartime agreement with Moscow, this would have been no safeguard against grave post-war difficulties. Similarly if any Austrian body had been formed in the Soviet Union, it would have been distrusted and disliked in the West. The disunity of the Austrian exiles may therefore have been lucky for post-war Austria.

The two most active elements among the exiles were the Habsburg Archdukes and their followers on one side and the Austrian Communists on the other. From 1941 onwards, in Britain and elsewhere, they formed a curious alliance in the Free Austrian Movement, which had loosely associated branches in many countries, including the Middle East and Latin America. The main bond which united monarchists and Communists from the start was determination to restore an independent Austria – the Habsburgs because this was a necessary step on the way to a restoration of the monarchy, the Communists – like their comrades inside Austria – presumably because Mossow wanted to weaken Germany in every possible way.

When the war broke out in 1939, Archduke Otto was in France, one of his younger brothers, Robert, was in London, and another, Felix, was in the United States. All were working together under Otto's direction for the formation of an Austrian representative body on the Allied side, and if possible for the establishment of an Austrian armed formation or 'Legion'. Towards the end of 1939 it looked as though the French government were moving towards recognition of an Austrian group in Paris – an idea regarded as rash and premature by the Foreign Office in London. But the French seemed unable to make up their minds about the degree to which the Habsburgs should be associated with the proposed body, over which Professor Richard Wasicky, of the Vienna University Faculty of Medicine, was to preside. By February 1940 prospects of official French recognition had faded; the proposed body disintegrated and, with the fall of France, most Austrians fled westwards.

The Foreign Office in London was extremely reluctant to become involved with the Habsburgs, largely because they did not want to upset President Beneš, now in exile in Britain, and still less to annoy Prince Regent Paul of Yugoslavia, who was maintaining an uneasy neutrality in the face of German pressures. In London, therefore, the Habsburgs were always frowned upon, and any idea that Archduke Otto should settle in Britain was seen with alarm. However, polite contacts were kept up with Archduke Robert; and his direct personal approach to Churchill in 1942 may have slightly hastened the process of formulating a British policy towards Austria. Churchill, who had a certain taste for monarchs, was less hostile to the Habsburgs than was Anthony Eden, who, as Foreign Secretary, noted on a Foreign Office minute on 4 December 1942: 'We want nothing to do with these Habsburgs. A.E.'[193]

When Archduke Otto went to the United States early in 1940, he had a considerable success. His brother Felix had already been campaigning for a Danubian federation under the Habsburgs. The British Embassy reported that Otto developed the idea of a 'United States of Central Europe' comprising not only Austria and Hungary but also Rumania, Bohemia, Moravia, Slovakia and possibly Croatia. In London, around this time, Archduke Robert was more modestly urging the B.B.C.'s Director General to broadcast in favour of the independence of Austria.

Early in 1941, Archduke Robert started a new initiative. About 1000 out of the roughly 10,000 Austrians in Britain (of whom around 90 per cent were Jewish)[194] had volunteered for service in the Pioneer Corps, but were dispersed in different units. The Archduke suggested they should be brought together in a specifically Austrian unit. However, since the idea stemmed from a Habsburg, the Austrian Socialists opposed it strongly and successfully, and it was abandoned.[195]

In the autumn of 1942, Otto was pressing for the formation of an Austrian Legion in the United States, while Robert renewed the attack in London (without success). In Washington, on 19 November, the Secretary for War, Henry Stimson, spoke in favour of an Austrian battalion in the U.S. Army, to 'demonstrate to Austrians all over the world the determination of the United States to free Austria. . .'[196] The U.S. State Department disliked the idea, but it found favour in the White House, and in January 1943 President Roosevelt spoke approvingly of it at a press conference. However, there was a storm of protest from anti-Habsburg Austrians and Americans of Czechoslovak or Yugoslav origin, and nothing happened. In London the Foreign Office had always thought the Americans were being rash, and felt duly relieved. From then on the Habsburgs played a less prominent role.

Attempts to set up a united Austrian organisation in London were profuse and confusing. As early as New Year's Eve, 1939, an 'Austria Office' was hailed by the *Sunday Times* as containing 'all that is virile and best' in the Austrian people as a whole, while next day the *Daily Herald* said that the 'Office' should shortly 'represent free Austria before the world'. However, both this and subsequent bodies were refused recognition by the Foreign Office, on the ground that they failed to represent adequately either Austrians abroad or Austrians inside Austria. When at the end of 1942 the 'Free Austrian Movement' (FAM) was formed, claiming to embody eleven out of thirteen Austrian groups in Britain, the Foreign Office decided to have 'informal contacts' with it, while still withholding recognition on the ground that it did not include 'important elements'.

The FAM was in fact dominated by Communists, with monarchists cooperating quite happily. The chief 'important elements' not included in it were the Left-wing Socialists – mainly R.S. – who became known as the Pollak Socialists after their leader in London, the former editor of the *Arbeiter Zeitung*, Oskar Pollak. They had close relations with the Labour Party, and since the Labour Party was represented in the War Cabinet and Ernest Bevin, in particular, took a close interest in them, the Foreign Office was careful not to leave them out of account. They were said to number around 200. There were also a few minor Christian Socials in London, who did not want to tie themselves to the FAM. Thus the two political parties which had been strongest in post-1918 Austria – in so far as they were represented in London – stood aloof from the FAM; and the same pattern was repeated in other capitals.

When therefore in April 1943 the Foreign Office prepared a paper on policy towards Austria, it noted: 'we are faced at the outset with the handicap that there is no Austrian government in exile representing the Austrian unity that has been destroyed . . . Nor is there the slightest prospect of building up a representative Austrian Council or Committee from the material available in the U.S.A. or elsewhere outside Austria . . . The Austrians themselves will have to throw up the first responsible government of restored Austria . . .'[197] The United States did not dissent.

In the Soviet Union, there was a small and active group of Austrian Communists, of whom the best known in the outside world was Ernst Fischer, the intellectual, writer and former Socialist; he was the chief broadcaster to Austria from Moscow. The official party leader was, however, an 'organisation man', Johann Koplenig. But the

Russians never seem to have tried to set up a more widely-based, if Communist-dominated, Austrian body in the Soviet Union. They were perhaps discouraged by the relative failure of Communists inside Austria to create a 'liberation movement' and the very limited achievements of the Free Austrian Movement in London and elsewhere. When the Russian armies advanced into Eastern Europe in 1944, Free Austrian committees were set up in the Bulgarian capital, Sofia, and apparently also in the East Hungarian town of Debrecen. But, apart from broadcasts from Sofia to Austria, very little use seems to have been made of them by the Russians.

One thing the Soviet Union had made clear before the war ended was that it did not like the Austrian Socialists. The Soviet periodical, *War and the Working Class*, in November 1943 attacked Renner for his 'capitulation' over the *Anschluss*, and also the 'London group of the notorious "Revolutionary Socialists"'. 'This group', it said, 'which yesterday favoured a Greater Germany and opposed Austrian independence, today is already hurrying to parcel out leading posts in the future Austrian State.' On 7 April 1945, as the Russian armies were approaching Vienna, the Soviet Communist Party newspaper, *Pravda*, wrote: 'some Social Democratic emigrés in London are already offering their services in the struggle to suppress Russian influence; in this way they want to make Austria again a bulwark against the East'.

It is likely that the Russians, knowing past Socialist strength in Austria, foresaw the resistance which Socialists might put up to Soviet policies in Austria. On the other hand they knew it would be quite unrealistic to attempt to form a combination of forces which excluded the Socialists. This may have been one of the reasons why the Russians, like the Western Allies, did not commit themselves to any one political body of Austrians in exile (apart of course from their inevitable commitment to Communists).

15 The Moscow Declaration on Austria, 1943

The initiative in working out a joint Allied policy towards Austria came from the British. At this time they were still blithely – in retrospect, blindly – self-confident in their power to play a leading part in shaping the design of post-war Europe. In particular, Churchill – in his spare moments – seemed to feel himself to be a master-architect.

The Foreign Office was much more slow and cautious in its approach to the Austrian question. It was surprised and a little shocked when on 12 November 1939, the French President Lebrun, in a message to the Dutch and Belgian monarchs, proclaimed: 'lasting peace can be established only by the reparation of the injustice imposed by force on Czechoslovakia, Austria and Poland'. A senior Foreign Office official noted: 'we [the British] have restricted ourselves in such statements to the Poles and Czechs. . . .'

During 1940, there was argument inside the Foreign Office over Austria. A minority view was expressed by Sir Robert (later Lord) Vansittart, at this time Chief Adviser and somewhat isolated: 'surely we have got very definitely to face and provide for the reconstitution of an independent Austria . . .' But the Department responsible for German and Austrian affairs retorted: '. . . the Austria of 1919 turned out to be an artificial creation . . . It may be that an independent Austria after this war will be even more artificial . . . It is too early to discern the shape of post-war Europe . . .' The Department's view prevailed.

Churchill had fewer doubts and stronger convictions about Austria than the Foreign Office. In his history of the 1919 peace conference (written in 1929) he had written that theoretically, the Austrian claim to join Germany, on the basis of the Wilsonian principle of self-determination, was difficult to resist. But, he went on, 'in practice it was loaded with danger. It would have meant making the new Germany larger in territory and population than the old Germany which had already proved strong enough to fight the world for four years. It would have brought the frontiers of the German realm to the summits of the Alps and made a complete barrier between Eastern and Western Europe.' Therefore, Churchill wrote, 'for the gravest reasons of European peace', it had to be excluded.[198]

Given this conviction that Austria must be independent, it was not surprising that Churchill, at the Mansion House on 9 November 1940, spoke of 'all the countries with whom and for whom we have drawn the sword – Austria, Czechoslovakia, Poland, Norway, Holland, Belgium; greatest of all, France; latest of all, Greece'. 'For all these', he went on, 'we will toil and strive, and our victory will supply the liberation of them all.' He followed this up on 17 January 1941 by mentioning Austria as one of the countries where the German occupation was building up hatred of the Nazi creed and the German name. In the following April, he spoke of millions of Germans spread over Europe, 'engaged in holding down Austrians, Czechs, Poles and many other ancient races they now bully and pillage'.

The Foreign Office remained cautious and reserved about Austrian independence, noting in January 1941 that many Austrians in Austria 'accept the union with Germany', and that 'any lead which we gave would only appeal to a minority and would antagonize the majority who would feel that we ourselves were seeking to impose a solution without taking Austrian views into account'.[199] But by the following September the Foreign Office was studying the idea of placing Austria in a federation: 'the solution which would probably suit us best is that of an Austria bound up with some sort of Danubian Federation . . . It is too early to say yet whether it will be practicable . . .'[200] Experts carefully examined all aspects of a federation. But in October 1941 the Foreign Secretary, Eden, was still cautious. In a letter to a fellow-minister, Leo Amery, who wanted Britain to encourage an association of East and Central European countries, he wrote: '. . . I feel that any attempt at this stage to sponsor a particular scheme will either disappoint our Allies or alternatively convince the Austrians and Hungarians that they must continue to cast in their lot with the Germans. My own feeling, and it is one which is fully shared with the U.S. Government, is that we should avoid commitments at the present stage of the war . . .'[201]

By this time a vitally important new factor had come into the situation: since June, the Soviet Union had been an ally. In December 1941 Eden went to Moscow to try to negotiate an Anglo-Soviet treaty. Stalin presented him with the draft of a secret protocol on future European frontiers, which provided that Austria should be restored, while the Rhineland and possibly Bavaria were to be detached from Germany.[202] Eden told Stalin: 'as regards the partition of Germany no decision has been taken either way by H.M.G. . . . We have not closed our minds to the consideration of a separate Bavaria or the Rhineland, and we are certainly definitely in favour of a separate Austria . . .'[203] There was also some discussion of federations in Eastern Europe. Stalin said: 'if certain of the countries of Europe wish to federate, then the Soviet Union will have no objection to such a course'.[204]

Eden therefore seemed to have taken a decisive step forward over Austria, while Stalin had indicated that he had an open mind over a federation. The British, however, were not yet ready to make a public statement about Austria. In December 1941 a group of Austrians in the

United States, including the conductor, Bruno Walter, and the writer, Franz Werfel, appealed to the British to declare that they did not recognise the *Anschluss*. The Foreign Office view, as revealed in a minute of January 1942, was: 'this does not seem to be desirable as yet . . .'[205]

One reason for caution in the Foreign Office at this time was that in the early part of 1942, negotiations about an Anglo-Soviet treaty were still going on. In April a British draft was sent to Moscow in which the idea of a federation in Eastern Europe figured fairly prominently. The Moscow counterdraft made no mention of this, and the Soviet Foreign Minister explained that 'the Soviet government had certain information to show that some federations might be directed against the Soviet Union'.[206] He was clearly referring to the discussions then going on between the Polish and Czechoslovak exiled governments in London about a federation of the two countries; this idea, in view of Soviet hostility towards the London Poles, did not please Moscow. In the event both the British and Soviet drafts were dropped and a totally different treaty, which referred neither to Austrian independence nor to federations, was signed in the early summer of 1942.

The Foreign Office remained reluctant to make any move over Austria. It wished to co-ordinate policy with the United States before any public statement was made. This annoyed Churchill; on 10 June 1942 he sent a personal minute to Eden: 'I do not propose to subject myself to any special inhibition about Austria. I certainly look forward to its liberation and thereafter to its re-establishment, either as a separate State or as the centre of a mid-Europe confederation.'[207]

In spite of this little outburst, Churchill refrained from any fresh public statement. But the efforts of the Foreign Office to co-ordinate policy with the United States lagged, perhaps partly because of the popularity of the Habsburgs at the White House. In July 1942 the U.S. State Department, without previous consultation with London, said that the United States had 'never taken the position that Austria was legally absorbed in the German Reich'. On 9 September Eden took a much more evasive line in the House of Commons: 'while H.M.G. could not commit themselves to any particular future frontiers in Europe, they equally did not regard themselves as bound by any change effected in Austria in and since 1938'.[208]

In December 1942, Archduke Robert set Churchill off on the warpath again, with a letter pressing that Britain should follow a more active policy towards Austria, especially over the question of an Austrian fighting unit. Churchill did not like the negative response proposed by the Foreign Office, and on 13 December sent a personal minute to Eden, saying that it would be a very good thing to have an Austrian unit if it could be managed without too much trouble, and adding: 'I am extremely interested in Austria and hope that Vienna may become the capital of a great Confederation of the Danube. It is perfectly true that Europe left Austria to her fate in a pusillanimous manner in 1938. The separation of the Austrians and South Germans from the Prussians is essential to the harmonious reconstitution of Europe . . .'[209]

The idea of Vienna as capital of a Danubian Federation must have alarmed Eden, who knew how much it would offend the exiled Poles and Czechs. In answer to a question in the House of Commons he said on 16 December: 'whether it will be possible or desirable to include Austria or Hungary within a federation based upon Poland and Czechoslovakia must clearly depend . . . upon the views of the Polish and Czechoslovak governments and people and upon the future attitude of the Austrians and Hungarians, who are fighting in the ranks of our enemies'. On 28 December Eden replied to Churchill's minute: 'I share your interest in Austria', he began, perhaps a little acidly, but went on to say that it was not easy to reach a decision on 'this complicated problem'. He opposed an Austrian–Bavarian confederation: 'I think we should work to wean

Austria from her traditional association with Germany.'
Confederations should be organic, not artificial growths.
Moreover, Eden wrote, 'a Danubian federation with its
capital in Vienna would cause consternation among our
Polish, Czech and Yugoslav allies'. An independent Austria
and perhaps Hungary might be included in a confederation based on Poland and Czechoslovakia, but account
must be taken of the wishes of the prospective partners.
'I do not see any future for the Habsburgs', Eden added.

Churchill, thwarted again, minuted tersely to Eden on
4 January 1943: 'In the circumstances I think it would be
better for you to reply to the Archduke Robert, saying that
I have passed his letter to you. W.S.'[210]

However, things were on the move. In January 1943 the
Political Warfare Executive, which was responsible for
propaganda to enemy and enemy-occupied countries, proposed that, to stimulate resistance in Austria, the government should make a statement saying that it would
welcome an independent Austria, 'playing its full part in a
reconstituted Central Europe', and urging that Austrians
'must make their contribution now, alongside their heroic
neighbours, the Czechoslovaks and Yugoslavs, to the
defeat of the common enemy'.[211] The immediate Foreign
Office response was negative, but its experts were set to
work and in February they produced a recommendation
that Austria should be restored as an independent state
but that the question of its inclusion in a Danubian federation should be left till later. The experts thought Austria
would be the natural leader of such a federation, but that
this was exactly what the other states of the area would
not accept.[212]

On this basis, the Foreign Office drew up a document in
April which noted that while the Czechs would not oppose
Austria's membership of a federation, the Polish exiled
leader, General Sikorski, had said that he would fear
Austria in an East European federation as a potential fifth
column. The Foreign Office paper concluded: 'the first step

must be the restoration of a free and independent Austrian State, standing alone'. But whatever international guarantees it might receive, this state would be weak and so a 'potential danger spot'; therefore, 'anything that can be should be done to strengthen Austria's international position . . . The way should be left open for her inclusion in whatever form of international or regional structures may develop in Central and South-east Europe.'[213]

In May 1943 Eden submitted this paper to the War Cabinet, arguing that with the turn of the tide of war, there were now better chances of embarrassing Germany by encouraging resistance and sabotage in Austria. He also proposed discussion with the U.S. and Soviet governments in the hope that a joint three-power declaration on Austria could then be issued.

Before the War Cabinet could consider the Foreign Office proposal, the Soviet Union made it known that it did not like federations. Already on 10 March the Soviet Ambassador, Ivan Maisky, had told Eden that Moscow was 'not enthusiastic' about federations in Europe, preferring a 'bloc of the United Nations', to be led by the Soviet Union and Britain.[214] On 7 June the Soviet Foreign Minister, Vyacheslav Molotov, sent a letter to the British Ambassador in Moscow saying that his government was 'unwilling to pledge itself' with regard to an East European federation, and also considered the inclusion of Austria and Hungary as 'unsuitable'.[215]

The War Cabinet, if aware of Molotov's move, took no account of it. On 16 June it agreed that the Foreign Office paper 'might be adopted as a broad statement of our policy in regard to Austria, for purposes of political warfare and preliminary discussions of post-war matters'. But the Cabinet also thought that a promise of independence might not have much appeal to Austrians, given the hardships the country had undergone during the inter-war period. There was therefore 'general agreement that we should aim at a Central European or Danubian group centred on Vienna'. Such a group, the War Cabinet said, should 'aim at combining the economic stability of the larger unit with the considerable degree of freedom, in purely local affairs, of the smaller national or racial units into which Austria-Hungary had broken up at the end of the last war'. But there must be great care in presenting this idea if jealousies and susceptibilities were not to be aroused.[216]

Clearly, Churchill had refused to budge from his belief that Vienna should be the centre of a Danubian federation. (Ernest Bevin may perhaps have supported him; eighteen months earlier he had been anxious to talk to the Pollak Socialists about Austria's place in a wider federation, though he had allowed himself to be dissuaded by Eden.)[217] Eden presumably felt it wisest to yield, or to appear to yield for the time being, and to try to overcome Soviet objections.

When, therefore, he approached the Soviet and U.S. governments in August 1943 with a proposal for a joint declaration on Austria – of which he submitted a draft – he recalled Molotov's letter of 7 June, but added: 'I should hope that this [Soviet] disapproval would not extend to the inclusion of an independent Austria and possibly a reformed Hungary in some confederation . . . on condition, of course, that any such confederation was in no way hostile to the USSR . . .' The British draft declaration was, however, tactful on federations: 'They [the three Powers] wish to see re-established a free and independent Austria, which shall enjoy, in association with those neighbouring states which will be faced with similar problems, that political and economic security which is the only basis for lasting peace.'

Nevertheless the British Ambassador in Moscow advised that there should be no reference to federations at all, because of the strained state of Soviet–Polish relations. Eden overruled him: he said that his proposal had received Cabinet approval, 'and in fact our Austrian policy . . . has been crystallised and approved in principle to a greater degree than in the case of most debatable areas in Europe . . .'[218]

In October, the U.S. State Department gave general approval to the Eden proposal, but said it would prefer to omit from the declaration any reference to 'association with neighbouring states', since the U.S. government had not yet committed itself on the subject of federations.[219] Otherwise the State Department suggested only small changes in wording.

From Moscow, there was no immediate reaction, but the Soviet Union agreed readily to the British suggestion that the proposed declaration should be one of the items on the agenda of the conference of the Soviet, British and American Foreign Ministers which had been fixed for October. Eden also submitted a draft declaration on federations in general, by which the three Powers were to say that 'they regard it as their duty and interest . . . to assist other European states to form any associations designed to increase mutual welfare and the general prosperity of the Continent'; they were also to promise 'not to seek to create any separate areas of responsibility in Europe' nor recognise such for others, 'but rather affirm their common interest in the well-being of Europe as a whole'.[220] This wording may well have strengthened Soviet suspicion that the British wanted an East European federation as a bulwark against Soviet influence; but the Russians did not object to discussing the British draft at the Three-Power Conference.

The Foreign Ministers – Molotov, Eden and the reserved and cautious Cordell Hull – met in Moscow on 19 October. Six days later Eden raised the draft declaration on Austria, as amended by the United States. Molotov said it was 'acceptable in principle' but needed small amendments; it was referred to a Drafting Committee. On 30 October this Committee reported agreement on a text which was accepted by the Foreign Ministers without further argument.

The changes made by the Russians were small. Eden commented: 'though we don't particularly like them, we and the Americans have accepted them'. The Russians had made the reference to Austria's neighbours still more vague, and had slightly sharpened the reminder to the Austrian people that they 'have a responsibility which they cannot evade, and that in the final settlement account will inevitably be taken of the part they play in resisting the German invader'.

Eden's proposal for a declaration on federations was smothered by Molotov in a speech of such statesmanlike wisdom that he was clearly covering up far more pungent reasons for rejecting it. The small countries, he said, would need time to orientate themselves to the new post-war situation; they should not be subjected to any pressure to join this or that new grouping; 'the premature and possibly artificial attachment of these countries to theoretically planned groupings would be full of danger . . .' Moreover, neither the emigré governments nor even the governments that would be set up after the war would be able 'fully to ensure the expression of the real will and permanent aspirations of their people'.

More candidly, Molotov said that some of the plans for federation reminded the Soviet people of the policy of the *'cordon sanitaire'* [protective belt] directed, 'as is known', against the Soviet Union, 'and therefore viewed unfavourably by the Soviet people'.[221] Eden denied any thought of a *cordon sanitaire* against Russia, but, in the face of Molotov's eloquence, yielded gracefully, and the proposed declaration on federations sank without trace.

Churchill, thwarted over a Danubian federation, still clung to the alternative of an 'Austria–Bavaria' federation, seemingly unaware of any conflict with the three-power declaration on Austrian independence, and mentioned it at the Tehran Conference in November 1943. Stalin, at that time eager to break up Germany, seemed deliberately to encourage Churchill. At Moscow in October 1944 Stalin even said he would be glad to see Vienna the capital of a federation of South German States.[222] At the Yalta conference 'Austria–Bavaria' again came up but was not seriously discussed, and lapsed with the eventual decision to maintain German unity.

Austria therefore emerged in 1945 as an independent and separate state, standing alone; all possibility of federation with neighbouring Danubian countries was finally ruled out by the fall of the Iron Curtain, dividing Soviet-dominated Europe from the rest of the continent. After the war, as Stalin showed in his dispute with Tito, he became more and more hostile to federations, even inside the Soviet power realm.

16 The Military Carve-up, 1945

In the closing stages of the war, the British government, and Churchill in particular, became more and more preoccupied with the advance westwards of the Russian armies and the prospect of the establishment of a Soviet empire in Eastern and Central Europe. A further worry was American reluctance to become involved in this part of Europe. In May 1943 Eden had noted 'the instinctive distrust of the Americans for any military operations which committed them further into Europe, except by a cross-Channel invasion'. Eden commented later: 'fear of entanglement in the Balkans and of British schemes to lure them there diverted the Americans from thoughts of Vienna and Prague and gave the Soviets too wide a field'.[223]

In June 1944 the argument between the British and the Americans became sharp. The British Chiefs of Staff were advocating a concentrated drive north in Italy which could lead to a further drive through Trieste and the Ljubljana gap to Austria. The Americans wanted to take troops from Italy for the assault on southern France designed to support the main Allied offensive in north-west France. Churchill argued the case with Roosevelt, who at one point suggested (perhaps maliciously) that both sides of the case should be put before Stalin.[224] Churchill replied that for long-term political reasons Stalin would obviously prefer the British and Americans to fight in France leaving 'East, Middle and Southern Europe' to fall naturally to his control.[225] Stalin was not consulted. Inevit-

10. Adolf Schärf, Socialist leader 1945–57

9. Leopold Figl, People's Party leader 1945–51

11. Adolf Schärf with Ernest Bevin, 1947

12. The Austrian Treaty signed at the Belvedere, 1955

14. Kennedy and Khrushchev received by President Schärf, 1961

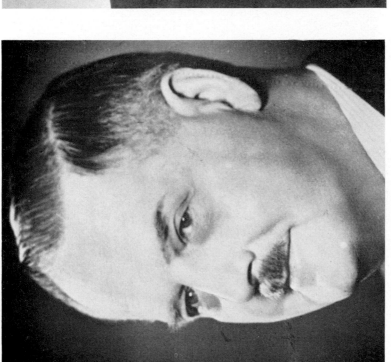

13. Julius Raab, People's Party leader 1951–30

16. Bruno Kreisky, Socialist leader 1967–

15. Josef Klaus, People's Party leader 1963–70

ably Roosevelt prevailed. Churchill wrote later: 'the army of Italy was deprived of its opportunity to strike a most formidable blow at the Germans, and very possibly reach Vienna before the Russians, with all that might have followed therefrom'.[226]

In September 1944 Churchill met Roosevelt in Quebec, and this time things went better. On 13 September he telegraphed to the War Cabinet: 'the idea of our going to Vienna, if the war lasts long enough and if other people do not get there first, is fully accepted here'.[227] When Churchill met Stalin in Moscow in the following month and concluded with him the 'percentage agreement' on spheres of 'predominance' in south-east Europe, Austria was excluded from its scope, remaining a sort of no-man's-land; Churchill kept a free hand to exploit the military situation as best he could. However, with depleted forces the Allied campaign in Italy was so difficult and slow that hopes of a drive into Austria faded.

At the Yalta conference in February 1945, Churchill and Stalin met again. Stalin – obviously assuming that the idea was by now militarily impossible – maliciously suggested that some British divisions should be transferred from Italy to Yugoslavia and Hungary and directed against Vienna. Churchill commented: 'it cost him nothing to say this now'.[228] On 1 April 1945 Churchill wrote gloomily to Roosevelt: 'the Russian armies will no doubt overrun all Austria and enter Vienna'.[229]

Churchill was too pessimistic. The Russians advanced on Vienna and were in full possession of it on 13 April, and then moved west up the Danube towards Linz. But Eisenhower, believing that Hitler and his most fanatical followers would try to hold out in a mountain stronghold near the Bavarian–Austrian border, sent the Third U.S. Army south-east down the Danube, and it reached Linz on 5 May, later meeting the Russians advancing from Vienna. The Seventh U.S. Army reached Innsbruck on 3 May, and sent a force south to the Brenner pass. At the same time the French crossed the Austrian frontier into Vorarlberg. The British in Italy had been delayed in the advance north-eastwards by the need to secure Trieste – partly as a supply port for Austria – against the efforts of Tito's forces to establish Yugoslav control there. But they crossed the southern frontier of Austria just before the German surrender on 8 May.

As the war ended, four 'liberating' armies were already on Austrian soil. But the Russians alone were in Vienna.

PART III

Austria Under Occupation,
1945–1955

17 The Renner Government and the Occupying Powers

Before the war had ended, a provisional Austrian government had already been formed in Vienna and approved by the Russian Commander, Marshal Tolbukhin; the Soviet Union had acted alone without obtaining the agreement of the Western Allies. Relations between the Soviet Union and the Western Allies over Austria were in fact badly strained. Fortunately, however, the Austrians did not know it. If they had, the Austrian political leaders would hardly have had the courage and self-confidence to try to take their country's fate into their own hands and to found a new Republic.

In April 1945, they believed that their country was being liberated, not conquered; that occupation by the victorious Allies would be short; and that full independence would quickly be restored to a united Austria. They could not see the two great dangers hanging over Austria: either that it would be absorbed as a whole into the Soviet power realm, coming under Communist rule in the process, or else that it would be divided, with the eastern half, and around half the population, falling under permanent Soviet control, and the western half integrating itself both politically and economically – perhaps also militarily – into Western Europe. The first of these dangers was lessened by the presence of the Western occupation forces in part of the country, and gradually faded. The second danger remained a very real one into the 1950s.

The part played by the Austrians themselves in establishing and preserving a genuinely democratic form of government, in maintaining the country's unity, and in resisting Soviet attempts to acquire an economic stranglehold, was important and probably decisive. In Czechoslovakia, where no Soviet troops were stationed after the end of 1945, the Communists succeeded in undermining and finally destroying a democratic system from within, with Soviet external support. If the Austrian Communists, with the help of the large Soviet occupation forces in Eastern Austria, had been equally successful, it would have been difficult for the Western Powers to take any action except perhaps to foster a separatist movement in western Austria and so divide the country irretrievably. It is in fact remarkable that Austria did not suffer the same fate as Germany or Korea.

The Austrian Socialists have claimed most of the credit for standing up to the Communists and preventing them from winning control over the workers so as to acquire an essential power base on which to erect a 'people's democracy' of the kind established throughout Soviet-dominated Eastern Europe, including East Germany, between 1945 and 1948. In other words, just as they prevented Austria from going 'Bolshevist' in 1918–19, so a generation later they prevented Austria from becoming a 'people's democracy'.

Austria's history in the early post-war years shows that there is a good deal of truth in this Socialist claim. But other factors were also important: in particular, a new-found sense of solidarity between the different social classes and different political parties, together with an unexpected – though sometimes wavering – loyalty of the western Lands to Vienna. The seven years of Nazi rule, followed by the shocks and hardships of military occupation in the post-war period, brought out the toughness, political ingenuity and organising ability which were ingrained in the Austrians but had been partially paralysed during the Hitler period.

Another very important factor was the generous economic aid given by the United States, first through UNRRA and later through Marshall Aid. This helped the Austrians to build up a stable and eventually thriving economy which was a solid base for political democracy. In addition the Western occupying powers, in spite of various errors of judgement, gave the Austrian government useful moral and political support and a good deal of sensible advice.

Finally, the Austrian leaders perceived and exploited the special position which Austria held from 1945 onwards as one of the sensitive points in the overall strategic and political confrontation between the Soviet Union and the West. They felt that they had to maintain good relations with both sides without making damaging concessions to either. Natural inclination and economic attraction might draw the Austrians to the West, but, strategically over-shadowed by the Soviet Union, they knew it would be fatal to give way entirely to natural inclination. So during the ten years of four-power occupation they evolved a new 'mission' for Austria – not, as in the past, as the bearer of Western or Germanic civilisation to the less advanced people of Eastern Europe, but as a connecting link between West and East, an interpreter and mediator between the two. In their conception of this mission there was an element of exaggeration and self-importance. But since Austrians clearly had a historically-rooted and deep-seated need for a 'mission' in Europe and in the world, the one which they chose after the Second World War was at least a useful and constructive one.

The Austrians who, between December 1944 and March 1945, had grouped themselves together in the Provisional Austrian National Committee had gone some way in their political planning for liberation. There was general agreement on returning to the 1920 republican constitution and on nationalising key industries, transport and banking. The future balance of power between the various political parties had not been discussed.

It was, however, obvious that the Russians were going to reach Vienna first. The Communists therefore expected to play a prominent role. They could claim that after the 1934 civil war they had won over workers from the Social Democrats, and that their outstandingly active resistance record strengthened their right to a big share of political power. It was said that when the Russians arrived, the Communists proposed that they themselves and the Social Democrats should each have 40 per cent of the posts in the new government, leaving 20 per cent for the Christian Socials; the Russians rejected this claim, believing that the Social Democrats were still considerably stronger than the Communists.

It is not clear whether the Russians arrived with any ready-made political plan for Austria. Adolf Schärf, the Socialist, believed that they had an exiled government in readiness in Yugoslavia.[230] There does not seem to be supporting evidence for this, though the Communist, Honner, was with Tito's forces.

What is certain is that the 74-year-old Renner put a new idea into the Russians' heads. He was living in retirement in Lower Austria, near the Semmering; because of violent behaviour by Russian troops in the neighbourhood, he went to protest to the local Russian commander, through whom he came into contact with high-level Russian officers who recognised his name as former Chancellor and a leading Right-wing Social Democrat. Thinking that he might serve a useful role, they consulted higher authority.

This idea might seem surprising. Renner was the type of Socialist most disliked by Soviet Communists and had been strongly attacked by Soviet propaganda during the war. (See p. 136 above.) But he was old, and could therefore (wrongly) be assumed to be feeble. Morover his 'capitulation' in 1938 over the *Anschluss* was exactly the sort of black mark in his dossier which, in Soviet eyes, could make him seem highly vulnerable and therefore likely to be a docile figurehead of a temporary transitional government which would pave the way for a full 'people's democracy'. In any case, it seems that Stalin himself was consulted and gave his approval to Renner's appointment, to head a provisional government.

Renner himself totally ignored the possibility that he might be unscrupulously exploited, and assumed that as in 1918 he was to form a government for all Austria, which would restore the pre-Dollfuss constitution and arrange general elections from which a fully representative government for a fully independent Austria would emerge. To maintain constitutional continuity, he at first planned, as President of the last Austrian parliament as it existed in 1933, to summon the old parliament and use it as the basis of the provisional government, thereby following the procedure used at the time of the collapse of the Habsburg Empire. But when the Russians brought him to Vienna in the second half of April, and he made contact with other political leaders and realised something of Austria's chaotic condition, he had to give up the idea.

Renner also had to yield to the Russians on some important points, giving the Communists greater representation in the government than he thought right, and, most reluctantly, giving them the key posts of Minister of the Interior and Minister of Education and Information. But to counterbalance this, he thought up the ingenious device of attaching two under-secretaries, representing the two other political parties, to serve under each Minister as watch-dog. The main economic posts, apparently on Soviet insistence, went to the Christian Socials (now re-christened the People's Party). This irritated the Social Democrats (now re-christened Socialists, to propitiate the Revolutionary Socialists, most of whom were ready to heal the 1934 split). But the Socialists' position was strengthened by another ingenious device of Renner's – the appointment of a 'political cabinet' of four ministers without portfolio, of whom his close friend, Schärf, was one.

Renner also resisted the Soviet intention that Austria should return to the constitutional position of 1938, which, as the Russians had perhaps failed to notice, meant a return to the 'Austro-Fascist' corporative state. Instead Austria was to go back to the pre-Dollfuss constitution.

By 26 April the government was formed. Renner knew that the Soviet Union was informing London and Washington and apparently assumed that their attitude would be favourable.[231] In fact, the British and Americans asked for time to consider the matter. But the Soviet Union was unwilling to wait, preferring to face them with a *fait accompli*. The Renner government was presented to the Austrian people, under Russian auspices, at a public ceremony at the Vienna Rathaus on 29 April.

The new government had as yet no idea that Stalin was at loggerheads with Churchill, and to a lesser extent Truman, over Austria. At the Yalta conference in February the Western leaders had put forward proposals for the demarcation of occupation zones in Austria. These were to be finally settled by the European Advisory Commission in London; but the Russians there were stone-walling. On 5 April Churchill sent a message to Roosevelt saying that since the Russians were on the eve of taking Vienna and no agreement had been reached, the West should take a 'firm and blunt stand'.[232] On 13 April Stalin suggested to the United States that Western missions should be flown to Vienna; but soon after he refused to allow them in until the E.A.C. had agreed on occupation zones.[233]

On 24 April, after Roosevelt's sudden death, Churchill took the matter up afresh with the new President, Harry Truman, urging that the Western armies should hold all the ground they could in northern Europe until the question of Vienna had been settled with the Russians; three days later he wrote to Stalin urging the need for agreement on occupation zones in Austria. By this time he was convinced that Stalin was deliberately stalling, to give time for the Russians to 'organize' Austria before the Western Powers got there.[234] The announcement from Moscow of the formation of the Renner government strengthened his suspicions and made him believe that Renner was simply a Soviet puppet. On 30 April, he sent a message to Stalin: 'we have been disagreeably surprised by the announcement . . . despite our request for time to consider the matter.'[235] He persuaded Truman to send a parallel message.

So relations between the Renner government and the Western Powers started off on the wrong foot. In June Western missions were permitted to visit Vienna but were then ordered out again by Marshal Tolbukhin. It was not until 4 July that zonal borders were agreed in the E.A.C. This made it possible for Allied troops to take up their positions in their respective zones.

Even after that, there was long and hard bargaining over Vienna. The Russians wanted the First District – the Inner City, where the main government buildings were located – to be part of the Soviet sector; they also wanted Vienna to be delimited by the old pre-Hitler boundary-line. The Western Allies wanted the Inner City to be under joint four-power control, together with the city boundary of the Hitler period, creating a considerably larger area. In the final deal, the West gave way on the city boundary but secured four-power occupation of the Inner City – a Soviet concession which had considerable importance later on, at times of Communist-instigated anti-government riots. The rest of the city was split into four sectors, with the Russians holding a good many of the traditionally working-class areas.

While this bargaining was going on, the fate of the Renner government hung fire. When the three Powers met at Potsdam in mid-July, the Western leaders said they would consider recognising it *after* their troops had been established in Vienna. By mid-August, this had at last been achieved. Even then, the Allied Council – intended to be the supreme authority in Austria – did not hold its first formal meeting until 11 September.

For nearly five months, therefore, the Renner government was dependent on the Soviet Union for political and practical support and was cold-shouldered by the Western Allies. In the Western zones, the Land governments that had been set up as early as April, on the same pattern of three-party cooperation as the Renner government in Vienna, were not recognised by the Western occupation forces, and had to be reconstituted and reduced to a (theoretically) advisory role.

This was because the Western Powers – particularly the British – had expected the defeat of Nazi Germany to leave a total political and administrative vacuum which would have to be filled by Allied Military Government. A draft directive for Austria in the 'post-surrender period', drawn up in September 1944, had said that 'some time is bound to elapse before sufficient Austrian representatives of the right type emerge to form a central administration'.[236] The directive was stern, even schoolmasterly, in tone: one of the purposes of the occupation would be 'to make clear to Austria that association with Germany has brought her to disaster, and to fortify her will not to renew that association'. But in Austria – unlike Germany – occupation was to be 'exercised in the interests of the country occupied, as well as in those of the United Nations.'[237]

The British had in fact failed to foresee first, that there would be a surprising number of Austrians – mainly members of the old political parties – ready to come forward and run the country's affairs competently, and next, that there was very little need of anti-Nazi indoctrination: seven years of rule by Hitler had done the job.

One of the prearranged Western policies was non-fraternisation with Austria. This provoked an angry note from Churchill to the Foreign Office at the end of June: '. . . this requires grave and urgent attention. We are dignified and insulting, the Russians are boon companions and enslavers. I never realized such follies were being committed.'[238] The policy was soon relaxed.

In one respect the Western Powers' insistence that the Provisional Government did not represent the Austrians was useful to Renner. The Russians wanted the Western Powers to recognise Renner. They must also have known that there was a movement in Tirol for forming a rival West Austrian government.[239] They therefore had to allow Renner to establish proper contact with the western Lands – which they had sealed off almost completely from Vienna – and to win the Western Allies' approval by broadening the base of his government. So representatives of all Lands and all 'democratic parties' were allowed to enter the Soviet zone and come to Vienna for a conference on 23 September; the Renner government was broadened to take in politicians from the Western Lands, notably Karl Gruber, the Tirolean leader, who took charge of foreign affairs. The conference agreed to hold elections throughout the country.

Thereafter, on 20 October, the Allied Council informed Renner of the recognition of his government by the four Powers: its authority was now to extend to the whole of Austria – though under the Allied Council's 'supreme authority'; it was 'empowered to enact laws applying to the whole of Austria provided that they shall first be submitted for approval to the Allied Council'.[240]

Renner's achievement had been remarkable, given the tension between Moscow and the West – the establishment of a central government for a united Austria, recognised by all four Powers, even if subjected to controls by the Allied Council which – as the next ten years showed – could at times be extremely irksome. It was moreover a government in which 'democratic' parties, in the Western sense, predominated; the Communists were in a minority even if they held two key ministries.

This achievement was presumably possible because the

Soviet Union still hoped that the Communists would eventually be able to come to power by undermining and disintegrating the other political parties. In particular, the Communists hoped to be able to swallow up the Socialists: their party manifesto of June 1944 had called for 'unity of the working class', for unitary trade unions, and for the gathering of the workers in a single united party.[241] More generally the Communists could be expected to use splitting tactics – by driving a wedge between the old enemies, the Socialists and Christian Socials (now People's Party), or by splitting each party from within. These tactics were used by Communists with devastating success elsewhere in south-east Europe, as also in East Germany; there seems little doubt that at this early stage the Soviet leaders still hoped to acquire control of all Germany, and probably of all Austria, by such means.

As soon as the first Austrian general election was held – on 25 November, before the first snows – Soviet expectations were severely checked. In spite of Communist control of the Ministry of the Interior and the Vienna police, the election was entirely free: the Russians had perhaps totally miscalculated Communist voting strength. In fact, the Communists won only 5 per cent of the votes and 4 seats in parliament. The People's Party were unexpectedly successful with 85 seats, and the Socialists won 76. After this crushing defeat, the Communists lost their key posts in the government, receiving as a sop the Ministry of Electrification; and from then on they had to use extra-parliamentary methods in trying to acquire power.

These methods included the Communist attempt to gain control of the trade unions, especially in the Soviet zone where industry was still mainly concentrated and where Soviet seizure of key industries offered special opportunities. There was also their attempt to detach the left wing of the Socialists, the former R.S.; and there was the abortive intrigue with the People's Party behind the back of the Socialists – the Communist Ernst Fischer's contacts with

People's Party leaders, including Chancellor Figl, in 1947.

There were also the Communists' rather half-hearted attempts to use mass demonstrations, combined with strike action, to overthrow the government or at least cause a breakdown of law and order which would justify armed intervention by the Soviet occupation forces.

Even short of armed intervention, the Russians could give the Communists powerful backing, ranging from prolonged political undermining of the central government's authority to practical help such as privileged paper supplies for propaganda, lorries for carrying demonstrators, and even the demonstrators themselves, supplied for the purpose from Soviet-controlled concerns. Moreover the Russians could give help by hinting that Austria would never get a peace treaty nor be freed from occupation until there was a government to Soviet liking – as was done in the Fischer–Figl affair.

It was therefore a remarkable achievement on the part of the Austrians and their political leaders that the Communists had so little success, and that a stable and relatively efficient democratic government remained in control throughout the ten years of occupation.

18 The Figl–Schärf Coalition and the Occupying Powers

Political stability in the post-war years was based on an entirely new element in the Austrian situation: the determination of the two big parties, the People's Party and the Socialists, to work closely together, inside the government. This was not easy. The Socialists neither forgot nor forgave the wrongs of the Dollfuss–Schuschnigg period during which their leading members had suffered some months of imprisonment, loss of jobs or pensions, and petty persecution. Nor did they intend to let the People's Party forget these things, and they insisted on full compensation and restitution. On the other side, some members of the People's Party still saw the Socialists as dangerously far to the Left, if not fellow-travellers with the Communists. The relationship between the two was never smooth, each party watching the other closely in case it gained an unfair advantage, and ready to retaliate quickly if it did; each was equally ready to exploit the other's mistakes.

Yet key men in both parties had had a common experience of prison or concentration camp under Hitler, or had come together in resistance, and this was a strong bond. So also was the urgent need to save Austria from near-starvation and from the very real threat to the country's independence and unity resulting from the occupation.

Austria was lucky in the two men who dominated the coalition formed after the 1945 election – Figl and Schärf. Once the election was over, Renner resigned as Chancellor and was then elected President – a post better fitted to his age. Figl, as leader of the party which now had an absolute majority in parliament, became Chancellor, and Schärf became Vice-Chancellor, and also leader of the Socialist Party. The People's Party did not want to carry alone the heavy responsibility and inevitable unpopularity of governing war-stricken Austria and so wished to continue the coalition. The militant wing of the Socialists would have liked to keep outside the government, as in Otto Bauer's day, but the leaders followed the old Renner line. Karl Gruber, of the People's Party, remarked that 'only co-responsibility could tame the radical wing of the Socialists'.[242]

Figl, a quiet, unassuming man, had been the leader of the Lower Austrian Bauernbund, or Christian Social-affiliated Peasant-farmers' Union. When the Russians came in, he headed the new Lower Austrian Land government. Partly by accident, he became the People's Party representative in the 'political cabinet' of the Renner government, and from this point moved up to become party leader, taking priority over the leaders of the two other interest groups which, with the Bauernbund, formed the structure of the party – the industrialists and businessmen grouped in the Wirtschaftsbund (Economic Union) under Julius Raab, a Christian Social who had once led the Lower Austrian Heimwehr, and the Catholic workers and employees grouped in the Arbeiter- und Angestelltenbund under Lois Weinberger.

In spite of his quiet manner and provincial background, Figl had a personality which impressed his colleagues and also foreign politicians. The American Secretary of State, Dean Acheson, meeting him a few years later, described him as 'a small red-headed man with sharp fox-like features and a red mustache', who 'handled the Russian occupation with irrepressible Austrian raillery and stubbornness'. 'What could not be prevented,' Acheson added, 'Figl did not oppose; but what could be frustrated he and his compatriots proceeded to confuse and bewilder until in many instances the Russians gave up in baffled disgust.'[243]

When Figl first became Chancellor, he had little experience of normal parliamentary politics; Schärf had had a great deal. He had made his career in the Social Democratic Party and, in particular, in the party's 'fraction' in the pre-1933 parliament. As a disciple of Renner, he had learnt a great deal from him. A strange but firm partnership grew up between Figl and Schärf; they were once called the 'good angels of the coalition'. They were capable of reaching compromises even on such highly sensitive issues, in terms of party politics, as the marriage law. The partnership lasted until 1953, when Figl was replaced by Raab, and a rather more difficult Raab–Schärf partnership was formed.

The long-term value of this period of 'co-responsibility' of the two once hostile parties was that it killed the old bogey of class war as a fight to the death, and the old stereotypes of the fanatical Socialist aiming at proletarian dictatorship and the wily but ruthless Catholic-capitalist out to destroy parliamentary democracy. Each party came to be seen as the representative of certain economic and social interests which might conflict but must ultimately be harmonised for the sake of the general interest of society as a whole. Class war was something to be waged not on the streets but inside the government itself.[244] It came to be generally accepted that consensus politics were the only form of democracy which would work in a small and exposed country like Austria.

The most difficult and delicate side of the coalition government's work, in the early years, was its relationship with the occupying Powers. The outcome of the election of November 1945 changed the attitude of the Western Powers: instead of regarding the government with suspicion and reserve, they became the champions of its right to run

Austria's affairs with the minimum of outside interference. The Soviet Union's attitude also changed: it became a stern and constantly nagging critic of the Austrian government, trying to cutail its powers and undermine its authority. It also pursued by various means the more far-reaching aim of changing the whole political system – in the first place by pressing for a totally new constitution. The result was a running battle between the Soviet Union and the Western Powers both in the Allied Council in Vienna and on the wider diplomatic front, fought with varying degrees of bitterness over the years of Austria's occupation.

There was a particularly sharp struggle in the economic field. At the Potsdam conference in July–August 1945 the Soviet Foreign Minister, Molotov, had demanded 250 million dollars in reparations from Austria, to be divided between the allies. The British and Americans said they did not want reparations and that under the 1943 declaration Austria should not be treated as an enemy country. Stalin then conceded that Austria should not be asked for reparations; but Molotov made this concession meaningless by demanding that Germany's external assets should be used for German reparations payments, all those east of a line from the Baltic to the Adriatic – which included eastern Austria – falling to the Soviet Union. The new British Labour Foreign Secretary, Ernest Bevin, was extremely suspicious and in 'a prolonged exchange' tried to extract from Stalin definitions of various types of German assets in various areas, but with little success.[245] Truman and Attlee yielded.

Probably not even Bevin saw what damaging use the Russians would make of this agreement, especially in Austria's case. After the *Anschluss*, Austrian properties of all kinds, especially those of great economic value, had come into the hands either of the German state or of German firms or individuals. All such property – regardless of pre-*Anschluss* ownership or the means by which

Germans had acquired it – was now claimed by the Soviet Union. Moreover it soon became clear that the Russians intended to use these 'assets' as a means of establishing an economic stranglehold on eastern Austria.

The Soviet occupying power took action against the Austrian oil industry immediately after Potsdam. In August 1945 it proposed formation of a Soviet–Austrian joint stock company for the oilfields at Zistersdorf, on the model already used by the Soviet Union in Rumania. The Soviet contribution was to be the property seized as German assets; the Austrians were to contribute 13 million dollars together with oil exploration rights throughout the whole of Austria for sixty years. A Russian managing director was to be in charge.

The Renner government had to deal with this Soviet demand alone, since the Allied Council had not yet come into operation. According to Schärf's account, Renner himself thought it necessary to accept it, and to establish close economic relations with the East. The Communists were naturally for accepting the Soviet demand, while the People's Party wavered. Schärf, however, insisted that no agreement should be signed with the Soviet Union until the Renner government had been recognised by all the Allies, and all the Allies had approved it. This view prevailed; the agreement was not signed, and the Russians also dropped a plan for an Austrian trade delegation to visit Moscow and sign a treaty for close economic cooperation. Schärf himself wrote later that the decision over oil was a decision over the future of Austria.[246] But it was only the beginning of a long struggle over the German assets, fought out partly between the Austrian government and the Soviet Union, and partly between the West and the Russians both in the Allied Council in Vienna and in the Austrian treaty negotiations of the following years.

The Allied Council started its career with a brief period of amity. At its first meeting on 11 September 1945 it gave formal recognition to the Socialist, People's and Communist parties as 'anti-Nazi and democratic' and therefore permitted to function throughout Austria. On 1 October the Council agreed that the 'democratic' press of Austria was to be given maximum possible freedom, subject to certain conditions, for instance, that public order should not be disturbed. There was to be no censorship. All this sounded well, but it did not prevent interminable wrangles between the Soviet and Western sides over what was or was not 'democratic', or insulting to an occupying power; and it did not stop the Soviet Commander from banning newspapers which he did not like inside the Soviet Zone. However, the relative freedom of the press meant that the Western Allies could publicise their side of the question in their disputes with the Russians, thereby keeping Austrians informed and, on occasion, giving the Austrian government much-needed moral support.

In mid-December 1945, the Figl government presented its first policy declaration to the Allied Council. This tried to define a new Austrian 'mission' in post-war Europe: 'Austria, which in its century-old cultural tradition has been oriented towards the West and has also always been the open door for the tremendously valuable contribution of the East to the entire culture of the world . . . is a key-stone in this respect for the whole of Europe. Every Austrian government must be aware of this respon-sibility . . .'[247] The Allied Council approved the declaration in general but deleted the description of Austria as a bridge between East and West – perhaps feeling that it was presumptuous.[248] On 18 December, the Council unani-mously recommended that the Figl government should immediately be recognised.

This, however, was the end of unanimity in the Allied Council on serious matters, for a long time to come. In late December there was a stormy meeting of the Soviet, American and British Foreign Ministers in Moscow. For the United States, James Byrnes raised the question of German assets in Austria, but without making any dint in the Soviet position. Britain had been pressing since November for the reduction of all occupation forces in Austria;[249] Byrnes raised this also in Moscow, but Molotov smothered it in accusations that the British were rebuilding the Austrian Army and forming White Russian units for use against the Soviet Union. Bevin strongly denied the charges. Molotov accused the Austrians of trying to 'insinuate Fascists' into the government.[250]

It was therefore not surprising that from the end of 1945 onwards, there was a series of unpleasant wrangles in the Allied Council in Vienna – over the Austrian currency reform and over German assets; over the need to treat Austria as an 'integrated economic unit' (which the Russians blocked in practice);[251] over Soviet complaints against pro-Western Austrian newspapers;[252] over the Austrian constitution, with the Russians demanding an entirely new one and the Western Allies successfully supporting the Austrian wish to keep the 1920 constitution as amended in 1929.[253]

The Americans began to take an increasingly firm stand: Austria, near starvation, was desperately dependent on outside aid which came – in inadequate quantities for the cities – through UNRRA, of which the United States was the chief prop and stay. The American representatives on the Allied Council in Vienna knew that the U.S. Congress must be convinced that this expenditure was worthwhile, and that Austria's rights as a 'liberated' country were being properly protected. It was in accordance with the logic of the times that if American money was keeping the Austrians alive, then the Austrians should have a political way of life of which Americans could approve.

19 The 1946 Control Agreement

The main struggle in the Allied Council in 1946 was over a new Control Agreement between the four occupying Powers. The issue at stake was whether the Austrian government and parliament were to conduct the country's affairs in a normal way, or whether they were to be the servants of the occupying powers, acting collectively or singly.

The first Control Agreement, signed by the four Powers on 4 July 1945, had been intended as an interim arrangement to be re-negotiated when the Austrian internal situation was ripe. In accordance with this first agreement, the Allied Council, when it recognised the Renner government in October 1945, said all legislation must be submitted to itself for approval. But after the election in November and the formation of a fully representative government, the time had come for a new agreement. The British Foreign Office set to work on a draft, which was completed in December. An explanatory memorandum of 13 December said that Allied policy should be to 'give Austria as much independence as is safe'.[254] But this was not very much: the Foreign Office draft provided that 'all enactments of the Austrian Parliament relating to Austria as a whole shall receive before they take effect the written approval of the Allied Council', which was to retain the power to veto any action by the Austrian government.

At the end of December, however, Bevin went to

Moscow for the meeting with the Soviet and American Foreign Ministers which showed that there was little chance of healing the growing split between the West and the Soviet Union over a whole range of European issues. At the same time the British in Vienna were increasingly conscious of the need to give the freely elected Austrian government a chance of governing. The British draft for a new Control Agreement, submitted to the Allied Council early in February, was noticeably different from the Foreign Office draft of December. Under Article 6(a), all laws and international agreements, other than agreements with one of the four occupying powers, were to be submitted to the Allied Council; if, however, within 21 days the Council had not stated any objection, the law or agreement could be published and put into effect. This meant that a veto could only be imposed by unanimous decision of the Allied Council; the Soviet Union, acting alone, would be powerless to exercise a veto.

On the side-lines, the Austrian Socialists were extremely active. A powerful plea for greater freedom for the Austrian government and parliament was made in a speech in Vienna in March by the veteran Socialist, Karl Seitz. At the British Labour Party's invitation, Vice-Chancellor Schärf and Dr Bruno Pittermann paid a private visit to London at the beginning of April, and presented a long memorandum to Bevin which spoke of the 'nerve war' waged by the Russians against the Austrians and put the question: is the eastern part of Austria to fall completely into the Soviet sphere of influence? It also complained of the Allied Council's existing power of veto over legislation and suggested a procedure close to that set out in Article 6(a) of the British draft submitted to the Council some weeks earlier.[255] Because of this, the Socialists later put forward a considerably exaggerated claim to the credit for the 1946 Control Agreement.[256] Their activities may, however, have had a certain influence.

During the debate in the Allied Council over the British

draft, all three Western allies eventually urged that if laws were not vetoed by the Council within 31 days they should be put into effect, while the Soviet Union insisted that they must be expressly approved by the Allied Council.[257] On the other hand, the Soviet Union did not want the Western Powers to be able to veto any agreement which it might want to conclude with Austria; it had not yet abandoned hope of an oil agreement. The Western Powers were at first divided on this second point; the Americans wanted the power to veto any such agreement. The Russians seemed to become confused over their priorities.

On 24 May a bargain was struck. The Russians got their way over agreements between Austria and one of the occupying powers: these were to be exempt from any veto. Over legislation, they made the concession which was to prove fatal to their efforts to control the Austrian government and parliament. In Article 6(a) of the new Agreement, a distinction was drawn between 'constitutional' laws and other laws. 'Constitutional laws' were to require the written approval of the Allied Council, so remaining subject to Soviet veto. In the case of all other laws, 'it may be assumed that the Allied Council has given its approval if within 31 days of the time of receipt by the Allied Council it has not informed the Austrian government that it objects to a legislative measure . . .'[258] They were thus veto-free.

There remained the question of how a 'constitutional law' was to be defined. The Allied Council's Executive Committee, meeting on 31 May, accepted a definition leaving the Austrian government a wide measure of discretion in deciding for itself what was or was not to be called a 'constitutional law'.[259] This, without any Russian objection, was passed to legal experts for final drafting. The new Control Agreement was approved by all four governments and signed on 28 June 1946.

From Soviet behaviour in the Allied Council almost immediately after the new agreement came into force, it

seemed that the Russians had quite failed to see the degree
of independence which the Austrians would gain from it.
In August they protested strongly against the Nationalisation Law passed by the Austrian parliament, which had
failed to exempt from its provisions the German assets
seized by the Soviet Union. (This was deliberate; the law
was largely designed to counter the Soviet Commander's
order of 5 July seizing all 'German property' – defined as
widely as possible – in the Soviet Zone.) The Soviet
General Kurasov accused the Austrian government and
parliament of 'an unfriendly act' and of violating the new
Control Agreement, and insisted on repeal of the law.[260]
The U.S. representative replied that the law did not violate
the new agreement: 'my government respects Austria's
right to nationalize industries throughout the country'.
(There was pleasing irony in American defence of a
nationalisation law to which Russia took strong exception.)
The British supported the American stand. The Soviet
representative could do nothing but express his 'deep
regret' at the Council's failure to reach unanimity.[261]

On 23 August the Russians tried a new attack, this time
on the definition of a 'constitutional law', arguing that this
had never been approved by the Council and should be
further discussed. But the Western representatives argued
that the definition had in fact been agreed by the Council's
organs, that they had signed the new Control Agreement
on this basis, and that they were unwilling to change it.
The Soviet Union was helpless.[262]

On 30 September there was a further wrangle – this
time over a new control agreement for the Vienna Inter-
Allied Command (VIAC). The Soviet Union said that the
Command's decisions must be unanimous; the British said
this would not be in the spirit of the new Control Agreement of 28 June. Both then and at later meetings, the
Russians argued that just because of the errors of the new
Control Agreement, the same mistakes should not be made
over the VIAC. They added that the Western Allies were

now trying, in the Council, to 'force on the Soviet Element decisions which are contrary to its interests'.[263]

All this suggests that there was a serious mistake somewhere in the Soviet decision-making process during the negotiations over the 1946 Control Agreement. It is significant that when in 1949 the U.S. Secretary of State urged a German control agreement on the Austrian model, the Soviet Union turned the idea down out of hand, on the ground that the crucial Article 6 of the Austrian agreement was unsuited to Germany.[264]

The importance of Article 6 to the Austrians was shown by the subsequent Soviet record. Between 1946 and 1953 the Soviet Union raised objections to over 550 non-constitutional laws, including laws on the restoration of property to Jews and other victims of the Nazis, price controls, railway fares and postal charges. They regularly objected to the Austrian budget as socially unjust. But they could not impose a veto. On security grounds, which enabled them to by-pass Article 6, they succeeded in banning civil aviation and the introduction of a television service.

Nor could Article 6 prevent the Soviet authorities from causing great difficulties to the Austrian government by holding up the issue of arms to the police and preventing proper police training, while at the same time pressing for the numbers of police to be cut down. This made the task of the Minister of the Interior (from the end of 1945, the Socialist, Oskar Helmer) particularly hard, especially when the Soviet Command appointed Communists as local police chiefs in the Soviet Zone and Vienna. The Russians also created an atmosphere of fear by arrests and kidnappings of Austrians for alleged activities against the Soviet armed forces; in particular, there was the kidnapping of Police Inspector Marek in 1948, against which Chancellor Figl protested to the Allied Council strongly – but ineffectually.[265] Where the Russians could claim that the security of the Soviet armed forces was involved, the Council was helpless.

They also had their moments of humour – whether conscious or unconscious is not clear from the official record. In December 1948 they backed the request of a party calling itself 'the Mountain Folk' for recognition. The Americans and British said its leader and only known member had been a Nazi Party member in 1933, and the party had not sufficient support to justify recognition. The Russians replied that 'adherents of this party would join it after it had been created'.[266] But no more was heard of the Mountain Folk.

20 The Communist Bids for Power, 1947–1950

In 1947 and 1950 the Austrian Communists, with Soviet support, organised strikes and riots which appeared to be attempts to overthrow or at least undermine the Figl government. The efforts were ineffective and Soviet support – partly because of the restraining presence of the Western occupying powers – was half-hearted. But this did not disprove that the aim was a change of government and a move towards a 'people's democracy'; similar methods succeeded in Rumania in 1945 and in Czechoslovakia in 1948.

The Spring of 1947 was a time when food supplies were unusually low. On 1 May Ernst Fischer, in the Communist daily, the *Volksstimme*, launched the slogan: 'an end to waiting – forward to action!' On 5 May workers in factories on the outskirts of Vienna went on strike, complaining of short food rations, and some marched to the city centre. A crowd of about 4000 gathered outside the Chancellery. Some shouted 'out with the hunger government'. At 1.25 p.m. Chancellor Figl received a deputation, but the crowd went on growing and some demonstrators made use of handy scaffolding to get inside the Chancellery. There were only 250 unarmed police on the scene; they had no hope of controlling the crowd. The Vienna Police President, non-Communist but ineffectual, appealed to the Vienna Inter-Allied Command for help; the Foreign Minister, Gruber, telephoned the U.S. Commander.

At the request of the British chairman, the VIAC met at

4 p.m. The Soviet commander said that the Police Presidents' appeal for help was 'provocatory, aiming at creating conflict between the Allies and the workers of Vienna'. The VIAC was still arguing whether or not to respond to the appeal when news came that the demonstration had broken up and help was no longer needed.[267] The simple fact that the Western Allies were at least prepared to consider intervention had clearly caused the Russians to pass word to the organisers to call the demonstration off. The Communist, Honner, told one dispersing group that if the government failed to recognise the gravity of the situation, 'it must go'.[268] But the attempt had failed. The Russians were not prepared to back the Communists up to the point of direct conflict with the Western Allies.

The Austrian government drew one conclusion – that it must speed up action to remedy the dangerous weakness, largely due to Soviet interference, of the Vienna police. With some difficulty the Minister of the Interior, Helmer, replaced the ineffectual Police President and removed the Communist who had real control of the force – Dr Dürmayer – to a post in Salzburg.[269] A further purge and strengthening of the police force followed. However, in the Allied Council the Russians continued to oppose the issue of arms to the police.[270]

After the fiasco of 5 May, the Communists turned to more subtle means of bringing about a change of government. In the same month, contact was established between Ernst Fischer and leading People's Party members, including Julius Raab, who were alarmed by the extremely depressing economic outlook – UNRRA aid was just ending and Marshall Aid had not yet been offered – and by separatist movements in the western Lands. Fischer proposed a reorientation of Austrian foreign policy and a re-casting of the government so as to remove men displeasing to the Soviet Union; this, he argued was the only way to get an Austrian treaty and economic aid. It was understood that the Communists were again to be given a strong position in the government and the Socialists were to be down-graded; the pro-American Gruber was to go. At one meeting, Figl himself was present. On Fischer's advice, the Socialists were kept in the dark.

However, Gruber found out what was going on and gave the story to an American news agency. This put an end to the Communist–People's Party contacts. The Socialists were very angry but decided to remain in harness with the People's Party. Gruber remained in office.[271] Some Austrians noted the almost simultaneous crisis in Hungary, where the Communist-manipulated split in the Small-holders' Party – in some ways the counterpart of the People's Party – led to the overthrow of its leader, Ferenc Nagy, and the establishment of Communist domination.

During 1947 the Communists also intensified their long-standing campaign for a united front of the workers, that is, for a merger of Socialists and Communists. They operated partly through the unitary trade union organisation established in 1945, and partly through their associates inside the Socialist Party – in particular, Erwin Scharf who, at the Socialist party conference in October 1947, came into the open with a resolution demanding joint action with the Communists and a sharper struggle against the People's Party. This was heavily defeated, and Erwin Scharf lost his post as the party third secretary; a year later he was excluded from the party and set up a splinter group of his own which fought the 1949 election in a 'Left Block' with the Communists, and later vanished. After 1947 the danger of a Communist-engineered split in the Socialist Party no longer existed.

This was a matter in which the occupying powers could not – openly – play any part. They were, however, very much concerned with the question of economic aid to Austria. In June 1947 the United States concluded a re-lief assistance agreement with Austria to tide the country over the difficult period after the end of UNRRA aid. The Russians objected to the agreement, claiming that it violated the 1946 Control Agreement, threatened Austrian independence and infringed the interests of other occupying powers.[272] The Americans could, however, argue that, since what was involved was an agreement between Austria and one of the occupying Powers, under Article 6 of the Control Agreement the approval of the Allied Council was not required. The Soviet Union had no right of veto.

The same argument could again be used over the much more important issue of Austria's acceptance of Marshall aid. When this was first raised in the Allied Council on 10 July 1947, the Soviet representative merely pointed out that Molotov had denounced and rejected the Marshall Plan, adding that he reserved his position. Presumably, too, the Russians at this point gave no firm instruction to the Austrian Communists: when Marshall Aid was discussed by the government, the one Communist Minister, Karl Altmann, raised no objection. When, however, the Cominform was created in the autumn with the express purpose of fighting the Marshall Plan, the Austrian Communists concluded that they could no longer stay in the government. Altmann found a pretext to resign on 19 November. Even the outward appearance of three-party government was at an end.

After this, it was inevitable that trouble should blow up when Austria became a member of the Organisation for European Economic Cooperation, created to plan the use of Marshall Aid. On 25 June 1948 the Soviet representative told the Allied Council that he could not recognise the legal validity of the agreement signed by Austria until it had been discussed by the Council. The British countered by saying that the Council should merely decide whether Austrian membership of the O.E.E.C. would assist her 'to recover that independence which the four Allies had pledged themselves to support'.[273] The Soviet objection was ineffective.

On 13 August, the Soviet representative objected strongly to the economic cooperation agreement between the United

States and Austria, implementing Marshall Aid. 'The Soviet Element,' he said, 'consider that the Allied Council must declare invalid the U.S.–Austrian agreement, which imposes on Austria cabalistic conditions, which violates the sovereignty and independence of Austria, and which is contrary to the Control Agreement . . .'[274] But because of Article 6, the Soviet Union could not veto it.

So Austria became a member of O.E.E.C., which brought it into the West European economic system, and received Marshall Aid, which laid the basis for the country's astonishing economic recovery and growth – and which also consolidated Austria's political stability as a Western-type parliamentary democracy. In all, between 1945 and 1955 Austria received 1600 million dollars in foreign aid, or six times the amount, in real terms, of the League of Nations loan to the first Austrian Republic.[275] This difference in the scale of foreign aid obviously is one part of the explanation of the higher level of Austrian achievement, both economic and political, in the second Republic.

The most serious Communist attempt to overthrow Austrian democracy was launched at a time of renewed economic difficulty and even hardship, just as the first phase of Marshall Aid (during which nearly half the total took the form of food supplies) had drawn to a close, and the second phase (1949–52), which was to concentrate on the reconstruction of industry, had hardly begun to get under way. Austria's problems were further complicated by the rapid rise in raw material prices caused by the outbreak of the Korean war in June 1950. In the early autumn, negotiations between the two sides of industry on wages and prices seemed to have got hopelessly bogged down. This produced serious discontent among workers.

The Communists thought the time ripe for action. They attacked the leaders of the trade union organisation for 'betraying the workers' interests' and declared that they must 'vanish'. They then called a general strike for 26 September, together with a march to the Inner City of

Vienna, ending at the Chancellery. On 25 September the Soviet City Command instructed the police authorities that they were not to bring any police from the Soviet Zone into the Inner City as reinforcements.

The Austrians nevertheless took certain counter-measures. Socialist workers were instructed not to take part in the march. And the government, instead of meeting at its usual hour of 10 a.m. every Tuesday, met two hours earlier, so that most Ministers had left the Chancellery by the time that the marchers arrived, at about 11 a.m. The marchers were addressed outside the Chancellery by the Communist leaders, Fischer and Honner. Figl, who had remained at his desk, refused to receive a delegation. This time – unlike the position in 1947 – the police were strong enough to keep order; the demonstrators left after about two hours.

The Communists did not give up. The next day, they sent 'Commandos' into the factories to get the workers to strike. One 'Commando' tried to storm trade union head-quarters. The trams were partially stopped; cement was poured into the tram-lines. In Lower Austria there were road blocks and blocks on level crossings. But the Socialist Party called on the workers to safeguard their work-places. By the end of that day, the Communist-led action had fizzled out.

On the first day of the troubles, a meeting of the Vienna Inter-Allied Command had been called by the U.S. Com-mander to 'consider the problem of maintaining order in the First District' (the Inner City). No Soviet representa-tive turned up. Three days later, on 29 September, the full Allied Council held a particularly stormy meeting. The American chairman, General Geoffrey Keyes, made two main charges against the Russians. First, over a long period they had intentionally 'interfered with the law enforce-ment agencies of the Austrian government', closing down its gendarmerie schools, refusing to permit the assignment of gendarmerie in the Soviet Zone, insisting on 'the retention of individuals legally removed by the Minister of the Interior' (that is, Communist police officials), and establishing Soviet-controlled works police in big undertakings.

Next, the American chairman made specific charges against the Russians of 'active encouragement and assistance' to 'the recent disorders': 'the Soviet occupation forces have deliberately, knowingly and with intent to discredit and interfere with the Austrian government, taken steps to encourage subversive minority elements in demonstrations and acts of violence'. Soviet army trucks, he said, had transported rioters; the Austrian police had been forbidden to move men from the Soviet sector to trouble-spots; a Soviet correspondent, claiming to be a Soviet officer, took part in the riots at the Chancellery; Russians prevented the Austrian police from dealing with workers from Soviet-controlled factories who had occupied the railway yards at St Pölten. A Soviet tank had 'fortuitously and conveniently' broken down on the railway tracks at Langenzersdorf. The American General then made a formal protest, backed up by the British and French, against the 'unilateral interference by the Soviet Element'.

The Soviet representative 'categorically rejected the invented and slanderous allegations', moreover, he said, 'the desire of the Austrian workers . . . to receive from the Austrian government the establishment of normal wages for their labour, and the seeking of normal living conditions, could not be considered "disorders".' There had, he added (correctly), been disorders in Linz, which was outside the Soviet Zone.[276]

The Austrian government followed up the Western onslaught on the Russians. On 5 October, Figl sent a letter to the Allied Council on the Soviet role in the disorders, and asked whether the occupying powers stood by their obligations under the 1946 Control Agreement. The American representative proposed that the Council should reply to Figl reaffirming 'its support for the freely elected Austrian government'. He added that the Secretary of

State, Dean Acheson, had told the Austrian government that 'the United States would take all proper action to fulfil its international commitments to Austria and, in particular, to ensure the maintenance of law and order in the areas of its responsibility.[277]

The Soviet representative continued to disclaim all responsibility for the disorders, in spite of circumstantial evidence offered by the Western side. Figl sent further letters; he made the charge that five district police chiefs on duty at the time of the disorders had obeyed not the Austrian government but the Soviet authorities. At a Council meeting on 10 November the Soviet representative, after renewed disclaimers, said that the Soviet Element 'respected the Control Agreement and . . . would continue to adhere to and implement agreements and decisions of the Allied Council'.[278] This looked like a slight climb-down. But the Western Powers took the further step of joint diplomatic action in Moscow. On 3 December, the American representative told the Allied Council that his government had 'made its attitude towards the illegal Soviet intervention in Austrian police and court affairs perfectly clear to the Government of the U.S.S.R.' As was now customary, the official summing up of the meeting was: 'in view of the disagreement, the Council took no decision'.[279]

The 'disorders' of September 1950 were the last Communist-organised, Soviet-backed operation of the kind. The Austrian government's refusal to be intimidated, the Austrian workers' refusal to follow the Communist lead, and the prompt and sharp reaction of the three Western powers, must have combined to convince the Russians that nothing could be achieved in Austria by such methods. And for reasons that were not altogether clear, they were unwilling to exploit their very strong military position. At any moment they could have cut the routes linking the Western contingents in Vienna with the Western Zones, as they did in the case of Berlin in 1948–9. They could equally have cut off the large, populous and economically important Soviet Zone from the rest of Austria, imposing a Soviet-controlled government by open force. But, presumably for wider strategic and political reasons, they did not attempt these things.

The Russians were of course hampered by the Austrian Communist Party's weakness and internal divisions. The official leader, Franz Koplenig, had spent many years in Moscow (1934–45) and was a safe and colourless *apparatchik*; Franz Honner, a former miner, had more character and more of a mind of his own; Ernst Fischer, a brilliant intellectual with Viennese sophistication and charm and a strain of Austrian patriotism, did not fit easily into the Soviet power apparatus (and eventually broke with the party after the Soviet invasion of Czechoslovakia in 1968). Yet the Rumanian Communist Party – to take one instance – was even smaller and weaker than the Austrian party, and was nevertheless placed in power by the Russians.

Austria, however, had the advantage that it was a particularly sensitive border area in the divided Europe of the post-1945 era. This fact combined with Austrian toughness and the Western presence to make Stalin hold his hand.

By the end of 1950 there was a new factor in the strategic balance in Europe which inevitably affected Austria. The Atlantic alliance, created in 1949, transformed itself into an integrated military system under American command, and the United States made it clear that West Germany was to be rearmed and brought into the system. This threw a new light on Austria's military potentialities. In the integrated defence system the territory of Western Austria could form a very useful bridge between American (and eventually West German) forces in southern Germany and their NATO allies, the Italians. The Russians must therefore have expected the Americans to wish to bring Western Austria into the NATO system, in some way. They must also have reflected afresh on the military value of Eastern

Austria to the Soviet defence system in Eastern Europe, which in 1955 was to be formalised in the Warsaw Pact.

The Austrians themselves were aware of the danger to their country from the consolidation of two opposing military blocs in Europe. Already in the autumn of 1950 the Soviet Foreign Minister, Andrei Vyshinsky, had told Gruber that the United States was 'preparing war against the Soviet Union' and that 'this was affecting the solution of every international question'.[280] The Austrians came to fear that one side or the other was planning to partition their country, like Germany. When Vice-Chancellor Schärf visited the United States early in 1952, he stressed the importance of maintaining Austria's unity. In May Chancellor Figl was in Washington, and made a strong impression on the Secretary of State, Dean Acheson, who paid a return visit to Vienna in July, intended to put heart into the Austrians. In September the British Foreign Secretary, Eden, also visited Vienna. These diplomatic journeys did something to show that the West was not planning to split Austria.

Nevertheless the Austrians – especially in Vienna and the Soviet Zone – were still uneasy and frustrated. Their country remained occupied (though the Western allies had reduced their troops to the minimum), and there was no prospect of the treaty which would liberate it from occupation.

21 The Austrian State Treaty and Austrian Neutrality

The negotiations about an Austrian State Treaty between 1946 and 1955 caused the waste of more man-hours of sheer boredom than any other Western–Soviet negotiation of the post-war years. This was because for long periods either one side or the other, or both – but more often the Soviet Union alone – had wider political or strategic reasons for delaying a treaty.

In the spring of 1946 the American Secretary of State, Byrnes, backed by Bevin, had urged Molotov to agree to start treaty discussions, and in June an American draft treaty was circulated. But Molotov was engaged in a political 'squeeze' intended to compel the Western allies to sign treaties with Soviet-occupied Rumania, Hungary and Bulgaria by refusing to sign a treaty with pro-Western Italy until they did. He therefore had no interest in an Austrian treaty at this stage.

By December 1946, with the other four treaties duly completed, the Soviet Union was ready to agree that work on the Austrian treaty should begin in January 1947, through Foreign Ministers' deputies. The deputies, meeting in London, found themselves grappling mainly with Yugoslavia's claims to a large slice of Carinthia, including the Land capital, Klagenfurt, and 150 million dollars in reparations. Czechoslovakia also asked for small frontier changes, but after bilateral Austrian–Czechoslovak contacts, these were dropped. The general outlook seemed reasonably good.

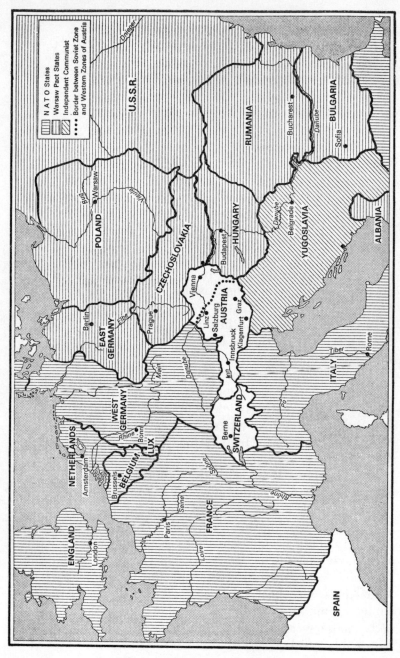

Map 2 Europe in 1955

When the four Foreign Ministers met in Moscow in the spring of 1947, however, Gruber and the Austrian delegation soon got the impression that the Western attitude had stiffened. There were sharp clashes over Soviet demands for large reparations from Germany which in practice could only have been paid by the Western Allies, who were therefore determined not to allow the Austrians to make economic concessions to the Soviet Union over German assets which would have had just the same effect. Moreover, after observing Soviet techniques in establishing Communist regimes in Eastern Europe, the Western side felt that given the near-starvation and economic disruption still existing in Austria, an early Western military withdrawal might leave the country an easy victim to a Communist bid for power.[281] The presence of John Foster Dulles, later President Eisenhower's Secretary of State, as member of the U.S. delegation representing the Republic Party, probably also contributed to the toughening of the Western attitude. Nothing was therefore agreed in Moscow except – on Bevin's proposal – to set up an Austrian Treaty Commission in Vienna to try to establish a definition of 'German assets' for treaty purposes. The Commission held eighty-five meetings in five months and achieved little.

In February 1948 the Foreign Ministers' deputies again met in London, this time concentrating on the German assets question – which meant Soviet claims for concession rights in Austrian oil for 50 years, 200 million dollars in respect of other German assets, Soviet participation in the Danube Shipping Company, and tax-free export of all Soviet profits. The Western side thought these demands would cripple Austria; in any case, preoccupied with forming the Western Union defence alliance and shocked by the Communist coup in Prague in March, they were in no hurry for an Austrian treaty.

A year later, the deputies again met in London. By this time, Tito and Stalin had quarrelled openly. The Yugoslavs now reduced their claims on Austria; but the Russians continued to back them. A year later again, in 1949, the Russians dropped their support; at the Foreign Ministers' conference in Paris in June, it was agreed that Austria should keep its 1938 frontiers. Considerable progress was also made over Soviet claims on Austrian oil and Danube shipping.

Yet again the negotiations came to a standstill, because of outside factors. The signature of the North Atlantic Treaty in April 1949 inevitably affected the Soviet attitude to the Austrian question – even though Chancellor Figl formally declared that Austria would maintain an independent position outside all military blocs.[282] By 1950 the Austrian government had come to the conclusion that Moscow did not want a treaty; it wished to keep troops in Austria partly to exert pressure on the recalcitrant Tito, partly to preserve the legal pretext contained in the relevant peace treaties for keeping troops in Hungary and Rumania, 'on Soviet lines of communication with Austria'. From the end of 1950 until the beginning of 1955, the Soviet Union had the further aim of using the question of an Austrian treaty as a political weapon in its fight to prevent the rearmament of West Germany as a member of NATO. In April 1955 the Soviet Prime Minister, Bulganin, in fact admitted to the Austrians that this had been the Soviet strategy.[283]

In early 1952, the West suggested a resumption of treaty negotiations. This was rejected by the Soviet Union on the curious ground that the Western Allies had failed to carry out their obligation under the Italian peace treaty to establish a Free Territory of Trieste. This was obviously a pretext rather than the real Soviet motive. Largely as a propaganda move – and not a very convincing one – the United States then put forward a 'short treaty', omitting all the contentious clauses, notably those on German assets. Inevitably the Soviet Union rejected it; it could not be expected to give up its economic demands for nothing.

This was discouraging for the Austrians. So the Foreign Minister, Gruber, turned to a new initiative intended to raise Austrian spirits – an appeal to the United Nations (of which Austria was not a member) for an early treaty. The Western Allies were unenthusiastic but eventually agreed. Gruber persuaded Brazil to sponsor the appeal; he wanted India as co-sponsor but Jawaharlal Nehru, though sympathetic, was unwilling. The appeal was discussed by the U.N. Assembly – in which Gruber was allowed to speak – at the end of 1952, with Latin Americans, Arabs and Africans showing marked sympathy for the Austrian plight; a resolution calling on the four Powers to restore a sovereign Austria was passed almost unanimously. But the practical effect was nil and the Austrian public was not much cheered.

However, Gruber's contacts with the Indians led to a meeting with Nehru in Switzerland in the summer of 1953. Krishna Menon, then Indian Ambassador in Moscow, was also present. The Indians said the Russians were worried over the question of a new *Anschluss* – which really meant that Moscow was afraid that Western Austria might somehow be drawn into the NATO alliance. Gruber said there was no question of an *Anschluss*, and the Austrian government had repeatedly said that Austria would not join any military bloc. Thereafter Krishna Menon raised in Moscow the idea of Austrian neutrality as the way to a treaty. Molotov said a neutrality declaration would be useful, but not enough.[284]

By this time Figl had been replaced as Chancellor (in April 1953) by Raab, who had been involved in the talks in 1950 with the Communist, Ernst Fischer, and who believed that his down-to-earth approach might prove successful where others had failed. In November 1953 the reputedly pro-American, anti-Soviet Gruber was replaced as Foreign Minister by Figl, with the Socialist, Bruno Kreisky, as State Secretary. Kreisky had spent twelve years in Sweden (1938–50) and was therefore convinced that neutrality was a practicable and even advantageous policy for a small state.[285]

On the Soviet side too there had been a change, and a far more important one – the death of Stalin in March 1953. This had been followed by a certain softening in the Soviet attitude in Vienna. In July a civilian, a prominent Communist, I. L. Ilyichev, was appointed Soviet High Commissioner; and certain long-maintained restrictions on Austria could at last be removed. Hopes rose.

But when the four Foreign Ministers met in Berlin in February 1954, the Soviet Union was still waging its battle to stop West German rearmament and therefore insisted on linking the question of an Austrian treaty with the German question. Figl and Kreisky declared to the Foreign Ministers that Austria would not enter any military alliance. This assurance was not very popular with the Western Powers;[286] and it failed to soften Molotov. The Soviet Foreign Minister wrecked all Austrian hopes by announcing that in any case occupation forces must remain in Austria until a German peace treaty had been concluded. This meant prolonging the occupation indefinitely, and the Austrians obviously could not accept it. The British Foreign Secretary, Eden, later wrote: 'I felt the deepest sympathy with the Austrians during these sessions, which were most unpleasant to sit through. Molotov behaved with a callous brutality, and although the little Austrian delegation took their punishment bravely, they were much dejected . . .'[287] In Vienna, the Soviet High Commission took up a threatening attitude to the Austrian government, accusing it of fostering Nazi and militarist activities; in May Ilyichev summoned Raab and Schärf and condemned them sharply for their supposed misdeeds.

In December 1954 Ilyichev made another unexpected move. He summoned an extraordinary meeting of the Allied Council to discuss a 'very important and urgent question', and accused the United States of violating the

1945 zonal agreement and the 1946 Control Agreement by stationing U.S. units in the French Zone, in Tirol, 'for the alleged purpose of safeguarding their communications passing through western Austria between West Germany and Italy'. This, Ilyichev said, was an attempt illegally to extend the U.S. Zone and 'to make use of the territory of western Austria for the purposes of the aggressive North Atlantic bloc'. The French and Americans replied that the American troops in question had been there for eight years and implied strongly that the Soviet charge was purely propagandist.[288] More probably the Russians genuinely feared that the Western Allies were thinking of incorporating Austrian territory in their strategic planning. Mikoyan was reported to have taken this line in private talks with Austrians in April 1955. At the same time, diplomats in Vienna thought that Moscow was seriously considering acting first and incorporating Eastern Austria into the Soviet bloc.[289]

Nevertheless, at a moment when the outlook for Austria seemed utterly bleak, the Russians suddenly hinted at a decisive change in their policy. In a speech to the Supreme Soviet on 8 February 1955, Molotov said that if all possibility of a new *Anschluss* could be ruled out, the occupation of Austria could be ended without waiting for the conclusion of a German treaty. The Austrians – in the face of strong Western scepticism – took this as a signal, and initiated diplomatic contacts in Moscow and Vienna, to probe Soviet intentions. The unexpectedly rapid result was that in April, Raab, Schärf, Figl and Kreisky – a powerful two-party delegation – went to Moscow. In four days, they reached agreement with the Soviet government.

On the first day, the Austrians carefully avoided using the word 'neutrality', sticking to their previous often-repeated pledge that Austria would join no military alliance. However, Molotov pressed them for a declaration on Austria's future foreign policy, making it clear that he wanted it to include a statement on neutrality. The

Austrians then overcame their inhibitions and declared that their policy would be permanent neutrality on the Swiss model.[290] (As early as 1947 Renner, then President, had written in favour of the Swiss model for Austria.)[291]

From then on, the talks went well, though there was tough bargaining with the redoubtable Mikoyan over the economic aspects of the treaty, especially oil. The Austrians had to concede more than they would have liked. But they obtained the crucial assurance from Molotov that he no longer insisted that the occupation troops should remain until there was a German treaty: he accepted the Austrian demand that the troops should leave by 31 December 1955.

Molotov also made another implied concession. Almost his opening remark in the negotiations was that the two political parties forming the Austrian delegation represented the overwhelming majority of the Austrian people; the Soviet government, he went on, had 'taken note' of this fact.[292] This came near to a formal statement that Moscow no longer had any intention of trying to change the Austrian régime or using Communists for this purpose.

Directly after the Moscow meeting, the Russians proposed a four-power meeting to conclude an Austrian treaty. The Western Allies, however, seemed curiously ill-prepared for this sudden breakthrough. They were particularly worried about one aspect of the Austrian–Soviet agreement. The Austrians had not only said that they would seek international recognition of their proposed neutrality; they also declared that they would welcome, and seek, a four-power guarantee of the inviolability and integrity of Austrian territory. The Western Allies disliked the idea of any such guarantee, insisting that it would give the Soviet Union a pretext for intervention in Austria, and warning the Austrians strongly against it.

More generally, they hesitated to accept Austrian neutrality. Dulles had always mistrusted neutrality and neutrals as providing an easy opening for a Soviet take-over. An American historian wrote later of 'what seemed in 1955 to be the United States' inability to cope with the idea of "neutralism"'; in the Austrian case, he added, 'the United States only grudgingly came to accept the idea of neutrality'.[293] In London, Harold Macmillan, then Foreign Secretary, put the question to the British Cabinet at the end of April. He noted that there was the disadvantage that the Soviet Union would exploit the pattern of a neutral Austria to lure Germany into a similar neutrality as a condition of reunification; on the other hand, the Austrians wanted a treaty and were ready to 'pay the price' of neutrality. The British Chiefs of Staff produced a strategic assessment: 'a neutral Austria, debarred from joining NATO or from giving transit to NATO forces, was acceptable only provided that its neutrality was made really effective and was guaranteed'. But the British were loath to involve themselves in a guarantee which might, conceivably, involve them in war, as in 1914.[294] The Cabinet gave Macmillan a more or less free hand.

In spite of Western misgivings, things moved fast. Diplomatic representatives of the four occupying powers completed a draft treaty at talks in Vienna, with the American, Llewellyn Thompson, extracting last minute concessions from the now compliant Russians, thereby bringing down attacks on Dulles in the Austrian press.[295] In May Dulles, Macmillan, Molotov and the French Foreign Minister, Antoine Pinay, met in Vienna. Molotov produced without warning a draft guarantee for the four Powers to sign; but, in the face of Western stalling, he dropped it. On 15 May the Foreign Ministers, together with Figl, signed the Austrian treaty in the Belvedere Palace, in a room overlooking the Inner City and St Stephen's Cathedral, while a vast and happy crowd waited in the gardens below. There were very few Western troops left in Austria; most had been withdrawn years before; all left by the end of October. There were still around 40,000 Soviet troops; they left before the end of September.

When the four Foreign Ministers met a month later in San Francisco, they took a relaxed view of the question of a joint guarantee to Austria: they agreed that if the Austrian parliament asked for one, they would all use the same text.[296] On 26 October 1955 the Austrian parliament passed a constitutional law declaring Austria's perpetual neutrality, which was therefore anchored not in the Austrian treaty, but in the free decision of the freely elected representatives of the Austrian people. Raab told parliament that the law would in no respect curtail the basic rights and liberties of the individual citizen, the freedom of the press or freedom of speech, nor was any obligation to maintain an ideological neutrality involved: 'our military neutrality includes no liabilities or restrictions in the economic or cultural spheres'. Raab added that Austria would welcome a joint four-power guarantee of the inviolability and integrity of its territory. He knew, however, that this would not be forthcoming because the Western Powers were unwilling. But Austria did obtain the desired international recognition of its neutrality by formally communicating the neutrality law to sixty-one governments which either explicitly or implicitly acknowledged it.

In December Austria became a member of the United Nations, a fully independent state among other independent states. This showed that Austrians interpreted their country's neutrality less rigidly than did the Swiss who regarded themselves as debarred from U.N. membership.

Many explanations have been given of the Russian decision to give up Austria. Some people thought that after Stalin's death there were two rival groups, the hard-liners around Molotov wishing to continue a tough anti-Western policy, the innovators around Khrushchev wanting to move towards a new phase of co-existence with the West. The rise of Khrushchev led to the defeat of the hard-liners and the decision to quit Austria.

Certainly the Soviet decision on Austria was linked with

the desire for a summit meeting with Western leaders. This had first been proposed by Churchill soon after Stalin's death in 1953, but the United States was reluctant to face a summit until West German rearmament was an accomplished fact, and from the start Eisenhower insisted on an Austrian treaty as one of his conditions for holding a summit. By the beginning of 1955, it was becoming obvious to the Russians that they could no longer hope to stop West German rearmament; the fall of Malenkov gave more power to Khrushchev; Khrushchev wanted a summit and was prepared to pay the price of an Austrian treaty.

Both Macmillan and Eisenhower seemed to incline to this explanation; and certainly Soviet acceptance of an Austrian treaty led rapidly to the summit. 'Because of the Soviet's action,' Eisenhower wrote later, 'and not wishing to appear senselessly stubborn in my attitude towards a Summit meeting . . . I instructed Secretary Dulles to let it be known . . . that we were ready. . .'[297] The summit was duly held within two months of the signing of the Austrian treaty.

Macmillan had also told the Cabinet that the Russians intended to use the model of Austrian neutrality as a pattern for other European states, notably Germany. This theory received some confirmation from Bulganin's speech at the founding conference of the Warsaw Pact in May 1955. He said that the restoration of the political and economic independence of a neutral Austria would be a significant contribution to the strengthening of European peace, and testified to the 'great potentialities' for promoting cooperation between states: 'it would be wrong to assume that this attitude is held by the Austrian government alone. There are quite a number of states, both in Europe and in Asia, which are adverse to joining aggressive military blocs.'[298]

In Europe, Moscow was anxious that Yugoslavia should abandon any idea of links with NATO either directly or through Greece and Turkey, with which it had signed a treaty of cooperation in 1953. Khrushchev was eager for reconciliation with Tito – which he achieved soon after the signing of the Austrian treaty. In the preliminary Soviet–Yugoslav contacts which led up to the Khrushchev–Bulganin visit to Belgrade, the Yugoslavs pressed strongly for an Austrian treaty. They already had good and even friendly relations with Austria, in spite of the territorial quarrel of the early post-war years; in 1951 Yugoslavia had declared an end to its state of war with Austria; agreement was reached on local frontier traffic and foundations were laid for regional cooperation and cultural exchanges with Slovenia.[299] In 1952, Gruber, as Foreign Minister, visited Belgrade. But more powerful than any general friendliness was the Yugoslavs' desire to see Soviet troops removed from their northern frontier, which could be achieved by an Austrian treaty. Yugoslav pressure may therefore have played a certain part in the Soviet decision to let Austria go.

In Asia, a great country strongly opposed to joining military blocs was of course India, in which Khrushchev was particularly interested, paying a long visit in December 1955. It would appear that Krishna Menon, as Ambassador in Moscow, had strongly urged Austria's moral claim to a treaty. India must therefore have had an influence on the Soviet decision.

As for the military arguments for and against giving up Eastern Austria, there was an obvious loss to the Soviet Union in abandoning territory in which Soviet troops covered most of the southern frontier of Czechoslovakia and the whole eastern frontier of Hungary, and from which they could threaten Yugoslavia from the north. But this was counterbalanced by the denial to NATO of Western Austria as a valuable land link between West Germany and Italy. Nevertheless, the Soviet defence chiefs would certainly have refused to relinquish Austria if this had meant relinquishing the right to keep troops in Hungary and Rumania. But this problem was overcome, the day before the Austrian treaty was signed, by the conclusion of the Warsaw Pact, providing a new contractual basis for the stationing of Soviet forces in Hungary and Rumania.

The Soviet leaders must therefore have concluded that on balance they gained more than they lost by signing the Austrian treaty. Yet the Austrians themselves must have played a fairly important part in determining the Soviet decision. They had shown themselves too tough and too alert to be easily dominated or seduced; they had shown themselves politically skilful enough to perform a fairly convincing balancing act between West and East; they had cultivated their international contacts with sufficient deftness to enable their small country to carry a certain weight in European affairs and even on a wider stage. Above all, through their direct approach to Moscow, they seemed to have convinced the Russians of their good faith in saying that they wanted Austria to be genuinely neutral and of their capacity to preserve this neutrality.

PART IV

Independent Austria, 1955–1972

22 The Last Decade of Coalition Government, 1955–1966

Austria could not have attained full independence in 1955 if it had not first achieved internal political and economic stability. This was necessary to convince the Russians, that hopes of overturning the Austrian political system were vain, and the West, that a neutral Austria could successfully stand alone and resist Soviet attempts at subversion.

The achievement of stability had been almost entirely the result of the cooperation between the two big parties, the People's Party and the Socialists. This had been forced upon them by the pressures of the occupation and by the hunger, cold and economic disruption of the early post-war years, later by the long-drawn-out struggle for a treaty. Neither party was strong enough to face these problems alone.

Cooperation depended on the growth of personal relations between leading men of the two parties. Between Figl and Schärf, between 1945 and 1953, there was a good understanding. After Figl's removal, largely through pressures inside his own party, relations between Raab and Schärf were colder; but Raab got on well with the Socialist, Oskar Helmer, Minister of the Interior in the post-war period, and this proved useful in times of strain. Raab also had excellent personal relations with the Socialist, Johann Böhm, who dominated the powerful trade union organisation (Österreichische Gewerkschaftsbund, or Ö.G.B.)

formed in 1945; this was especially important during the first efforts to establish a rational wages and prices policy.

In spite of shared responsibilities and personal contacts, the coalition was never very amicable. To lessen interparty jealousies and local friction, there was the curious and elaborate system of *Proporz*, or proportional representation of the two parties, according to electoral strength, not only in the federal government and the parliamentary committees, but also in the Land governments and in local government down to a low level, and in nationalised industries and other official or semi-official institutions such as radio and television. This system was much criticised, and ridiculed, in later years, but served a useful purpose and gave practical experience of government and administration to a wide segment of politically-minded Austrians.

The Foundations of Economic Policy

The main work of the coalition government – apart from the special problems of the occupation and the treaty – was to agree and carry through economic policies. The economic problems facing Austria in the post-war decade were much the same as those facing other non-Communist European countries. There was first the period of emergency relief, then the period of recovery through Marshall Aid, and then the burst of economic growth and sudden prosperity with the accompanying dangers of overheating and recession. What was remarkable about Austria was that economic policies were hammered out by a process of hard bargaining between the two big parties both inside the government itself and through organisations closely linked with the government machine.

This process was inevitably difficult. The People's Party represented the interests – which sometimes conflicted – of the industrialists, businessmen and shopkeepers, peasant-farmers, and white-collar workers; it was the party of the self-employed. The Socialists represented the much more homogeneous interests of the industrial workers. The

People's Party was the natural channel for demands for low taxes (which meant a low rate of government expenditure), a balanced budget, a low rate of wage increases and relatively high food prices. The Socialist Party was a natural channel for demands for high wages, low food prices and a high rate of government expenditure for social purposes (necessitating high taxes). The Socialists were naturally more in favour of State intervention in the economy than the People's Party, but the People's Party – as heir to the historical tradition of the Christian Socials – was fearful of liberal *laissez-faire* economic policies and willing to accept a rather paternalistic role for the government.

In the immediate post-war years, the Austrian economy was in such grave difficulties, and so entirely dependent on outside economic aid – mainly, in one form or another, from the United States – that economic argument inside the coalition government was kept within narrow limits; there was moreover plenty of advice, control or direct interference from one or other of the occupying powers. The Russians seemed to have little interest in restoring the Austrian economy – while sniping at the Austrian government for its economic inadequacy – and a great deal of interest in acquiring control of as large a section of Austrian industry as possible. One result of this was that the bulk of American aid went to western Austria, since the Americans could then be certain that it would not simply find its way into Soviet hands. In consequence, the industrialisation of the predominantly agricultural western Lands, especially Upper Austria, which had already been launched by Hitler for war purposes, was carried a long way further. Linked with this was a steady movement of population from Soviet-occupied Eastern Austria to the West, for both political and economic reasons, with important long-term consequences for Austria's social and economic structure and for the balance of strength between the two big parties.

The short-term effect of Soviet economic policies – or behaviour – was not only to keep the two big parties together but also to drive the coalition government into the Americans' arms. The acute food shortage in Vienna and the surrounding area of the immediate post-war years resulted partly from Soviet requisitioning, partly from the farmers' natural hoarding instincts, partly from the barriers erected (mainly by the Russians) between the different occupation zones. The Austrian government turned inevitably to the Americans who alone seemed able to help effectively (though the British also gave aid amounting to £10 million). A kind of economic alliance was established between the coalition government and the Western allies, who tried to defend the government against Soviet attempts to take over Austrian industry as 'German assets'[300] and Soviet demands for the 'economic disarmament' of Austria, entailing restrictions, for 10 years, on the production of iron ore, pig iron, aluminium and nitrogen, also steel smelting.[301]

It was the Americans – together with the British – who first pushed the coalition government towards a firm wages and prices policy, in the autumn of 1946. This was at a time of social unrest caused by shortage of food and clothing, which the Russians were using to discredit the Austrian government. The American representative told the Allied Council that the Austrian government should establish and maintain a planned and unified control over the price and wage structure of the country, with a view to preventing disparity between price and wage increases.[302]

This American–British recommendation – slightly unexpected, at that time, from the United States – can be seen as the starting point of an important development in Austrian economic and political life. The first phase was the successive wages and prices agreements – five in all – negotiated annually between 1947 and 1951, not inside the government, but between Raab, as President of the

Federal Economic Chamber, and Böhm, as President of
the trade union organisation. The first agreement, in
August 1947, followed a period during which wages had
risen by 45 per cent and the cost of living had risen nearly
90 per cent in 12 months. The aim was to keep down wage
increases on the one side, and on the other to fix the price
of food, coal, electricity, gas, railway fares and clothing
and to control rents. At the same time, to keep a fair
balance, unemployment benefits and old age pensions were
raised and income tax was made more progressive so as to
ease the burden on wage-earners. In 1949, according to
the International Labour Office, Austria devoted a bigger
proportion of the national income to social purposes than
any other country except Germany and the Saar.[303]

The bargaining each year was difficult. The wage increases normally were fixed at a lower percentage than
the price increases. The relative docility of the workers
was due partly to the personal authority of Böhm and to
Socialist Party discipline, partly to the large-scale unemployment of the period: in February 1950 the figure was
195,000, or nearly 10 per cent of the registered labour
force, rising to 215,000 in the following two years and to
285,000 in 1953. The low rate of wage increases was com-
pensated in some degree by special welfare measures such
as the 'nutrition benefits' for children and workers in 1948.
The price controls were a good deal less effective than the
wage controls, and the cost of living continued to rise,
especially after the fifth and last wages and prices agreement.

The Raab–Böhm agreements were criticised in later
years as having delayed a return to normal economic
conditions. But both big parties were jointly responsible.
The Socialists could correctly claim that the agreements
had done a great deal to maintain social peace and prevent
strikes;[304] while the People's Party could claim that they
were essential to counter the inevitable inflationary trend
of the time.[305] In the longer view, the agreements laid the

basis of the 'social partnership' which later took the form of the Parity Commission for Wages and Prices, regarded by Austrians as one of their special achievements.

The wage–price agreements of 1947–51 were interlocked with successive measures aimed at stabilising the currency at a realistic rate. This was inevitably a piecemeal process, made particularly difficult by the need to obtain the Allied Council's approval, which caused damaging delays and made the required secrecy impossible. Although the Socialists strongly favoured currency stabilisation, the direct responsibility lay with the People's Party Ministers who held the chief financial and economic posts in the government. They had to contend with critics inside their own party who were seeking to safeguard private savings or who found the existence of several exchange rates, or black-market rates, very advantageous. On the whole, however, the middle class suffered a good deal less from the post-1945 currency measures than from the effects of Seipel's recovery programme after the First World War.

The agreements caused particular discontent in an important section of People's Party supporters, the peasant farmers, who contended that the prices fixed for farm produce were too low. They put strong pressure on Chancellor Figl – regarded as their own special representative – who responded with measures such as additional premium payments on bread grains.

However, the balance of power inside the People's Party was shifting away from the peasant farmers, its traditional source of voting strength, towards the industrial and business interests grouped around Raab's Wirtschaftbund, or Economic Union. The drift away from the land was accelerating, and although the Bauernbund, or Peasant-Farmers' Union, remained numerically the strongest of the economic interest groups which composed the People's Party, its weight in Party decision-making inevitably dwindled, all the more because of the surprising spurt made by Austrian industry from 1953 onwards. As the political power of the farmers waned, so also did Figl's standing in the People's Party. It was then natural that Raab should become the party's dominant figure.

The Raab Era

Raab dominated Austrian politics for eight years. He was a solid, silent man who seldom revealed his thoughts or shared his plans even with close party colleagues. His habit of acting on his own without discussion inevitably caused friction, especially as he grew older. He had, however, a typically Austrian sense of humour and earthy turn of phrase which won him affection as a father figure – though he could use sarcasm as a sharp political weapon. He also had massive common sense, at least in economic affairs and party politics. The Socialist, Schärf, paid tribute to his 'remarkable realism', which enabled him to look beyond the limits of his businessman's mentality.[306] In his attitude to the Socialists, he got on with individuals as well as he could, though he could never get on terms with Schärf's successor as party leader, the agile and fluent Bruno Pittermann. His basic view was: 'I would rather have the Socialists at the same table in the government than have them in the streets.'[307]

Raab became Chancellor after a prolonged crisis between the two big parties. With the phasing-out of Marshall Aid in 1952, the Americans were pressing the Austrians to stop inflation and balance the budget – to learn to live on their own resources without the generous aid of the post-war years. At a time when there were a quarter of a million unemployed, the Socialists feared that the People's Party would revert to the methods of the Seipel era, to financial orthodoxy, cuts in government spending and a low level of economic activity. Certainly Dr Reinhard Kamitz, who became Finance Minister in 1952, seemed inclined to this course. The Socialists themselves wanted full employment and economic expansion.

The negotiations over the budget between the two

parties in the autumn of 1952 reached total deadlock. The government resigned. In the following February elections were held in which the People's Party lost three seats while the Socialists gained six – winning more votes than the People's Party, though still one seat behind it in parliament (73 to 74). The Socialists claimed that under the *Proporz* system, these results showed that they should have more power inside the government and in other government-controlled bodies. The People's Party tried to resist this argument and diminish Socialist influence by bringing into the government the small party of the Right – at that time the Electoral League of the Independents, formed four years earlier to provide a home for less implicated Nazis, which had won fourteen seats. This did not suit the Socialists: they had originally fought for the right of the 'Independents' to form a party because they wanted to stop their votes from strengthening the People's Party and perhaps giving it a permanent absolute majority; but they did not now want them in the government. They therefore rejected the idea; so also did the President, the veteran Socialist, General Körner; so also did the Allied Council.

The People's Party had to yield. Raab replaced Figl as Chancellor, and the two-party coalition was resumed. The system of *Proporz* was maintained in the government, but the Land governments and district councils were freed from it.

Under Raab's leadership, the two parties managed to find common ground in economic policy, in a big investment programme and intensive promotion of exports. Raab and Kamitz became exponents of the 'social market economy' propounded by the West German Economics Minister, Ludwig Erhard, the creator of the German 'economic miracle'. This aimed to get the best of both worlds by linking a free market economy with a system of progressive taxation which was to provide the money for advanced social welfare policies in social insurance, pensions, housing and agricultural support. It was brilliantly successful in West Germany; Austria, helped by the world economic situation, achieved a similar success, with a period of rapid expansion from 1953 to 1957. A recession at the end of 1957 was quickly overcome.

The conclusion of the Austrian treaty in 1955 brought special economic problems and new political difficulties in relations between the two big parties. It had become the custom for a Socialist Minister to have charge of the nationalised industries, as counter-weight to the People's Party's control of the Finance and Trade Ministries. As a result of the treaty, the Soviet Union (against payment in goods) returned the oil industry, the Danube Shipping Company and other Soviet-held concerns to Austria. If these were now to become part of the Socialist domain, Socialist power would be very much strengthened.

As a consequence of the 1946 nationalisation law and subsequent measures, together with the return of the Soviet-held concerns, the nationalised sector of the Austrian economy was a very important one, though still smaller than the private sector. It included oil, iron and steel, electricity, shipbuilding and chemicals. The 1968 figure for those employed in the nationalised sector was 107,500, or 18.2 per cent of all industrial workers.[308] In addition the three biggest banks (the Creditanstalt Bankverein, the Österreichische Länderbank and the Österreichisches Creditinstitut) were nationalised, which meant the indirect nationalisation of a number of concerns producing manufactured goods which were financed by these banks.[309]

Control of this vast economic empire was therefore a matter of great concern to the two big parties. The Socialists believed it right to acquire for the party the strongest possible power base in the state; they were also ideologically committed to the progressive nationalisation of industry – a commitment which they found more and more embarrassing during the late 1960s and early 1970s.

The People's Party did not want the Socialists to gain more power and, although it had approved the 1946 nationalisation law as a defence against Soviet grabbing, its most influential elements were committed to the belief that private enterprise was more efficient than state-controlled enterprise.

The concerns returned by the Soviet Union also presented special short-term problems; some were in such poor condition that it was hard to fit them in with more modern and efficient industries. In the oil industry, in particular, the Russians had over-produced, so that there was a steady decrease in production in the years following 1955; 2.3 milliard schillings of new investment was required to restore the industry.[310]

The quarrel between the two big parties over the nationalised industries, especially oil, was the main bone of contention in the election held in May 1956. By this time the Electoral League of the Independents had fallen apart and had been replaced, as the small party of the Right, by the Freedom Party, founded in November 1955. This never managed to win as many seats as its various predecessors. The election result showed a popular trend towards the People's Party, which gained eight seats. However, the Socialists also gained one seat; the losers were the new Freedom Party, which won eight fewer seats than its predecessor, and the Communists, who lost one.

Raab therefore formed a new two-party coalition government in which the balance of cabinet posts favoured the People's Party by ten to eight. The *Proporz* system was continued, though subjected to increasing criticism in the independent press, particularly for its application to radio and television. A compromise was reached on the nationalised industries: they were taken away from the control of a Socialist Minister and brought together in a single holding company, the Industry and Mines Administration, with a Board formed by Ministers representing the two big parties. They thus became a battleground for sharp inter-party rivalry, and the new arrangement did not prove successful; the necessary reorganisation and large-scale investment could not be carried through. Three years later the nationalised industries again came under direct government control, this time under the Chancellor's authority.

The really important and lasting achievement of this period was the formation in 1957 of the Parity Commission for Wages and Prices. (See p. 208 above and p. 230 below.) Its original role was as a mechanism for crisis management during a time of spiralling wages and prices and strike action; but, as a consequence of its later development, it came to be described as 'almost the optimum concentration of power in Austria'.[311]

Although the 1956 election had shown a clear though modest swing in favour of the People's Party, the presidential election of the following year showed that Austrians still did not wish to commit themselves collectively to one or other of the big parties. Ever since the Second World War the President had been a Socialist – first Renner, then Körner. Since 1951 the President had been elected by direct popular vote, not through parliament, in accordance with the 1929 amendment to the 1920 constitution. Körner died in January 1957. The People's Party had high hopes of winning the presidency from the Socialists; but Raab himself was not willing to stand – if he had, he might well have won handsomely – so they put forward a distinguished surgeon as candidate. The Socialists put forward Schärf, who won by 100,000 votes. This was regarded in People's Party circles as a personal defeat for Raab, whose authority began to wane from then on.

The Socialist Move to the Centre

The Socialists, heartened by Schärf's victory, replaced him as Vice-Chancellor by the party leader, Pittermann. They also set out to re-think their party's policy in fundamental

terms. A commission to draw up a new party programme
was headed by Kreisky. He had been influenced by his
long years of first-hand contact with the moderate, gradual
and highly successful Social Democracy of Sweden.
Austrian Socialists had also had close contacts since 1946
with the British Labour Party and had observed the British
Labour government's theory and practice in creating a
welfare state.

The Austrian party's action programme of October 1947
– drawn up at a time when the Communists were pressing
for a merger with the Socialists – had stressed that the
Socialist Party was fundamentally democratic, rejecting
any form of one-party system and believing in the free
interplay of forces between political parties. It was therefore intended both to draw a sharp dividing line between
Socialists and Communists, and also to clear up the
damaging ambiguities of the party's Linz programme of
1927 which, though intended to establish its basically
democratic character, had included revolutionary-sounding
phrases in order to keep the radical left wing happy.[312]

The Austrian Socialists had also taken an active part in
drawing up the programme for the reborn Socialist International which, issued in 1951, recognised that socialism
could be based not only on Marxist theory but also on
humanitarian or religious foundations, and that its aims
were social justice, growing prosperity, freedom and world
peace. Through the International, in the following years,
the Austrians had kept in close touch with West European
and Scandinavian socialists.

By 1957 the party leaders were ready for a further step
to broaden the Socialists' political appeal by seeking
middle ground. The Austrian electoral system of strict
proportional representation made it difficult for either of
the big parties to win an absolute majority in parliament;
if the Socialists were ever to achieve this aim, they would
have to move out from their bastion of power, the industrial working class, and penetrate the middle class and the

white-collar workers, and make themselves acceptable to the Catholics.

Until then, it had seemed that the Socialists' traditional anti-clericalism had survived – though in softened form – the Hitler period and the occupation. When Renner died at the end of 1950 there was an unpleasant squabble over reports from Catholic sources that before his death, he had returned to the Catholic faith. The Socialist Party hotly denied these, seeing them as an insult to the dead leader. In the 1947 party programme, the Socialists had declared that religion was a private matter; there should be freedom of faith and religious practice – but no support for religious instruction from State funds. Given the privileged position of the Church in pre-Hitler Austria, this Socialist attitude seemed hostile to devout Catholics, and was in strong opposition to the People's Party call, in 1945, for religious instruction in schools.

It was true that the People's Party, after 1945, did not want to be as closely identified with the Church as the Christian Socials had been, and the Austrian Bishops on their side said they did not want any links with any political party. Nevertheless it was generally accepted that the People's Party and the Church were close to one another, and many people still regarded the Socialists as hostile to the Church.

By 1957, Schärf – a life-long anti-clerical – saw the need for a change. On becoming President he said that he would do all he could towards a settlement of relations between State and Church; he was glad there was now a new climate. Also in 1957, there were contacts between the leading Socialists, Pittermann and Franz Olah, and Church dignitaries.

The ground had therefore been prepared for the new party programme worked out by the commission under Kreisky, which was finally adopted after long and heated debate in May 1958. This contained very little of the old doctrinaire Marxism; it was markedly conciliatory towards small businessmen, Catholics and even the Catholic Church itself. It declared that socialism and religion were not opponents: 'every religious man can be a Socialist'.

This development in the Socialist attitude made it possible for the two big parties to reach a compromise on the long-disputed question of the 1934 Concordat, which had been concluded by Dollfuss and had given the Church far-reaching privileges, but had been repudiated by Hitler. The Raab government made an approach to the Vatican; but Pope Pius XII had himself negotiated the 1933 Concordat and was stiff in his attitude. After his death in October 1958, things moved ahead and, after delays caused by internal party wrangles, a new agreement with the Vatican was signed in June 1960 – by the Socialist, Kreisky, now Foreign Minister. Two years later the question of religious instruction in schools was settled in agreement with the Vatican. All that was left outstanding was the marriage law which remained a bone of contention into the 1970s. In practice the post-*Anschluss* National Socialist marriage law of 1938, permitting divorce for all, including Catholics, continued in operation.[313]

In spite of this convergence between the two big parties over the Church question, relations were becoming more and more competitive and more and more strained. After the People's Party's success in the 1956 election, the question had been raised whether or not the 'big coalition' should be continued. In May 1959 there was a fresh election in which the future of the coalition was the main issue. The People's Party leaders said it should continue but change its method of work – by which they meant a weakening of the *Proporz* system and of the power of the Socialists. The Socialists, on their side, accused the People's Party of trying to break up the coalition and rule alone. However, the election result made continuation of the coalition a necessity: the People's Party lost three seats and the Socialists won four – and also more votes than the People's Party. The Freedom Party increased their seats from six to eight. The Communists disappeared from parliament, apparently for good.

This meant that there was virtually a dead heat between the two big parties. The Socialists regained confidence and demanded increased power in the government. The People's Party was distressed that the popular trend had been reversed and indulged in heart-searchings and internal disputes. The negotiations for the formation of a government were long and difficult. In the end the Socialists for the first time acquired the post of Foreign Minister, for Kreisky, and Socialist State Secretaries were appointed for Finance, Trade and Defence. The nationalised industries, by an ingenious arrangement, were placed under the Chancellery – that is, under the auspices of the Chancellor – but under the immediate control of the Socialist Vice-Chancellor, Pittermann.

The People's Party seeks Renewal

The 1959 government was the last of the Raab governments, and was regarded as transitional. It was assumed, inside the People's Party, that Raab's time was drawing to a close. In February 1960 he was replaced as party leader by the Styrian, Alfons Gorbach, a more yielding and conciliatory personality who had the prestige of three years in Nazi concentration camps. A new party programme was worked out, and presented by Josef Klaus, then Land Governor of Salzburg; it aimed to give the party a new look and win back the voters who had strayed in 1959. It proposed reforms in many fields, including the development of Austria's economic structure, the school system, workers' participation through profit-sharing and so on. An Institute for Applied Social and Economic Research was set up.

Towards the end of 1960, Raab let it be known that he intended to resign; and in the Spring of 1961 a new government was formed under Gorbach. He brought in two of the People's Party's bright younger men, Josef Klaus (then 50), as Finance Minister, and Karl Schleinzer (then 37), as Defence Minister, both Carinthian-born.

The election of November 1962 showed that the People's Party was making some slight headway in winning support with its new look. It gained two seats, while the Socialists lost two, which gave the People's Party a lead of five seats over its rival. The Freedom Party kept its eight seats. The Socialists had been somewhat handicapped by the activities of one of its prominent members, the mercurial and sometimes unaccountable Franz Olah, then President of the trade union organisation (the Ö.G.B.), who was pursuing a scheme to form a 'small coalition' between the Socialists and the Freedom Party, under his own leadership, using somewhat doubtful methods for this purpose. But the official Socialist policy was continuation of the big coalition. This also seemed to be the general Austrian wish.

The People's Party, however, wanted a shift in the balance of power inside the government, in its own favour. In particular, they wanted to get back the Foreign Ministry (from Kreisky) and majority control on the boards of all nationalised industries. The negotiations lasted until March 1963, and only ended after President Schärf had personally intervened.

In the new Gorbach government, Kreisky remained Foreign Minister and Olah became Minister of the Interior. Of the prominent younger People's Party representatives, Schleinzer remained in office, but Klaus left – a withdrawal which advanced his upward political progress. He had turned his back – in his own words – on the 'Viennese' and the Establishment, but a group of young friends, mainly in the western Lands, spontaneously started a 'Klaus Come Back' movement,[314] putting him forward – against Gorbach's wishes – as candidate for the position of People's Party leader. This move was strongly opposed by Klaus's fellow-reformer, Schleinzer.[315] Nevertheless Klaus won at the Klagenfurt Party conference in September 1963, and became party leader – for the time being, without a government post.

This situation could not last long. Gorbach suspected Klaus of intriguing against him, called for a vote of confidence in himself from the party leadership, and was defeated. Klaus was chosen to become Chancellor in Gorbach's place, and formed a government from which most of the older generation of People's Party politicians were excluded.

Klaus and his younger colleagues were impatient with the 'big coalition' but the parliamentary situation seemed to permit no alternative. Moreover in April 1963 the Socialist, Schärf, had been elected by a sizeable majority for a further term as President; and this was taken to mean that most Austrians still wanted a balance between the two big parties, and that the swing in favour of the People's Party in the 1962 election might not continue.

Klaus's first government was therefore still a coalition, with the Socialist Pittermann as Vice-Chancellor. But the partnership between the two big parties was becoming more and more strained and difficult. The new generation of People's Party leaders were eager to end it, but could not do so until they had won the necessary seats in parliament.

The Socialists were determined to maintain the coalition – while defending their interests as toughly as possible inside it – hoping that there would in time be an electoral swing back in their favour. Pittermann once explained the Socialist attitude to Klaus in Sarastro's words in the *Magic Flute*: 'I will not force you to love, but I will not give you your freedom.'[316] At the same time the Socialists continued a desultory flirtation with the Freedom Party. The People's Party resented this as a threat to break the big coalition and replace it with a 'small coalition', and therefore as an act of bad faith.

*

The Habsburg Problem

The People's Party was particularly resentful about the cooperation between the Socialists and the Freedom Party in the long dispute over Otto Habsburg's demand to return to Austria. In the early 1960s, this somewhat unreal issue strangely dominated the Austrian scene. The Austrian treaty of 1955 had banned a Habsburg restoration. But Otto Habsburg, wishing to return to Austria as a 'private citizen', made repeated declarations renouncing his claims as a member of the House of Habsburg. The question of the return of certain property to the Habsburg family was also involved.

The cause of Otto Habsburg's return was popular with a section of the public and of the press. The People's Party leadership was on the whole favourable, feeling that association with the Habsburgs would strengthen the party's prestige. The Socialists were strongly opposed, partly on quite sound political and international grounds, partly because the issue could be used against the People's Party. The question which no one could answer was whether Otto Habsburg, if he came back, would try to play a political role, on the Austrian stage or a wider European stage; to judge by his record from the 1930s onwards, even if he had finally abandoned all hope of a return to monarchy, he would find it hard to keep out of politics.

There was a sharp division inside the coalition government; no answer was given to Otto Habsburg's formal declaration of renunciation made in 1961. The matter came before the Constitutional Court, which declared itself not competent to deal with it. It then came before the Administrative Court of Justice, which in May 1963 declared that Otto Habsburg's declaration was satisfactory – in other words, that he could return to Austria.

At this point the Socialists and the Freedom Party – the natural heir to the anti-Habsburg tradition of the German Nationalists – drew together: in parliament, on 4 July

1963, they joined in voting against Otto Habsburg's return, in opposition to the People's Party.

The People's Party leaders saw this as yet further proof that the Socialists (especially Olah) were intriguing with the Freedom Party to form a small coalition. The Habsburg affair further complicated the negotiations for the formation of the first Klaus government, which only succeeded after Otto Habsburg had undertaken not to return during the lifetime of the existing parliament. The dispute continued to simmer during the last phase of the coalition, embittering relations between the two big parties still more. It was only settled after the big coalition had been buried, with Otto Habsburg's unsensational and innocuous return. The prolonged dispute had perhaps been useful in convincing him that he had no chance of playing a political role; the fact that his return created so little stir showed the degree of maturity which Austrians had attained.

The end of the Coalition

The coalition ended at last as a result of the election of March 1966, which for the first time gave the People's Party its heart's desire – an absolute majority over the Socialists and the Freedom Party. It won four seats while the Socialists and the Freedom Party each lost two. Klaus and his supporters had campaigned on their claim to govern Austria alone, with the appeal: 'give us a clear majority'. They had criticised the coalition as outworn, a device which had robbed parliament of its true functions; Austria, they argued, should have a democracy of the classic Western type. In this the People's Party was supported by the independent press and by some influential West German journals such as the *Spiegel*.

The Socialists on their side campaigned for a continuation of the coalition – if possible under Socialist leadership. They suffered for their tactical error in failing to repudiate firmly a Communist pledge of support – which gave the People's Party the chance to raise the old bogey that the

Socialists were Red at heart. They also suffered from the aftermath of the troubles which had blown up over Olah, because of his idiosyncratic behaviour and suspected scandals in the background. These had finally led to his exclusion from the Socialist Party in November 1964. Olah, who had been very popular with some sections of the workers, tried to start up his own 'Democratic Progressive Party' and fought the 1966 election, failing to win a seat, but taking 148,000 votes away from the Socialists. This rather distorted the electoral picture.

The People's Party leaders therefore could not be sure that the general mood was in favour of ending the big coalition. There had been signs that Austrians still wanted to keep the two big parties in balance: when President Schärf died in February 1965, another Socialist, Franz Jonas, Mayor of Vienna, was elected in his place, in preference to the former People's Party leader, Gorbach. So Klaus, after the 1966 election, did not immediately set out to form a one-party government. After receiving his mandate from President Jonas, he opened negotiations for a new coalition, but set tough conditions which it would be hard for the Socialists to accept – a reduction of power for the Foreign and Interior Ministers (Socialists), more power for the Lands, more power for the People's Party in the nationalised industries, and more power for parliament whenever the two big parties could not agree.

The Socialists debated among themselves, with Pittermann holding that the party should go into opposition while Kreisky wanted to keep the coalition. Pittermann won the day, and telephoned the news to Klaus. At last Klaus was 'free'.[317]

Within a few hours, Klaus presented his new government – the first one-party government in post-1945 Austria. Twenty-one years of coalition had come to an end.

23 Economic Policy-Making: Austria's 'Elastic Band'

When in 1966 Austrians found themselves, for the first time in a generation, with a one-party government, many felt afraid. Some of the middle class feared that the Socialists would go 'into the streets', and that there would be strikes, demonstrations and class war. Some Socialists feared that the People's Party would make use of its political monopoly to force its will – or the will of the big industrialists – on the workers, and to rob the Socialist Party of its hard-fought positions of power in political and economic life.

These things did not happen. Austria's remarkable peace and quiet, its freedom from strikes and industrial action and other forms of social unrest, were maintained intact. Economic policy, in real terms, continued to be decided on the basis of negotiation, bargaining and compromise between the various economic and social interest groups, with remarkable smoothness. In consequence, Austria became more and more prosperous.

This was possible because during the last decade of two-party coalition government, the main focus of economic decision-making had shifted from the government itself to the leading interest groups as represented *outside* the government, in particular to the Parity Commission for Wages and Prices created in 1957.

The Parity Commission was the nodal point of the dense, complex web of overlapping economic organisations which had grown up alongside government and parliament, closely linked with them by political and personal ties, but separate from them.

There was the hierarchy of Economic Chambers. These traced their history back to the year of European revolution, 1848, and to the Chambers of Commerce established by law in the Habsburg Empire in its aftermath; their role was to advise the government on problems of industry and trade. Twenty years later, the government delegated certain functions to the Chambers, which were also authorised to send delegates to the Austrian Upper House. After the collapse of the Habsburg Empire a new law was passed, in 1920, establishing the position of the Chambers in the new republican Austria; and after the Second Republic was formed, a further law was passed, in 1946.

A highly complex system grew up. Under the Federal Economic Chamber in Vienna there are six 'professional' sections, including industry, commerce, transport and tourism; there are also nine Land Chambers, each with six 'professional' sections. Membership is compulsory by law; in this the Austrian system is like that of the six founder countries of the Common Market, but not Britain. The Chambers are financed by the subscriptions of member firms; their governing bodies are elected by members, directly at the lowest level, above that indirectly. In 1970 the total number of member firms was 284,000.[318]

The Chambers must be consulted by the government on economic and financial legislation and policy. The State delegates certain duties to them, for instance, in respect of vocational or professional training. The Economic Chambers also actively promote foreign trade, doing the work which elsewhere is usually allotted to government officials and diplomats; in 1970 there were around 90 Austrian trade centres in all continents, over 60 of them staffed by highly efficient experts trained and employed by the Chambers.[319] But perhaps the key role of the Chambers is the negotiation of collective contracts with the representatives of the workers. Both in this field and in their dealings with the government, they regard it as an important function to harmonise conflicting interests of individual firms or sections so as to present a united front. Politically, the Economic Chambers are dominated by the People's Party through its Wirtschaftsbund, or Economic Union, though Chamber elections are contested by small Socialist and Freedom Party groups.

On the workers' side, the counterpart of the Economic Chambers, as 'autonomous corporations' based on public law, are the Chambers of Labour. These arose from the demand of the workers to have representative bodies of the same legal standing as the Economic Chambers. They were established after the collapse of the Habsburg Empire by a law of 1920. When the Dollfuss–Schuschnigg 'corporative state' was introduced in 1934, it was intended that they should somehow be fitted into its framework, but little was done. They vanished under Hitler, were revived in 1946, and were consolidated by a law of 1954. All manual workers and non-manual employees automatically belong, and pay dues to the Chambers – including foreign workers who have been at least one year in Austria. All dues-paying members elect the governing bodies of the Chambers. Each Land has its Chamber and in Vienna there is the Federation of Chambers of Labour. The Chambers do not represent senior civil servants, doctors, dentists or similar professional groups, who have their own organisations. The Chambers of Labour are politically dominated by the Socialists, but there are also People's Party, Freedom Party and Communist 'fractions'.

Alongside these two networks of Chambers, based on public law and compulsory membership, there are two 'voluntary' organisations. By the side of the Economic Chambers there is the Industrialists' Association (Vereinigung Österreichischer Industrieller), representing about 80 per cent of private industry, with 3600 members in 1971 – or around one-eighth of the total of the Economic

Chambers. This is because the Industrialists' Association mainly represents the interests of large industries, while the Economic Chambers represent all firms, taking particular care of small and medium-size undertakings – which the big industrialists call parish pump politics.[320] The nationalised industries do not belong to the Industrialists' Association, except in so far as individual directors, usually People's Party men, may wish to belong on an individual basis. Politically, the Association is close to the People's Party; its President (1971), Mayer-Gunthof, was also Vice-President of the People's Party's Wirtschaftsbund. But some of its members tend to think that the People's Party is too soft on such issues as workers' participation, preferring the tougher Freedom Party.

The other 'voluntary' organisation is the extremely powerful trade union organisation, the Ö.G.B., which operates alongside the Chambers of Labour. It was founded in 1945; in the First Republic, there had been no unitary organisation, but two or more – the Socialist 'free unions', the 'Christian' unions, linked with the Christian Socials, later the Heimwehr-promoted unions known by Socialists as 'yellow' unions. After 1934 the 'free unions' led a semi-illegal but still active existence, until all unions were abolished by Hitler in 1938.

In 1945, when the Soviet Armies had just entered Vienna and fighting was still going on nearby, former trade unionists, Socialist, Christian and Communist, combined to set up a single united organisation, for which they obtained the Soviet commander's approval. The circumstances of its origin partly explain the Ö.G.B.'s extraordinarily centralised, even authoritarian character. The Communist Party, in its 1944 manifesto, had called for a unitary trade union organisation. This type of organisation could therefore be expected to please the Russians, who probably expected that it would soon come to be dominated by the Communists and so serve as a transmission belt for Communist, or Soviet, control.

This, however, did not happen. Against opposition from both People's Party and Communists, the Socialists insisted that all union posts should be filled, not through inter-party agreement, but through elections from the very start.[321] The outcome was that they successfully thwarted all Communist moves to take command, and themselves maintained unquestioned control by perfectly democratic methods.

Although the Ö.G.B. is a voluntary organisation, about two-thirds of all workers and employees belong to it (in 1971, just over 1,500,000) – an unusually high proportion in non-Communist continental Europe. The Ö.G.B. is in legal terms a 'juridical person'. But the sixteen unions which form its constituent parts are not. This means that while a union can negotiate a collective agreement, in strict legal terms the Ö.G.B. must sign it. Moreover, it is the Ö.G.B. which decides questions of demarcation between unions, which are mainly, though not entirely, organised on an industry-by-industry basis; the big exception is the Union of Private Employees, which is the second largest. However, in any one undertaking there can be only one manual workers' union and one 'white-collar' union.

The main source of the Ö.G.B.'s power over the unions is its financial control. In principle, each trade unionist is a member of the Ö.G.B.; his own union collects his subscription and passes it on to the Ö.G.B., which then retains most of the money for general purposes but returns a certain proportion – usually about 18 per cent – to the union concerned. The Ö.G.B. claims that this system enables it to maintain strong supporting institutions for the benefit of all unions, for instance, in the fields of research, welfare, education, leisure activities and an emergency fund for use in strikes (which seldom occur). The system is also supposed to prevent competition or antagonism between unions, and to even out the differences between strong and weak unions.[322] Strikes can only be called by the decision of the leaders of the union concerned, and the Ö.G.B. must be informed.

Great stress is laid on the 'supra-party' character of the Ö.G.B. This means that in the Ö.G.B., the unions and works' councils, elections are contested by a Socialist 'fraction', a Christian Workers' (or People's Party) fraction, and a Communist fraction (since the party split of 1970, by two rival Communist fractions). It is reckoned that around 70 per cent of all trade unionists are Socialist (1971). But both Socialist and non-Socialist leaders see big advantages in the Ö.G.B.'s supra-party status. It gives the (Socialist) President (a post held by a series of strong personalities – Böhm, Olah, Anton Benya) a powerful position in relation both to the government of the time and the Socialist Party; he can expect to be one of the country's chief economic policy-makers, and therefore to play a special political role. Since 1945, one of the Ö.G.B.'s three Vice-Presidents has been a People's Party representative – Erwin Altenburger, a People's Party member of parliament who has also held government posts. In an interview in September 1971, Altenburger said that in spite of the raging seas of internal politics, the Ö.G.B. had been able to remain an island of calm; united, it had been able to safeguard its members' interests.[323]

The division of labour between the Chambers of Labour and the Ö.G.B. is not clear, and there seems to be a good deal of overlapping. But broadly speaking the Chambers of Labour concentrate on questions of legislation affecting workers' rights and welfare – on which they must be consulted – and on highly efficient economic and social research. The Ö.G.B. also expects to be consulted by the government on legislation, but it concentrates on relations with the employers over wages, conditions and general economic policy. Both the Chambers and the Ö.G.B. conduct educational work. For instance, in 1971, the Vienna Chamber of Labour ran evening classes in an enormous range of subjects, from Christian symbolism to the Culture and Ideology of India, from the Unknown Self to Astronomy.

Farmers and peasants have their own representative organisations, the Chambers of Agriculture, which first grew up in the various Lands and were then grouped together in 1953 in the ponderously-named Conference of Presidents of the Chambers of Agriculture. This 'Conference' often plays a bigger role in shaping agricultural policy than the Ministry of Agriculture.[324] The Chambers represent approximately 130,000 farmers and peasants and their families. In Chamber elections, the People's Party's Bauernbund (Peasant-Farmers' Union) is dominant.

Almost every economically active Austrian, therefore, is represented not only politically, in parliament, through one or other of the political parties, but also economically through a Chamber and probably also a 'voluntary' organisation. All these various bodies hold regular elections at various levels, either on a country-wide basis or at Land level or at local level; in the factories there are works' council elections. The average Austrian must therefore spend a good deal of time voting. However, he, or she, may find the task quite simple, since in very many cases candidates are affiliated in some way with the political parties, so that it should be possible to vote on the same party ticket in all circumstances. Nevertheless there are sometimes unexpected election results, so that clearly party loyalties are not entirely rigid in all contexts.

There is another factor which makes the dense network of economic organisations seem even more complicated, though in practice it may simplify things. There are many cases of 'personal union', that is, of one person holding two or more posts at the same time in different parts of the network. A man may be a member of parliament and an active trade union official: after the 1971 election Benya, the Ö.G.B. President, saw no reason why he should not simultaneously be First President (Speaker) of parliament, though he did lay down the active leadership of the metal-workers' union. The Vice-Chancellor in the government was also an Ö.G.B. Vice-President. There was a similar practice in the People's Party; the President of the Federal Economic Chamber, Sallinger, was a prominent People's Party politician. Analysis of the 1971 parliament showed that out of ninety-three Socialists, all but a dozen were government officials or officials of the Chambers, trade unions or works councils; of the People's Party members, one-half were officials of one kind or another, one-quarter peasant-farmers, and one-quarter belonged to the free professions; in the Freedom Party, however, only two out of ten were public officials.[325] The best way up the political ladder was a research job in one of the economic organisations.

Partly as a result of their extensive research activities, these organisations adopted a policy of operating on the basis of 'objectivity' and informed analysis rather than political ideology. It is therefore regarded as both legitimate and desirable for them to set strict limits to conflict between different interest groups and to seek a not very clearly defined 'common good'. They therefore work in a different atmosphere from the two big political parties which, even when coalition partners, regarded each other almost as enemies. Their mutual antagonism has been described as a kind of Freudian complex, a trauma inflicted during the First Republic, when the two big parties formed two totally self-contained sub-cultures mutually opposed in the economic, social, geographic and religious fields.[326]

The economic organisations do not suffer from this 'Freudian complex'; and perhaps for this reason they have tended to become more and more the organs of economic decision-making, first through the Raab–Böhm wage–price agreements, from 1957 on through the Parity Commission for Wages and Prices. This resulted from agreement between the People's Party Chancellor, Raab, and the Socialist Ö.G.B. leader, Olah, and was launched through a more or less informal government decision which was no more than an 'invitation' to the four big economic organisations to examine jointly the justification for wage demands and price increases in terms of their effect on the Austrian economy as a whole.

The Parity Commission has therefore no basis in public law; it is a voluntary body which can make recommendations but cannot issue orders. Yet it came to embody the 'Social Partnership' and became so powerful that in the second half of the 1960s some people feared that it might usurp the proper functions of government and parliament, becoming a sort of second government; others admired it as a uniquely Austrian achievement and the foundation of Austria's surprising success in securing rapid economic growth and full employment with what was by general European standards a remarkably low rate of inflation. It was also seen as a powerful protector of social peace, securing Austria against a return to the 'class war' atmosphere of the First Republic.

The four economic organisations making up the Parity Commission are the Economic Chambers and the Conference of Presidents of Chambers of Agriculture on the one side, and on the other, the Ö.G.B. and the Chambers of Labour. The one side is therefore linked with the People's Party, the other with the Socialists. Perhaps with the purpose of maintaining symmetry, the Industrialists' Association is not included – though it is well represented indirectly through the Economic Chambers with which it is closely linked by various 'personal unions'. The government itself is also represented, through the Chancellor and the Ministers for the Interior, Trade, Industry and Social Administration, and either the Chancellor or the Minister of the Interior takes the chair. The government representatives, however, do not vote; their role is rather to hold a watching brief, leaving the negotiation – or haggling – and harmonisation of conflicting interests to the economic organisations. This, however, is mostly done at informal meetings of the four organisations held just before the formal meetings of the Commission, so as to present a united front to the government representatives.[327]

The economic organisations, both in the Parity Commission itself and in its subordinate sub-committees for Prices and for Wages, have to reach their decisions by unanimity. This, somehow, they manage to do. The Commission, like the economic organisations themselves, has its own teams of experts in the Advisory Council for Economic and Social Questions set up in 1963, and they presumably help in the achievement of 'objective' and 'factually-based' decisions. Since the upward revaluation of the West German Mark in 1969, the Commission has also concerned itself with currency matters and the impact of monetary policy on the economy.

The idea that the Parity Commission could achieve independent power as a sort of dictatorship of the interest groups, apart from the government or even opposed to it, seems very exaggerated – as exaggerated as the idea that the important role of the economic organisations is a sort of hangover from Dollfuss's corporative state. The underlying reality which rules out any sectional dictatorship is the very close web of informal personal relationships which in a small country like Austria, with Vienna as its magnetic centre, plays a vital part in the whole process of decision-making, and makes frank, private discussion between political opponents frequent and easy.

Klaus has given two instances of this practice, in his memoirs. When he became People's Party leader in 1963, he invited the Ö.G.B. leader, Benya, to come and talk. Klaus said to him: 'you represent one and a half million trade unionists, and there are several hundred thousand of my supporters among them; I represent 2 million People's Party votes, and there are several hundred thousand trade unionists among them. For their sake, ought not cooperation between us to be possible?' Benya, according to Klaus, agreed. In 1966, as Chancellor in the new one-party government, Klaus again asked Benya to come and see him, and (at a time of economic stagnation combined with full employment) suggested that a ceiling of 6 per cent should be set on wage increases in the coming year. Benya thought 6.5 per cent would be the right figure, but urged that there should be no formal agreement and, above all, that nothing should be published.[328] The agreed figure was subsequently confirmed as correct by the Organisation for Economic Cooperation and Development.

In 1971, the O.E.C.D. praised Austria's prices and incomes policy, 'laid down largely on an informal and voluntary basis by the government and the social partners', as no less important than the 'classical' instruments of monetary and fiscal policy. The result, the O.E.C.D. said, had been that wages had risen only 'moderately'; the trade unions had been prepared to tolerate a rapid increase in profits so as to permit increased industrial investment; in some cases wage demands had been kept down to maintain a firm's competitiveness in export markets; and consumer prices had been kept down with the help of government controls.[329] The picture of social peace in 1971 was remarkable: strikes had involved only 2430 workers and total working hours lost were 212,000, the lowest figure in 20 years.[330]

It was therefore not surprising that when in 1966 Austria switched from two-party coalition to one-party government, the Parity Commission proved that it was not simply a projection of the coalition into economic life, doomed to collapse when the coalition vanished. Instead, the Commission acted as a stabilising factor at a time of political change, and continued this role when the People's Party gave way to a Socialist government.

One expert observer wrote: 'the Social Partnership is an elastic band, which holds together not only the big economic organisations, but in a certain measure also government and opposition. It . . . has the function of building a consensus and guaranteeing social peace.'[331]

The same observer however also suggested that the Social Partnership might stifle initiative and innovation: 'it is the expression of a society which is afraid of conflict and fears the rule of the majority'.[332] Given Austria's rate of economic growth at the beginning of the 1970s – 5.5 per cent in 1971, or 2 per cent above the average for the O.E.C.D. countries,[333] this warning seemed over pessimistic in the economic field – though perhaps not, in the long run, in the political field. That, however, was a question for the future, when a generation had grown to power which no longer suffered from Freudian complexes and was not scarred by the traumatic experiences of the past.

24 Austria and the Common Market

Austria, heavily dependent on foreign trade, followed the birth and growth of the European Economic Community with close and anxious attention, seeing from the start that it must achieve a close link with it sooner or later.

After 1945, the Austrians had no choice, if they wished to remain independent, but to seek economic ties with the West. In September 1946 Renner – true to the ideas which he had held a generation earlier – had thought that Austria's trade policy should be directed to the East.[334] When Figl became Chancellor at the end of 1945 he said in his first government declaration that 'the geographic and economic structure of Austria make necessary the cooperation of this state with the immediate neighbouring states, especially Czechoslovakia, Hungary and Yugoslavia . . .'[335] But it quickly became clear that this course could not save Austria from economic disaster. The Russians made it very difficult for Austria to import essential goods from Hungary and Czechoslovakia; at the same time they exported goods from the Soviet-controlled industries of Eastern Austria to the neighbour states without submitting them to Austrian controls, thereby causing Austria considerable losses over the ten years of the occupation.

Marshall Aid and Austrian membership of the Organisation for European Economic Cooperation turned Austrian eyes from the East to the West. When post-war restrictions were lifted, it was inevitable that Austria's trade with

West Germany should grow particularly fast; there were links dating back to the Hitler period and beyond. By 1958 half of Austria's exports went to the six Common Market countries, and over half its imports came from them; one-tenth of Austria's exports went to other West European countries, and one-eighth to the Comecon countries (the Soviet Union and the East European states).[336]

Therefore when the Common Market came into existence, Austria had very strong economic reasons for wishing to join. On the other hand, it was only a short time since the State Treaty had been signed. Austria was anxious to keep on the right side of the Soviet Union: Soviet benevolence was of particular value in 1958, when Raab, Figl, Pittermann and Kreisky visited Moscow and obtained a Soviet offer to give up 50 per cent of outstanding deliveries of oil, together with other concessions. It was not clear how strict an interpretation Moscow would try to place on Austria's self-imposed neutrality, nor how far it would push the argument that since West Germany belonged to the E.E.C., Austrian membership would be a form of *Anschluss*.

On political grounds, therefore, the Austrians wanted an alternative to full E.E.C. membership. When in 1958 Britain was pressing for the creation of a wider European Free Trade Area around the E.E.C., Austria favoured this solution. But negotiations were broken off by General de Gaulle soon after his return to power in France. Austria then joined the other non-E.E.C. countries – Britain, the three Scandinavian countries, Switzerland, Portugal – in forming the much looser European Free Trade Association in November 1959. This had no political aims or institutions so that Austria's neutrality raised no problem. It was the common hope of the EFTA countries that their move would lead to fresh negotiations with the Common Market; but it did not.

The EFTA link was never popular in Austria, least of all

with the People's Party, which had much stronger ideological links with the Christian Democratic parties of the
Common Market countries than with the Socialist-minded
Scandinavians or with the British. The Socialist leader,
Pittermann, on the other hand, had an ideological aversion
to the 'capitalist' E.E.C. Kreisky – then Foreign Minister –
defended Austria's membership of EFTA as enabling it to
avoid economic isolation, improving its position vis-à-vis
the Common Market, securing a certain compensation for
the discriminatory effect of the E.E.C. Common External
Tariff, and preparing for wider European integration.[337]
The Freedom Party – the natural protagonist of close ties
with West Germany – campaigned in 1961 for Austria to
quit EFTA.

When in 1961 Britain and Denmark applied for membership of the Common Market, Austria was faced with a
difficult problem. A few months later, in December 1961,
Austria and Switzerland together applied for association
with the E.E.C. under Article 238 of the Rome Treaty. At
the same time Austria declared that association must exclude all political implications and must not harm its trade
with Eastern Europe. Austria also told the E.E.C. Council
that Austria must be able 'in case of threat of war' to
suspend certain provisions of any treaty of association, or
even to denounce it. In spite of these Austrian precautions,
the Soviet Union sent a stiff note to Vienna, declaring that
association with the E.E.C. would be incompatible with
neutrality, and drawing attention to the State Treaty provisions on the *Anschluss*. Czechoslovakia later chimed in
with a similar note.

At the end of June 1962, when Chancellor Gorbach
visited Moscow, Khrushchev said that Austria's entry into
the Common Market would violate the treaty and took a
tough and negative stand. Gorbach pleaded that Austria's
highest aim was 'a strict maintenance of our freely-
undertaken perpetual neutrality and loyalty towards our
obligations under the State Treaty ... As long as we who

sit here decide the political fate of Austria, this will guide our conduct.'[338] Khrushchev was apparently unimpressed. Both then and later Soviet leaders refused to distinguish between entry into the E.E.C. and association with the E.E.C. At the same time, the Russians seem to have dangled alternative carrots under Austrian noses: in the autumn of 1962 the National Bank Governor, Dr Kamitz, said in New York that there had been 'invitations to take part in Comecon'.[339]

France, under de Gaulle, was cold towards the Austrian approach to the E.E.C. When de Gaulle received Foreign Minister Kreisky in February 1960, he told him that it was more important to safeguard Austria's political position than to bind it to the E.E.C.; he advised patience and the strengthening of bilateral relations with the individual Common Market countries.[340] When Chancellor Gorbach visited Paris in the summer of 1962, de Gaulle gave him no promise of support about the E.E.C.; instead he gave him an 'assurance' that France, in following a policy of reconciliation with West Germany, had made it a condition that there would never again be an *Anschluss*.[341]

In January 1963 de Gaulle vetoed Britain's entry into the Common Market. Once again Austria had to face a difficult problem. On 26 February the coalition government agreed to try to continue negotiations for association. The six E.E.C. governments were formally notified on 9 March, and in April the E.E.C. Ministers agreed to study various possible ways of Austrian participation in the Common Market.[342]

This 'go it alone' policy was well understood by Austria's EFTA partners. In practice, Austria's trade with EFTA was flourishing: exports more than doubled (10.5% to 22.9%) between 1958 and 1968, while exports to the E.E.C. sank from 49.6 per cent in 1958 to 40.4 per cent in 1968. But imports from EFTA increased more modestly from 11.2 per cent to 18.1 per cent, while imports from the E.E.C. expanded still further, from 54.3 per cent to 57.4 per cent.

As for the Comecon countries, Austria's exports grew over the same period from 12.4 per cent to 14.9 per cent, while imports dropped slightly from 10.8 per cent to 9.8 per cent.[343] In spite of shifting trends, the underlying fact was that Austria was far more heavily dependent on trade with the E.E.C. than any other EFTA country.

The Austrian attempt at single-handed negotiation with the E.E.C. met with constant frustration. It was 1964 before the E.E.C. Commission presented a report on the matter to the Ministers, who then gave a mandate for the opening of negotiations. But the E.E.C. became too involved with its own internal crises and the partial French boycott to devote much attention to Austria. In January 1965 the Moscow newspaper *Pravda* attacked Austria's E.E.C. approach, claiming that it might once again submit itself to the dictatorship of those forces which had already once pushed Europe to destruction.

The Austrian government had by this time come to believe that the Soviet Union's hostility to the Austrian approach to the E.E.C. was influencing de Gaulle,[344] who was already planning his state visit to Moscow in the following year. When Klaus visited Paris, together with his Socialist colleagues, in June 1965, he tried to appeal to de Gaulle on the grounds that the General's concept of 'Europe from the Atlantic to the Urals' must surely hold a place for Austria, and went on to ask for his support in the negotiations with the E.E.C., perhaps also in reassuring the Russians. De Gaulle replied with the utmost courtesy that Austria should look south-eastwards, in accordance with its historic role: '*Vous etes Danubiens*'.[345] Prime Minister Pompidou, too, advised Klaus to develop relations with the Danubian states.

From this it was clear that de Gaulle had no intention of intervening on Austria's behalf, either in Brussels or in Moscow. Desultory talks went on in Brussels in the autumn of 1965 and the early months of 1966, without result. During the election campaign at the beginning of

1966, the People's Party played with the idea of quitting EFTA – as a pro-E.E.C., anti-Socialist gesture – but then thought better of it. In the summer, the Soviet President Nikolai Podgorny visited Austria and expressed Russia's 'icy rejection' of the E.E.C.: Austria, he said, must keep well away from it.[346]

In December 1966 the French Foreign Minister, Maurice Couve de Murville, told the E.E.C. Ministers that there must be a further examination of the question whether a special agreement with Austria would be advantageous to the Community and whether, in view of the overall European situation, it was free from political objections: had Soviet objections been considered?[347] In February 1967 Klaus went to Moscow and again pleaded Austrian good faith over the E.E.C.; again he came up 'against granite'.[348]

During 1967, the British Labour government made a new approach to the E.E.C. The French now had a fresh reason for delay over Austria. When Pompidou and Couve de Murville visited Vienna in the autumn, they said that Austria's approach should be considered in the framework of the wider enlargement of the Common Market, so there could be no decision over Austria until a decision had been reached over Britain.[349]

By this time yet another apparently insuperable obstacle had been placed in Austria's path. In July Italy, because of Austrian-based terrorist activities in South Tirol, declared a veto on negotiations for Austria's association with the E.E.C. This blow was followed by de Gaulle's second veto on Britain, towards the end of 1967, which removed the hope that Austria's problem could be solved in the wake of British entry.

Austria had to start yet again. The Klaus government tried to pursue the idea of a special tariff-cutting arrangement which the French at one time seemed to favour as a harmless alternative to the enlargement of the E.E.C. This move soon came to a dead end. It was two years before a real new start could be made, partly as a result of Austrian–

Italian reconciliation over South Tirol, but mainly because de Gaulle had retired and his successor, President Pompidou, was moving towards acceptance of Britain and other candidate countries into an enlarged E.E.C.

In December 1969 the Hague summit conference of the Six, summoned by Pompidou, opened the way for negotiations not only with Britain and the other candidates for full membership but also with those EFTA countries which were not applying for membership. Austria quickly established contact with the E.E.C. in the hope of obtaining a special interim arrangement for 30 per cent across-the-board tariff cuts, to tide things over until the time was ripe for a wider and more far-reaching agreement. When Kreisky succeeded Klaus as Chancellor in April 1970, Austria continued to pursue this aim. But although there seemed to be no ill-will on the part of the Six, their extremely slow methods of work, together with their preoccupation with the more urgent problems of entry terms for Britain and the other full candidates, eventually made it obvious that Austria could not hope for rapid results.

It was not until June 1971 that the E.E.C. Commission could complete proposals for a free trade zone in industrial products between the enlarged E.E.C. and the EFTA 'neutrals', Austria, Sweden and Switzerland. This delay had one advantage: it gave the Austrians time to continue pacifying the Russians; and when the Trade Minister, Josef Staribacher, saw Kosygin in Moscow – also in June 1971 – he came to the conclusion that Austria need no longer fear difficulties from the Soviet side.[350]

In December 1971 the E.E.C., having completed negotiations with Britain and the other full candidates, turned to negotiations with the three 'neutrals' and the other EFTA countries concerned. The aim was to conclude an agreement which would come into force at the same time as the Common Market was enlarged on 1 January 1973.

In addition to industrial free trade, Austria wanted

special arrangements on agricultural exports. This was of some importance. In 1970, agricultural exports formed 5 per cent of Austria's total exports; 62 per cent of these (chiefly meat and dairy produce) went to the E.E.C., mainly West Germany, and 18 per cent to EFTA countries, the two combined therefore taking 80 per cent.[351] Since Austria had a large deficit in its agricultural trade with the E.E.C. and EFTA, it wanted to maintain and expand its exports as far as possible. During the negotiations it emerged that Italy and Holland wanted access to Austria and the other EFTA countries for *their* agricultural exports, but that France was reluctant to allow reciprocal access to the E.E.C. for the agricultural exports of Austria and the other EFTA countries, for fear of upsetting the E.E.C.'s Common Agricultural Policy.[352]

The main obstacle in the negotiations was, however, the demand of the Six to exclude a group of 'sensitive products' from the proposed free trade arrangements so as to protect certain industries of the Six. These included special steels, paper, non-ferrous metals and aluminium, which meant that about 20 per cent of Austria's exports to the E.E.C. would suffer.[353]

In February 1972 Chancellor Kreisky toured the capitals of the Common Market countries and Britain to press Austria's case, with particular attention to Paris. The West German Chancellor, Willy Brandt – an old friend of Kreisky's – visited Vienna in the following May and reaffirmed his support for a fair, reasonable solution taking account of Austria's interests.[354]

Finally, after the usual crises (the last caused, to Austria's great indignation, by Britain) the E.E.C. signed agreements with Austria and the other EFTA countries not seeking membership at a multiple ceremony on 22 July 1972. The agreements provided for free trade in industrial products accompanied by 'safeguard mechanisms'. Tariffs on 'sensitive products' were to be reduced over a longer period than that set in the overall programme of tariff cuts.

On agriculture, the partners declared 'their readiness to foster, so far as their agricultural policies allow, the harmonious development of trade in agricultural products'. The E.E.C. and Austria were to set up a joint committee, to meet twice a year, to manage the free trade arrangements. This was an institution which Austria could regard as lacking all political content and therefore in no way infringing its neutrality.

In addition, Austria obtained privileged treatment in that it also signed the long-sought and elusive interim agreement with the E.E.C., providing for a 30 per cent reduction in tariffs, to come into effect on 1 October 1972. This was described in Brussels as a 'bonus' for Austria, giving it an important head-start in the general process of tariff-cutting, destined to lead to free trade in a market of about 300 million people by the 1980s.

Austrian patience and obstinacy were at last rewarded. Kreisky said in Brussels that the long delay had 'not been of advantage to Austria's economic relations with the states of the Community'. Nevertheless Austria's economy had progressed: 'we are entering this close relationship with the states of the E.E.C. well-prepared, and I believe we shall be in a position to make a valuable contribution'. In the Austrian parliament a few days later the People's Party leader, Schleinzer, attacked the agricultural provision as totally inadequate; but he hailed the agreement as a 'historic success'.[355]

Austria's whole long and frustrating approach to the Common Market showed very clearly the limits – and the possible scope – of its neutrality, declared two years before the Common Market was born. Soviet opposition to any link between Austria and the E.E.C. was outspokenly, repeatedly and sometimes threateningly expressed. It stemmed partly from Moscow's overall opposition to the E.E.C. and its desire to keep it as restricted and isolated as possible. But it must also have been prompted by the wish to stop the Austrians drifting any further towards the West and to frighten them into putting a very strict interpretation on their neutrality.

The Austrians kept their nerve and refused to panic. Since they had declared their neutrality of their own will and rejected outside guarantees, they could legitimately say that they alone had the right to interpret it. So, while they tried to avoid provoking Moscow and to provide every reasonable assurance, they refused to let themselves be deflected. Austria's economic future was at stake and they believed throughout that they could reach their goal without giving Moscow any excuse for serious intervention. They counted on the Soviet Union's surprising capacity for accepting an accomplished fact, once it was accomplished, even if it had been protesting strongly against it until the last moment. The Soviet party leader, Leonid Brezhnev, fulfilled this expectation when early in 1972 he suddenly switched to a much more conciliatory attitude towards the E.E.C.

French coldness towards Austria's approach to the E.E.C. throughout the 1960s raised another problem of Austria's international position. It seems clear that de Gaulle did not only wish to please the Russians by freezing the Austrians. While mindful of Austria's imperial past, he perhaps still saw Austria as a 'second German state', as Dollfuss and Schuschnigg had seen it, with the potential long-term danger for France that might flow from this fact; and that was why he so strongly stressed his opposition to any new *Anschluss*. He had an even more immediate reason to fear an increase in German strength than the Russians. Germany's growing economic and financial power within the Common Market – and its superiority in numbers – was a serious worry to the French during the latter 1960s. If seven million Austrians were to be thrown into the balance alongside the Germans, the French would feel still more threatened.

Austria's 'German-ness' was therefore still a political factor which could create problems in its external relations.

Enlargement of the E.E.C., accepted by France as a means of diminishing Germany's predominance, also reconciled it to a link with Austria. But neither the French nor the Russians were likely to forget Austria's 'German' past quickly.

A problem looming up at the beginning of the 1970s was whether Austria would in practice be able to remain aloof from the E.E.C. institutions. Under the impulse of the E.E.C.'s enlargement it seemed possible that its existing institutions might be strengthened or new ones created to deal with foreign policy and ultimately defence. The Austrians had always said that they could not belong to the E.E.C. institutions since this would violate their neutrality. Chancellor Kreisky, in Paris in February 1972, said that Austrians would not be able to join a monetary and economic union in an enlarged E.E.C. He added, however, that, provided that Austrians took their decisions autonomously, they would be able to adapt themselves to the evolution of Community policy, or harmonise their legislation with Community legislation so as to facilitate cooperation.[356]

This typically Austrian 'pragmatic' solution might work well for a time, but it would deprive Austria of a direct voice in the making of E.E.C. decisions which could have a big impact on its economy, even perhaps its international position and its security. The best hope for Austria was that East–West *détente* in Europe might produce a new situation in which the negative aspects of its neutrality would fall away.

25 The South Tirol Dispute

The South Tirol dispute was one of the most troublesome problems that faced successive Austrian governments between 1945 and 1969. It divided two countries which, in post-1945 Europe, should naturally have been on good and friendly terms. There were times when the Italian and Austrian governments were both anxious to end it; but internal politics, especially in Italy, made it particularly difficult to achieve a compromise which would not be denounced as betrayal by the more nationalist elements on the two sides, above all in South Tirol itself.

There was also a certain difference of approach between political parties in the two countries. The Italian Christian Democrats had to pay heed to their own right wing and to those further to the Right; it was easier for Social Democrats such as Giuseppe Saragat to be conciliatory; but they had much less power. In Austria the People's Party was much more immediately involved in the dispute than the Socialists. The Land of Tirol was a People's Party stronghold, and the South Tirol People's Party, which completely dominated the political life of the German-speaking minority in Italy, was allied with its Austrian sister party. As Schärf remarked, if South Tirol had returned to Austria, the People's Party's parliamentary majority would have been considerably strengthened and would perhaps have become permanently consolidated.[357] The Socialists, with their main weight in Eastern Austria, were less emotionally and politically implicated in the dispute. Yet no Socialist politician would have wished or dared to risk the charge of being lukewarm or negligent over South Tirol.

In practice, the Austrian parties worked well together, up till the final moment of agreement with Italy. The Austrian record was marred by the terrorist activities of extremists, whom the authorities could very probably have taken stronger measures to suppress. But Austrian diplomacy was tenacious, patient, resourceful and ingenious. In the end a compromise was achieved which was reasonably satisfactory to the South Tirolers and broadly acceptable to public opinion in both Austria and Italy. In comparison with similar apparently insoluble national quarrels elsewhere during the period, remarkably few lives were lost in spite of the strong feeling on both sides.

The Austrians were, and remained, convinced that they were fundamentally in the right, and that by all principles of self-determination the 200,000 German-speaking inhabitants of South Tirol should have belonged to Austria, as they had done for centuries. If the 1919 peace settlement had perpetrated an injustice, that was no reason why things should not be put right after the Second World War. At the first sitting of the newly-elected parliament in December 1945, Renner, laying down the post of Chancellor, stated Austria's claim to South Tirol. The Figl government, formed immediately afterwards, reaffirmed the claim in its first policy declaration. During 1946, the government was more occupied with South Tirol than with the Austrian treaty. In February an Austrian memorandum on South Tirol was submitted to the Allied Council to be passed to the four governments.[358]

When the Allied Foreign Ministers started discussing the Italian peace treaty, it soon became clear that Austria could have no hope of regaining South Tirol, in spite of all the eloquence of the Tirolese Foreign Minister, Gruber. Austria could therefore only aim at securing special treatment for the South Tirolers.

The Western Allies were not unsympathetic to the Austrians. At the first meeting of the Allied Council in Vienna on 11 September 1945 the French representative,

General Béthouard (presumably mindful of the fact that Austrian Tirol formed part of the French occupation zone) said that he considered that 'the Southern Tirol should be incorporated in the whole of the Tirol'.

In Britain, Bevin wanted first and foremost to get Austria re-established as an independent state – that is, rescued from the threat of Soviet domination – and therefore wished to avoid delays over South Tirol. Speaking in the House of Commons on 4 June 1946, he said that at the Moscow Conference in 1943 'it was decided that it was pre-*Anschluss* Austria that we were guaranteeing to restore'; when therefore it had been proposed at the London Conference of Foreign Ministers that 'she be so re-created', Bevin had agreed, while making a reservation that there might be minor frontier rectifications in Austria's favour. 'I still think so,' Bevin added. 'We have got here a mixture of economic and ethnic considerations', he went on, and he urged that there should be a 'sensible arrangement' between Austria and Italy.

Churchill, however, was free from the restraints of power. As Opposition leader, he allowed himself to be carried away: why, he asked, cannot the natives of that mountainous and beautiful land be allowed to say a word about their destiny on their own behalf? Why can they not have a fair and free plebiscite. . . ? 'No quarrel remains between us and Austria,' Churchill went on. 'Every liberal principle which we proclaim . . . would be impugned by the assignment of the South Tirol to Italy against the wishes of its inhabitants.'

The exigencies of treaty-making with the Soviet Union and the desire to anchor Italy firmly to the Western sphere of influence prevailed with the British Labour government. The Americans for their part were subjected to the activities of powerful Italian pressure groups in the United States. Even minor frontier rectifications were rejected.

Gruber, with remarkable good sense, realistically accepted the inevitable and worked out with the Italian

Foreign Minister, the Christian Democrat, Alcide de Gasperi, the agreement of 5 September 1946, providing that Italy should grant political autonomy to South Tirol, together with concessions over the use of the German language and in the cultural field. This agreement was attached to the Italian peace treaty as an Annex, to which one article of the treaty specifically referred.[359] The border of the proposed autonomous area was discussed, and de Gasperi gave Gruber an assurance – or so Gruber believed – that the area would not be extended (so as to take in more Italians) against the will of the South Tirolers.[360]

The Soviet Union and the East Europeans, together with the Austrian Communists, hotly attacked the Gruber–de Gasperi agreement – in Gruber's view because they did not want a quick normalisation of Italian–Austrian relations which would make it more difficult to absorb Austria into the East European system.[361] Gruber himself thought that through the agreement, 'much was gained when all might have been lost'.[362]

Then the trouble started. The Italian interpretation of the Gruber–de Gasperi agreement removed most of its value from the Austrian standpoint. The Italians extended the autonomous area to include the whole of the province of Trentino as well as the predominantly German-speaking Province of Bolzano (Bozen). The result was that there were more than twice as many Italians as German-speakers in the area; moreover, Italian settlers were encouraged to move in. Political autonomy therefore had quite a different meaning. The South Tirolers were disappointed and grew angry. The Austrian government felt that it had the right and duty to intervene, since the Gruber–de Gasperi agreement, annexed to the Italian treaty, had the status of an international agreement. The Italians argued that they had carried out the agreement and that what happened after that was a purely internal Italian affair.

In 1956 the Austrian government formally proposed to Italy the formation of a joint commission of experts to examine all disputed questions arising from the agreement. Italy refused. In 1958 the South Tirol People's Party raised the matter in the Italian parliament; the Land parliament of (Austrian) Tirol backed the South Tirolers' move. As internal pressures were rising, Foreign Minister Kreisky aired the dispute in the U.N. Assembly in 1959. The Italian Foreign Minister denied Austria's right to intervene in Italian affairs. However, in 1960 the Assembly passed a resolution calling on the two parties to resume negotiations on differences arising from the execution of the Gruber–de Gasperi agreement. In case of failure, they should resort to the Hague Court or seek another mutually acceptable solution of the dispute.

From this the Austrians got some satisfaction, since the United Nations had at least recognised their right to have a say in the South Tirol question. But there was no immediate progress. The next nine years were taken up with sporadic Austrian–Italian discussions at various levels and varying degrees of warmth or coldness. These were punctuated by anti-Italian terrorist acts on a fairly small scale – carried out by extremists in South Tirol. These were countered by Italian accusations of negligence on the part of the Austrian government and repressive measures which caused fresh indignation among South Tirolers and in Austria itself.

The most hopeful point of the Italian–Austrian contacts, before 1969, was at the time of the meetings of the (Socialist) Foreign Ministers, Kreisky and Giuseppe Saragat, during 1964. Agreement seemed near. But there was a fresh wave of terror acts; and Saragat became President of Italy and so ceased to be the Italian negotiator over the South Tirol. The impulse was lost. When Chancellor Klaus and Kreisky visited Rome in December 1965, they felt that Saragat's attitude was unchanged but that his good will had almost no practical effect.[363]

As a result of the apparent deadlock, extreme right-wing groups in Austria, otherwise of only marginal importance, saw their chance to exploit the situation. The key figure appeared to be a junior academic at Innsbruck University – Norbert Burger – who had some support in Tirol and Upper Austria and links with kindred extreme right-wing groups in West Germany. (Burger later tried to form his own National Democratic Party and contested the Lower Austrian Land election in October 1969 and the general election of 1970 – with no success.)

The Italians believed – as they had always done – that the Austrian authorities were failing to take energetic measures to stop terrorists from using Austrian territory as a base for action in South Tirol. To put pressure on the Austrians, they imposed their veto on the Austrian–E.E.C. negotiations in 1967. Austria declared there was no connection between the two questions, and urged the Italians to stop obstructing progress towards a South Tirol settlement.

In spite of this confrontation, there were hopeful elements in the situation. In particular, the leader of the South Tirol People's Party, who was also Provincial Governor – Silvius Magnago – had talks with the Italian Prime Minister, Aldo Moro, aimed at clearing the way for a settlement. This required courage; he had earlier been the target of a bomb attack and he had to reckon with a great deal of trouble inside his own party. Nevertheless he persuaded his party to accept a 'package deal' offered by the Italian government and intended to improve the South Tirolers' position, on condition that Italy would reach agreement with Austria on means of giving this deal an international 'anchor', so as to guarantee that this time it would be carried through. Italy, however, did not wish to accept this condition, maintaining that the package was an internal Italian affair.

Eventually, during 1968, with Kurt Waldheim as Austrian Foreign Minister, the idea of an international 'anchor' was dropped. Instead, the 137-point package, giving more powers to Bolzano Province (South Tirol) in the economic and cultural fields and in public order, was linked with a detailed 18-point 'calendar of operations'. Successive Italian steps to implement the package deal were to be locked in with public statements by Austria designed to remove the Austrian–Italian dispute from the international arena.[364]

On 20 October 1969, the South Tirol People's Party approved the plan. A month later the South Tirol Land assembly also gave its approval. On 30 November, in Copenhagen, the Italian and Austrian Foreign Ministers, Moro and Waldheim, concluded their agreement: this was the starting-gun for the 'calendar of operations'. On 15 December, Chancellor Klaus fulfilled Point 4 of the calendar. He declared in parliament that during the period of the implementation of the package deal, expected to be about four years, the Austrian government would not raise the South Tirol question in an international forum.

The debate that followed was unusually heated and emotional. The former Foreign Minister, Kreisky, who had worked so hard between 1961 and 1966 to reach an agreement, made a statesmanlike speech; but he and the Socialist Party, together with the Freedom Party, voted against the government. This, however, was clearly part of the game of party politics, as played not only in Austria but in other Western countries as well. The Austrians, in spite of twenty years of coalition, had not forgotten the game.

When Kreisky became Chancellor a few months later, the policy of reconciliation with Italy was continued. If for no other reason, this was necessary for Austria's fresh approach to the Common Market. At the end of 1970 Magnago, the South Tirol leader, received the Robert Schuman prize at Strasbourg for his services to South Tirol and to Europe.[365]

A year later, in November 1971, President Jonas paid a State visit to Italy to seal the new friendship between the two countries. This was the first time that an Austrian

Head of State had visited Italy since the Emperor Francis Joseph met King Victor Emmanuel II in 1875. To mark the occasion, President Saragat amnestied a handful of South Tirolers imprisoned for terrorist acts. The visit was a gala occasion; the two Presidents expressed warm hopes for their countries' future friendship. The Italian Foreign Minister promised Italy's support for Austria's approach to the E.E.C. The South Tirol dispute was ended – as far as could be seen, permanently.

26 Single-party Government: from People's Party to Socialists

Austria's first one-party government – the People's Party government of Josef Klaus – lasted for its due legislative period, and then rather surprisingly suffered defeat. Its four years in office, from 1966 to 1970, had outwardly been successful. In external relations, the South Tirol dispute had been settled, and Austria had been able to launch a new and more hopeful approach to the Common Market; Klaus's policy of 'active neutrality' had stood up well to the severe test of the invasion of Czechoslovakia by the five Warsaw Pact countries in 1968.

The Austrian economy overcame the stagnation of 1967 and surged ahead in 1968 and 1969. The long-term economic plan, drawn up by the People's Party's leading economist, Dr Stefan Koren, laid a sound basis for further economic growth in the 1970s. Koren's starting point was that budgetary and monetary policies alone could not solve Austria's problems; there must, he argued, be a far-reaching restructuring of Austria's industries, through formation of larger units, regional development, a government investment programme, further reorganisation of nationalised concerns, an expansion of sources of energy, and improved technical training. The plan for industry was matched by a 'Green Plan' for agriculture, aimed at adapting it to the requirements of the market, with particular reference to the exigencies of the Common Market agricultural system.

The Socialists paid the Koren plan the compliment of

producing an economic programme of their own, in 1968, which had many likenesses to it. The Socialist plan, however, laid especial emphasis on the retraining of workers to secure high mobility of labour in a rapidly changing economy, and on the need for more research and development. On the ideological side, the Socialists continued their steady move towards middle ground by proclaiming their faith in a democratically organised mixed economy, with planning and competition as guiding principles, based on the co-existence of different types of ownership; to satisfy the party's Left wing, there was some emphasis on *Mitbestimmung*, or workers' co-determination, as a means of democratising the economy.

The People's Party government did not confine itself to economic reform: it also put through legislation in the fields of higher education and housing, and reorganised radio and television. Agreement was reached on reducing the working week, by 1975, from 45 to 40 hours. Klaus could claim with some justice that his government had contributed to the rapid development of a 'welfare society'.[366] Nevertheless, from the autumn of 1967 onwards, the Socialists steadily won successes in Land and local elections. By the beginning of 1970, the People's Party's chances of success in the pending general election were rated only as roughly equal to the Socialists'.[367]

The reasons for the People's Party's failure to win greater popularity and prestige during its four years of power were many and varied. Klaus's personality did not impose itself on the public in the same way Raab's or Gorbach's. He was apparently regarded as too rigid and academic in his approach. He acquired the reputation of a pronounced 'clerical'; he was a member of the influential Catholic student organisation, the C.V. (Cartellverband), which for half a century had proved so efficient in placing its members in key positions in public life. He himself said later that he had erred in exposing his 1966 government to the criticism that it was 'militantly clerical', because of its C.V. membership (even though this could not be said of three of its ministers, Schleinzer, Koren and Kurt Waldheim).[368]

Klaus also came to be regarded as an over-zealous reformer or crusader for his favourite causes – the liberation of 'the State' from undue interference by interest groups, which must not be allowed to become a sort of second government, and the restoration to parliament of some of its rightful power of decision which had lapsed during the past twenty years. He condemned three things which he saw as the hallmarks of the coalition – 'the unholy *Proporz*, the unholy *Junktim*, and the veto'. The system of strict proportional representation of the two big parties in all fields had, he thought, been carried to absurd lengths, in the filling of posts, the allotting of public funds, even the composition of delegations travelling abroad, which had inflated Austrian representation at international conferences to the point of ridicule. The *Junktim* was the practice by which before one party would agree to a proposal made by the other, it would demand a corresponding concession from it on some totally unrelated matter. The 'veto' meant the custom by which all government decisions had to be reached unanimously – which enabled a single minister or interest group to block action indefinitely.[369]

Klaus's declared aim was that all posts should be filled on the basis of merit alone without regard to party allegiance, and that every issue should be decided on its own merits. The State must no longer be the prey of the parties or other interest groups; government and parliament must set the common good as the highest political aim. Ministers should be politically responsible to the Chancellor rather than the servants of interest groups.[370]

Such ideas were popular in some quarters, especially with the non-party press. But in practical terms it was very hard to change a system so strongly entrenched – the close interconnexion, through established custom, personal ties and 'personal union' between government, parties, interest groups and parliament. Any attempt to realise Klaus's aims inevitably provoked strong opposition, from the interest groups, from Socialists fearing to lose established political and economic positions of power, and from inside the People's Party itself.

In practice, Klaus did not seriously change previous custom. In his 1966 cabinet there was an obvious system of *Proporz*, if on a new basis: instead of proportional representation between the two big parties, there was now *Proporz* between the Lands, with the Western Lands strongly represented. There was also *Proporz* between the interest groups which formed the People's Party – the Workers' and Employees' Union, which moved into the foreground, the Peasant-farmers' Union, the Economic Union, and also the People's Party-dominated Federal Economic Chamber. Parallel with the government, the Parity Commission for Wages and Prices continued to be just as powerful – perhaps even more so, in that it replaced, in one very important field, the now defunct coalition.

On the other hand, parliament, from 1966 on, did genuinely become rather more active and lively, since decisions were taken there which had previously been taken in the various 'coalition committees'.[071] Yet a great deal of advance consultation between the parties still went on *before* legislation came before parliament, especially on key issues such as the budget. It was even said that the Klaus government continued to act as though the coalition were still in existence. Dramatic confrontations in parliament seemed to have elements of shadow-boxing or play-acting.

Klaus's greatest trouble – in narrow political terms – was probably the disunity inside the People's Party which – apart from the early years of Raab's leadership – seemed to suffer from a plague of leadership struggles and internal intrigues. This was no doubt partly because the party was a fairly loose coalition of differing, even divergent, interest groups, and was dependent on them for financial support.

Klaus thought that he himself also suffered from being a man of the Western Lands, not a member of the Vienna political Establishment.[372] In general the People's Party suffered from the lack of a clear political ideology and internal party discipline – two things which the Socialists managed to maintain in spite of internal disputes.

Another reason for the People's Party failure in the 1970 election was that the Socialist Party had evolved in a direction which made it better able to capture the uncommitted or floating voter. After the Socialist setback in 1966, there was a shake-up: more attention was paid to the Lands, which came to have more influence on party policy; and at the 1967 party conference, Kreisky, backed by delegates from the Lands, replaced Pittermann as leader. Kreisky, in opposition to Pittermann, had favoured continuation of the big coalition and was determined to keep open the option of renewing it.

Under Kreisky's leadership, the Socialists set out to steal some of the People's Party thunder – for instance, through their economic programme, increasing use of economic experts and research techniques, reasonableness and pragmatism, a conciliatory attitude towards the Church. They also set out to extend their geographic base from Vienna and Eastern Austria into the Western Lands.

Changes in the social and economic pattern of Austria were making political allegiances more fluid. By the end of the 1960s the drift away from the land had reduced the number of Austrians working in agriculture and forestry to just under one-fifth. Many of those who had left the land had gone, not into the heavy and manufacturing industries, but into service industries such as tourism, commerce or insurance. The outcome was that the service industries absorbed nearly two-fifths of the working population, compared with a little over two-fifths in the heavy and manufacturing industries. In one sense, therefore, the struggle between the two big parties could be seen as a struggle for the political allegiance of the growing sector of the service industries, which could not be regarded as the traditional or ideological preserve of either.

The Socialists' move to the middle involved a sharp repudiation of Communist support: their tacit acceptance of it in 1966 had proved a bad mistake. In October 1969 they officially declared their unyielding and uncompromising opposition to 'Fascism and Communism'. In any case, the Communists were a spent force; the party split over the 1968 Soviet invasion of Czechoslovakia, and Ernst Fischer, who had openly condemned it, was expelled from the party in the autumn of 1969. Even the party's chief stronghold, the Communist 'fraction' inside the Ö.G.B., was split. In these circumstances, the People's Party could no longer convincingly use Red bogey propaganda against the Socialists who had, moreover, shown during their years of opposition that they had no intention of going into the streets or launching strikes; they had played the game of parliamentary opposition according to accepted rules.

Kreisky's personality was a particular asset to the Socialists. He had the quick wit, fluency and neat turn of phrase of the Viennese middle-class Jewish intellectual, the width of vision of a man who had spent 12 years living abroad (in Sweden) and had then served for 13 years first as State Secretary and then as Minister for Foreign Affairs. He had an air of easy authority and relaxed self-confidence. At the same time he had a long record of service to the Socialist Party: he had been prominent in the Socialist Youth in the early 1930s, when he had acquired his first experience of leadership. He was arrested by the Schuschnigg government in 1935, later released; arrested again by the Hitler régime at the time of the *Anschluss* in 1938 and sent to concentration camp, again later released. On his return to Austria after his years of exile, he was at once close to the seats of power, working closely with the veteran Socialist, President Körner, before moving to the Foreign Ministry in 1953. Above all, his dispassionate, pragmatic approach, with its stress on economic advance and modernity, was well suited to the mood of the late 1960s and early 1970s. In 1970, he was 59 – old enough to be a reassuring father-figure, young enough to claim leadership of a modern Austria.

In spite of favourable omens, the Socialists' approach to the election of March 1970 was cautious. Their leaders said they were for a return to the big coalition; their attack on the People's Party concentrated on rising prices (though the rate of increase was very moderate) rather than ideological issues. The Freedom Party – now mainly the party of a disgruntled section of the middle class – obviously thought poorly of the Socialists' chance of success: at the beginning of 1970, its leaders said they would on no account form a coalition with the Socialists, though they would with the People's Party.

The People's Party itself hoped and campaigned for an absolute majority. Nevertheless, important sections of it, particularly the industrialists – and all those who preferred to have half the cake all the time rather than all the cake for part of the time – wanted a return to the big coalition. Their feelings were reciprocated by the trade union leaders, especially Benya, who felt that coalition government fitted the requirements of the Parity Commission more neatly than did a one-party government.

In the event the Socialists, somewhat to their own surprise, won more votes than the People's Party, and seven seats in parliament, so that they emerged with 81 seats to the People's Party's 78, while the Freedom Party held a key position with 6 seats.

The Socialists were therefore close to an absolute majority, but had not reached one. This posed the question, whether to return to a big coalition, or try to form a small coalition. The scale of the Socialist success and the People's Party setback made a big coalition seem inappropriate, though many people in both parties, and in the general public, would have liked one. It would have been more logical for Kreisky to form a small coalition with the Freedom Party, in spite of ideological differences, just as his friend Willy Brandt, now West German Chancellor, had formed a coalition with the small Free Democrat Party a few months earlier. But this was ruled out by the Freedom Party's pre-election pledge not to enter a coalition with the Socialists on any account – which its leaders must now have regretted bitterly.

A small coalition of People's Party and Freedom Party was another possibility. Klaus himself regarded this as unrealistic and withdrew from the negotiations (and subsequently from the party leadership). The interparty negotiations led nowhere. In the end Kreisky, with encouragement from President Jonas, a fellow-Socialist, formed a Socialist government based on a minority in parliament. (The position of Foreign Minister was, however, kept as a non-party post, under the diplomat, Rudolf Kirchschläger, with whom Kreisky had worked closely on the South Tirol question when he himself had been Foreign Minister.)

Kreisky could only hope to carry on parliamentary business if he could count on the votes of the Freedom Party; and he established an understanding with its leader, Friedrich Peter, that these would be forthcoming. The position was, however, inevitably uneasy. The Freedom Party expected some form of political reward. This was provided through a new electoral law which made the system of representation in parliament still more strictly proportional and increased the number of parliamentary seats from 165 to 183; it was calculated to improve the electoral chances of the Freedom Party.

The Socialist government, in spite of its lack of a majority, was able to carry through its legislative programme without much trouble, helped by the fact that the People's Party was sensitive to any charge of obstructionism. Of the bills presented to parliament, 86 per cent were passed unanimously, while a further 3 per cent were passed by a combination of Socialist and People's Party votes; only in the case of about 10 per cent did the People's Party oppose the government.[373] Legislation included such controversial social issues as homosexuality and divorce.

Nevertheless the minority government did not last long. For one thing, the Freedom Party, having won its reward in the form of the new electoral law, was eager to strengthen its parliamentary position; its leader, Peter, was reported to have warned Kreisky that he would not prolong his tacit support.[374] For another thing, the People's Party was in trouble. The retirement of Klaus after the 1970 defeat had left it with unsolved leadership problems and bitter internal quarrels, which were not settled until Karl Schleinzer heavily defeated his rival and opponent, the economist, Professor Koren, at the party congress in June 1971. Schleinzer, a 47-year-old Carinthian who had made his way upwards as an agricultural expert and representative of peasant-farmers' interests, and who was regarded as right wing and sympathetic to the Freedom Party, still needed time to find his feet and establish his authority. His agricultural background placed him in the tradition of Dollfuss and Figl, and seemed a little anachronistic in the 1970s. A further difficulty for the People's Party was its lack of money. Because of its decentralised structure, which enabled its constituent 'economic organisations' to keep part of their members' subscriptions for their own purposes, it depended considerably on the contributions of the industrialists; and in the summer of 1971 they were unwilling to produce more money only 15 months after the last election.[375] The weaknesses of their opponents therefore tempted the Socialists to an early election.

Above all, Kreisky felt increasingly confident. The re-election of the Socialist, President Jonas, in the Spring of 1971, in a contest with the distinguished People's Party candidate, Kurt Waldheim, together with other electoral successes showed that opinion was running in favour of the Socialists. The economic situation was good. Austria's growth rate in real Gross National Product had been second only to Japan, among O.E.C.D. countries, in 1970.

The currency was strong: in May 1971 the Austrian schilling was revalued upwards by 5.05 per cent – which created an upsurge of self-confidence among Austrians. There was inflation, but it was relatively mild, running at 4.7 per cent in 1971, compared – as Kreisky pointed out – with 6.3 per cent in Switzerland and over 9 per cent in Britain.[376]

Kreisky therefore could see every advantage in striking the People's Party before it recovered strength, and, following Harold Wilson's example in 1966, calling an election to strengthen the Socialists' parliamentary position. So, exploiting the People's Party's clumsy tactics in dragging out the customary interparty negotiations on the budget for the coming year, Kreisky claimed that it was impossible to work on the basis of the existing parliament and called for its dissolution which, with the support of the Freedom Party, he obtained.

Thereby Kreisky regained full freedom of manoeuvre. In the light of the outcome of the election, he could either form a Socialist government with a parliamentary majority, or a renewed big coalition, or a small coalition with the Freedom Party, now eager for the rewards of office. During the election campaign, he consistently soft-pedalled the idea of a single-party government; while exploiting every weakness of the People's Party, he carefully kept open the option of a big coalition, knowing that many Austrians, especially trade union leaders and big industrialists, still hankered after a return to the cosy security which this offered. The Freedom Party, as an alternative and more manageable, though somewhat embarrassing, coalition partner, was handled by Kreisky with marked restraint.

The election, held on 10 October, produced a result which surprised most observers – an absolute majority for the Socialists, who won 93 seats against 80 for the People's Party and 10 for the Freedom Party. What was more, the Socialists won just over 50 per cent of the votes – which in a country such as Britain would have given them a much bigger parliamentary majority. Their successes in the Lands which had been traditional People's Party strongholds – Styria, Carinthia, Salzburg, Vorarlberg, Upper Austria – were of particular long-term importance. Although Kreisky's majority was only three seats – in practice, two, since the Socialists had to provide a non-voting Speaker – he formed his second all-Socialist government with full confidence in the future.

Between 1966 – the start of single-party government – and October 1971 the Socialists' share of the votes had risen from 42.5 per cent to 50.22 per cent; the People's Party's share had fallen from 48.35 per cent to 42.98 per cent; the Freedom Party's had remained steady around 5.5 per cent.[377] The Communists and other extreme Left groups had ceased to exist in real terms. It seemed possible that Austria was moving towards a prolonged spell of Scandinavian-type social democracy in an increasingly prosperous mixed economy.

If so, it was a surprising outlook for a country where nine-tenths of the population were professed Catholics, even if only one-third of them were regular churchgoers; which had been torn by party strife, even bloodshed, in the inter-war years; and which bordered on three Communist states. Even if the swing to the Socialists were to be reversed, the first five years of single-party government suggested that there was little danger of a return to the political instability of the past. Having once tasted the pleasures of calm and prosperity, Austrians would not quickly tire of them.

27 Austria in the 1970s

The Economic and Social Outlook

Austria moved into the 1970s well placed to compete successfully with the advanced industrial nations of Europe. At the end of 1971, the head of the Austrian Economic Research Institute forecast that the rate of economic growth would continue to be above the European average; that in 1972 Austria would overtake Britain in terms of Gross National Product per head, and at the end of the 1970s would catch up West Germany and Switzerland. The Austrian growth rate, which was 7.1 per cent in 1970, was 5.5 per cent in 1971, and was expected to run at 4 per cent in 1972, compared with an estimated 3 per cent for the European countries belonging to the Organisation for Economic Cooperation and Development.[378]

A report by the O.E.C.D. on Austria's industrial policy, published in 1971, pointed to the need for further structural changes, aimed at promoting the development of modern growth industries; for more research and development; and for increasing productivity through vocational training and greater mobility of labour. These were all problems which the Austrians had discovered for themselves and were tackling with energy.

The Austrian schilling was one of the strong currencies of Europe. Following the upward revaluation of May 1971, the prolonged international monetary crisis later in the year caused little excitement in Austria. In late December the Austrian schilling was revalued by a further 2.27 per cent.

The Austrians continued, however, to worry over the

rising price spiral. The 1971 figure of 4.7 per cent was well below the (O.E.C.D.) European average of 6½ per cent. But the European figure was expected to go on rising, perhaps more rapidly. For Austria, heavily dependent on foreign trade, it was difficult not to 'import inflation'. They themselves credited their relative success in keeping inflation at bay to the Parity Commission for Wages and Prices. All parties were agreed on this, even though one or other might from time to time carp at the Commission's unique power. An attempt by the Kreisky government at the end of 1971 to strengthen long-standing provisions for government control of the price of certain key goods and services produced indignant cries of alarm: it was accused of trying to undermine or even destroy the famous 'social partnership', based on consensus, and to substitute for it the rule of the majority – which might be tolerable, even desirable, in parliament, but must not be permitted in the really important field of economic life. Kreisky almost certainly had no such intention; a last-minute compromise was patched up before the end of the year.

The Austrians' admiration for the Parity Commission was also shared by outside experts. The O.E.C.D. described it as 'a body of particular importance' and as 'typically Austrian in character'; it did not dissent from the Austrian view that it was 'one of the important and effective instruments for sound development and relatively great price and wage stability'.[379] Another O.E.C.D. report, in September 1971, said that 'with progress towards a more flexible fiscal policy and with a further development of the unique institutional arrangements for price/income determination, prospects for sustained and balanced growth were favourable'.[380]

Nevertheless the Parity Commission was effective only because the Ö.G.B. – the trade union organisation – had such a remarkably strong hold on the workers. The O.E.C.D. pointed out in 1971: 'Austrian wage levels are still lower than those prevailing in neighbouring European

countries, and it is natural that Austrian workers should
feel a strong desire to 'catch up' progressively with the
workers of these other nations.'[381] On the other hand, the
O.E.C.D. also pointed out that social benefits were higher
in Austria than in many other European countries; the
proportion of the G.N.P. which was devoted to social
security was 18.2 per cent in 1968. This was said to be the
highest proportion in Europe.

The trade union leaders – the Ö.G.B. – at the end of
1971 put full employment at the head of their list of
aims.[382] This seemed odd. There had in fact been full
employment since 1960; the real problem of the 1970s was
shortage of labour. This was particularly acute in Vienna;
as a consequence, 137 firms moved away from the city
between 1965 and 1969. From the early 1960s, foreign
workers had been brought in on the basis of a yearly agreement between the 'social partners' on the maximum
figure – that is, with the approval of the Ö.G.B. In 1971
there were 160,000 foreign workers in Austria; almost
58,000 were in Vienna alone – an increase of 13,000 on the
year before.[383] In Vienna, of the total of socially insured
workers, 7.8 per cent were foreign workers; in Vorarlberg,
the proportion was as high as 19.8 per cent, in Salzburg,
9 per cent, in Burgenland, as low as 2.1 per cent. Live
births to foreign parents in 1971 were 4.1 per cent of the
total, with the figure as high as 14 per cent in Vorarlberg,
9 per cent in Vienna, and 5 per cent in Tirol and Salzburg.[384] These figures had to be set against the fact that
Austria had a very low birth rate and that the natural
population increase in 1971 was 0.15 per cent or one-third
of the world average.[385]

The vast majority of foreign workers came from the
south-east, mainly Yugoslavia and Turkey. A few came
from further afield: the shortage of nurses in Vienna was
so acute that it was planned to bring about 50 trained
nurses from Korea in 1972.

Many foreign workers lived in ghetto-like conditions;

they were not popular among Austrians. The Viennese resented – among other things – their habit of gathering at big railway stations in their free time – presumably gravitating to the point nearest home. The Socialists in Vienna tried to take steps to break down the barriers and bring foreign workers and their families – if they were planning to stay in Austria – into normal contact with Austrians. They made a special effort with the children; plans were made for teaching Turkish and Serbo-Croat to school-teachers in 1972. In February 1972 Kreisky invited Socialist leaders from West Germany, Switzerland and Italy to a meeting to discuss common problems, one of which was the social problem of the foreign workers. 'They must not become the "black men" of Europe,' Kreisky said.

The other side of the picture was the danger of a brain drain of young Austrian scientists and technicians to rich German-speaking countries such as West Germany and Switzerland, also to the United States. In 1971, however, this had not reached serious proportions.

Other social problems facing Austria were shared by most European countries. Austrians were highly conscious of the whole environment and pollution complex; they hoped to be in the vanguard in devising anti-pollution methods. In spite of Austria's advanced social welfare system, poverty and housing were still tasks to be tackled. Kreisky, in his government declaration of November 1971, placed below the poverty line 360,000 people receiving supplementary benefits and 60,000 widows. In housing, he said that Austria came low in the European league: 2.8 million Austrians, he went on, were living in dwellings which did not come up to modern standards.[386] (In 1961, 63.6 per cent of dwellings had running water, and 29.6 per cent had a bath.)[387] The suicide rate and car accident rate were high. Austria also held the European record for deaths resulting from alcoholism.[388] These were, however, problems which Austrians faced self-critically and constructively.

One of the chief social and political problems of the 1920s and 1930s had faded away. The old tension between Vienna and the Lands had largely relaxed. The Lands had ceased to be so strongly agricultural. Between 1950 and 1965, nearly half a million workers had left the land, and the process was continuing.[389] The contribution of agriculture and forestry to the G.N.P. in real terms had shrunk from 10.5 per cent in 1960 to 7.7 per cent in 1970, while earnings from agriculture, by 1970, represented only 5.2 per cent of total national earnings.[390] This steady decrease in the importance of agriculture had been accompanied by the rapid growth of new industries in the Western Lands.

Nevertheless, the average Viennese was, in the mid-1960s, still better off than other Austrians (though Vorarlberg and Salzburg ran Vienna close) and twice as well off as the average Burgenlander.[391] Similarly, there were more university graduates in Vienna than in other Lands – nearly five times as many as in the Burgenland.[392] As elsewhere, the educational system favoured the children of middle-class parents. Successive governments aimed to carry out regional development policies and to create greater equality of opportunity in education, but the process was inevitably slow.

Vienna remained the great international cultural centre of tradition, followed at some distance by Salzburg. The impressively rebuilt Vienna Opera House offered mainly the established classics up to and including Richard Strauss, with an occasional performance of *Danton's Death* by the contemporary Austrian composer, Gottfried von Einem. There was a plentiful supply of Viennese operetta. The serious theatre again offered either the classics, whether foreign or Austrian (Grillparzer, Schnitlzer, Nestroy), or well-established contemporary foreign dramatists such as Dürrenmatt. The chief fare of the concert-halls, too, was the classics, with some emphasis on Mahler and Bruckner. Bookshops gave the most prominent display to the works of foreign authors, whether in the original or in translation. The general impression was that Vienna was like a camel living on its extremely richly-stored cultural hump. But, with its opera-houses, concert-halls, theatres, galleries and museums, it had an enormous amount to offer the intelligent tourist, if rather less for young people seeking novelty and experiment.

The tourist industry was of great importance to Austria as a whole, as a vital element in the balance of payments, nearly equalling the deficit in foreign trade. In 1971 receipts from tourism grew two and a half times more than the G.N.P. West Germans predominated among the tourists. There were also around 6000 Americans living in Vienna, many of them retired people.

The overall picture was that Austria was moving into the 1970s in conditions of economic prosperity and growth and social peace which were above the European average and were in some respects outstanding.

The Political Outlook

In spite of outward shows of hostility, the two big parties seemed to have reached a state of equilibrium and a certain mutual understanding. Neither seriously suspected the other of planning to seize permanent power, however often dark warnings might be uttered. Given the stabilising factor of the 'social partnership', the parties could allow themselves occasional firework displays of mutual enmity.

The Socialists could not count on a long uninterrupted period of office. The changes in Austria's social structure had narrowed the traditional power-base of the People's Party without broadening the power-base of the Socialist Party in any solid or dependable way; instead, it had expanded the class of floating voters, estimated at 5 per cent to 7 per cent of the total. The Socialists owed their success in 1971 partly to two temporary factors: Kreisky's personal authority and political appeal, and the internal troubles of the People's Party. In the mid-1970s the situation might therefore change. Austrians moreover tended to be influenced by political trends or swings in Western Europe, especially in West Germany. But it looked as though the two big parties would be prepared to alternate in power without disrupting the basic political calm. In the event of an economic crisis – which, if it came, would probably be caused by external factors – it seemed extremely likely that the two parties would return to a big coalition, or even a 'government of concentration' including the Freedom Party, in order to weather the storm.

One important question was whether the workers would remain as loyal to the trade union leadership and the Socialist Party as in the past; whether there might not be a 'shop-floor' movement towards the far Left, perhaps accompanied by a move of younger and more militant Socialists in the same direction. Several factors were likely to work against any such development. One was the intensive educational work of the Socialist party and the trade union leadership, aimed at explaining the hard economic realities of life to the rank and file. Another was the workers' preoccupation with economic security rather than changes in the existing system; according to opinion polls in late 1971, they took small interest in the Ö.G.B.'s demand for 'co-determination' or workers' participation in industry.[393]

Finally, living next door to two Soviet-dominated Communist states, Hungary and Czechoslovakia, Austrians were, either consciously or unconsciously, extremely wary of any move towards the far Left.

Austria's Place in the Outside World

The Austrians, having chosen neutrality as the price of freedom, were determined to put their own interpretation on it, and to retain the initiative in shaping their own foreign policy. Their neutrality was to be 'active', not passive. They regarded themselves as practising a more real neutrality than Finland, whose freedom they thought to be curtailed by its security treaty with the Soviet Union.

Austrians made no secret of the fact that their natural sympathies lay with the West and that their way of life was basically a Western way of life. At the time of the Soviet suppression of the 1956 uprising in Hungary, they did not conceal their feelings and gave shelter generously to tens of thousands of Hungarian refugees, some of whom settled permanently in Austria and easily integrated themselves into Austrian life. The Soviet invasion of Czechoslovakia in 1968 caused even stronger feelings in Austria; Austrian journalists and television reporters did outstanding work in getting the news and pictures to the outside world; once again, Austrians gave shelter to the rather smaller number of refugees from Czechoslovakia, most of whom moved on westwards.

During the 1968 crisis, the Austrians moved certain army units to the Czechoslovak frontier, as a precautionary move or warning gesture. In all discussions of plans for army reform – hotly debated in late 1971 – the universal assumption was that any possible attack on Austria would come from the Soviet Union. In such an event, Austria would have little chance of putting up a successful defence, and the government was said to be in favour of the idea of declaring Vienna an open city, perhaps other big towns also. But it was regarded as essential that Austria should be able to put up some sort of defensive action on the frontier and try to regain lost territory: this would be necessary as at least a symbolic demonstration of determination to defend Austrian neutrality. At the same time, politicians argued that a sound economy or a healthy and contented society were the best weapons of defence. Socialists also argued that just as the workers had defeated the Communists in 1950, so in future they would be the country's best defenders.

From the time of the state treaty onwards, the Austrians

consistently tried to cultivate good relations with the
Soviet Union, and – apart from the dispute over the E.E.C.
– they had some success. Visits were exchanged, top-level
discussions took place, and trade made progress. Even
more energetically, Austria tried to cultivate good relations with the East European States, with five of which it
had been linked more or less closely in its imperial past.
On the political side, the 'Club of Nine' was formed in
1965, with the aim of grouping together small NATO and
Warsaw Pact states and neutral countries, with the
Austrian Foreign Minister as presiding genius, for the
pursuit of good neighbourly relations. The project seemed
harmless enough and made some headway; but, although
it seemed in line with the Soviet policy of peaceful co-
existence, after a few years Moscow frowned and the
'Club' withered.

In the economic field, Austria made much more progress,
concluding bilateral agreements with the East European
countries and doing everything practicable to expand
trade, in the face of the many restrictions and obstacles
imposed by the Communist governments' tight system of
controls, their chronic lack of hard currency, and the
resulting necessity for barter deals. By the end of 1971
Austria had gone a long way towards liberalising imports
from the East European countries and was hoping they
would reciprocate by opening the door wider for Austrian
exports. They were also hoping for progress towards some
form of multilateral payments system; and they were exploring the field of 'economic cooperation', which meant
cooperation between individual concerns. As a result of
these efforts, in 1971 around 13 per cent of Austria's exports went to the Comecon countries (without Yugoslavia)
and 9 per cent of its imports came from them.[394] This was
a far higher share than in the case of the West European
countries where the figure was well under 5 per cent. It
was therefore important, not only politically, but also on
hard economic grounds, for Austria, in its relationship with

the E.E.C., to retain full freedom in its trade with the Comecon countries.

An advertisement placed in the *Financial Times* in December 1971 by the leading Austrian bank, the Creditanstalt-Bankverein, proclaimed: '*A Bridge between East and West*. . . . Situated as it is on the Danube, our country has fulfilled this important function for many centuries but the significance of Austria's role as mediator in Europe has never been greater than at the present time . . .' The bank went on to offer its services in the business field, in this role. Austrian political and business leaders had high hopes that Austria's 'mediating' role could be used to good advantage. It certainly had first-hand knowledge and long-standing ties with Eastern Europe. But the West Europeans, during the 1960s, were already eager to make their own contacts with the East, and in most cases were capable of doing so. This was particularly true of the West Germans; and with the success of Chancellor Brandt's *Ostpolitik* at the end of the 1960s, it became clear that Austria's services were not much in demand. There were difficulties and disappointments over projects for pipelines linking the Soviet Union through Austria with west or south European countries. On the other hand, most American firms establishing subsidiaries in Austria did so because 'for geographical and human reasons Austria is the best launching-pad for exports to the East'.[395] Other foreign companies establishing themselves in Austria may have had the same motive.

Austrian efforts to make Vienna a great international meeting-place had considerable success – starting with the Khrushchev–Kennedy meeting in 1961, and progressing to the American–Soviet Strategic Arms Limitation Talks of the late 1960s and early 1970s, though in this case Vienna alternated with the rival neutral capital, Helsinki. The Austrians would have been less than human if they had not also secretly hoped that Vienna might become the meeting-place of the long-projected and long-delayed European

Security Conference. This was a proposal for which the Austrians had strong natural sympathy, believing it might soften the East–West division of Europe and ease relations with the East European states – though they were too realistic to be anything but sceptical about any hope that it might lead to a liberalisation of relations between Moscow and its East European subordinates. Also, although theoretically favourable to mutual armed force reductions in Europe, they were realistic enough to see the dangers of any arrangement which would leave the Soviet Union still in a position to dominate Eastern Europe without any check from American forces in the West.[396] Nevertheless, as early as June 1970 Austria sent a memorandum to all European governments, the United States and Canada proposing that the question of force reductions should be added to the conference themes already proposed by the Warsaw Pact. This proposal was not at the time popular in Moscow or Paris, but it at least staked Austria's claim to play an active part in preparing the conference.

Partly as a result of Austrian efforts, Vienna became the permanent seat of two United Nations institutions – the International Atomic Energy Agency and the International Development Organisation, for which vast new buildings were projected in 1971. Vienna also became the headquarters of the oil producers' organisation, OPEC, of which Austria was a member, and which brought Austria into close contact with the Arab oil-producing states.

As other irons in the international fire, Austria could look with satisfaction on the election of a former Foreign Minister, Dr Lujo Toncic-Sorinj, as Secretary-General of the Council of Europe in Strasbourg, and the appointment of a young Socialist, Janitschek, as Secretary of the Socialist International at its London headquarters.

The biggest success for Austria in the foreign field was however the choice of another former Foreign Minister, Kurt Waldheim, as U.N. Secretary-General in succession to U Thant in December 1971. Austrians saw this as a reward for their policy of 'active neutrality'. Austrian diplomacy had cleared the way for it by timely establishment of diplomatic relations with Communist China earlier in the year, and by voting in favour of Peking's admission to the United Nations and against Nationalist China in the autumn. So when it came to the crunch, Waldheim was the only candidate against whom none of the five Powers capable of exercising a veto had any serious objection. A Chinese veto cast in the first round of voting was seen as nothing more than a sop to the non-European candidates; it was not repeated in later votes. Fortunately, too, Waldheim spoke good French; he was therefore favourably regarded by France, which feared that French was steadily losing ground as a world language.[397]

Waldheim himself said that his election showed that the international community respected 'our neutrality, our willingness to mediate between East and West, between the industrial nations and the developing countries, . . . our efforts in the humanitarian and peace-keeping field.'[398]

Austria's place in the world seemed well assured. But under the surface there remained a deeper question: whether, in the Europe of the 1970s, there was a place for a small country, wishing to be genuinely independent, but heavily dependent on other European countries for its economic well-being, even its survival.

In 1971 the Foreign Minister, Rudolf Kirchschläger, remarked that the limits of Austria's neutrality would be overstepped if fundamental economic decisions for Austria were taken not inside the country, but elsewhere.[399] In parliament after the signing of the agreements with the E.E.C., Kirchschläger said that these in no way affected Austria's neutrality policy: this was too firmly directed towards *détente* and peace for it to change the existing balance of power.[400] Yet if during the 1970s, in what Kreisky called 'the era of great continental and subcontinental markets', Austria were to be drawn more and more closely into the E.E.C.'s orbit, then it might have to face serious problems – particularly if progress towards *détente* was long delayed.

Special problems might also be posed by its single biggest trade partner, West Germany, which still took a rather big brotherly attitude towards little Austria with its 'Germanic' past. In 1971 West Germany already dominated certain sections of Austrian industry – the extreme case was the electrical industry where 60 per cent of the workers were employed by foreign-owned companies, primarily West German.[401] (Kreisky was, however, well aware of the political dangers involved and early in 1972 declared that West German purchase of the Mandl arms factory was out of the question.)

The outlook for the 1970s was therefore that Austria would have to continue to walk along a political knife-edge, if it was to survive as a small, independent, neutral country in the heart of Europe, up against the East–West line of division. But the Austrians could be expected to exercise their proven toughness and ingenuity to safeguard the freedom, social peace and prosperity which they had won for themselves.

Notes

PART I

Chapter 1

1. Karl Renner, *Österreich von der Ersten zur Zweiten Republic* (Vienna: Verlag der Wiener Volksbuchhandlung, 1953) p. 15.
2. Otto Bauer, *The Austrian Revolution* (Leonard Parsons, 1925) p. 74.
3. Ibid., p. 72.
4. T. G. Masaryk, *The Making of a State* (George Allen & Unwin Ltd, 1927) p. 270.
5. Oscar Jaszi, *The Dissolution of the Habsburg Monarchy* (University of Chicago Press, 1929) p. 447.

Chapter 2

6. C. A. Macartney, *The Habsburg Empire 1790–1918* (Weidenfeld & Nicolson, 1969) pp. 519, 654; *The Social Revolution in Austria* (Cambridge University Press, 1926) pp. 41 ff.
7. Macartney, *The Habsburg Empire, 1790–1918*, p. 683.
8. Bauer, *The Austrian Revolution*, pp. 138–9.
9. Otto Bauer, *Bolschewismus oder Sozialdemokratie* (Vienna: Verlag der Wiener Volksbuchhandlung, 1920) pp. 116, 120.
10. Macartney, *The Habsburg Empire*, p. 797.
11. Ibid., p. 655.

Chapter 3

12. Bauer, *The Austrian Revolution*, p. 54.
13. Ibid., p. 66.
14. Walter Goldinger, *Geschichte der Republik Österreich* (Vienna: Verlag für Geschichte und Politik, 1962) p. 13.
15. F. L. Carsten, *Revolution in Central Europe 1918–1919* (Temple Smith, 1972) pp. 26–9.

Chapter 4

16. Bauer, *The Austrian Revolution*, pp. 90–2.
17. Carsten, *Revolution in Central Europe*, pp. 84–6.
18. C. A. Macartney, *The Social Revolution in Austria* (Cambridge University Press, 1926) p. 99.
19. Ibid., p. 100.
20. Carsten, *Revolution in Central Europe*, pp. 78–107.
21. Bauer, *The Austrian Revolution*, p. 166.
22. Macartney, *The Social Revolution in Austria*, pp. 145–6.

Chapter 5

23. *Documents on British Foreign Policy*, 1st series (H.M.S.O.) I 432–3.
24. Harold Nicolson, *Peace-Making* (Constable, 1933) p. 351.
25. Winston Churchill, *The World War – The Aftermath* (Macmillan, 1941) p. 229.
26. *DBFP*, 1st ser. I 118.
27. Macartney, *The Social Revolution in Austria*, p. 109.
28. *DBFP*, 1st ser. I 402.
29. Ibid., pp. 512 ff.
30. Bauer, *The Austrian Revolution*, p. 123.
31. Ibid., p. 124.
32. *DBFP*, 1st ser. I 654.
33. Bauer, *The Austrian Revolution*, pp. 122 ff.
34. *DBFP*, 1st ser. I 30.
35. Ibid., p. 118.
36. Renner, *Österreich von der Ersten zur Zweiten Republik*, p. 39.
37. *DBFP*, 1st ser. I 81.
38. Ibid., XII 292–3.
39. Ibid., pp. 146–7.
40. Ibid., I 571–2.
41. Ibid., p. 454.

Chapter 6

42. *DBFP*, 1st ser. XII 137.
43. Ibid., p. 321.
44. Ibid., pp. 333–4.
45. Ibid., XII 321.
46. Goldinger, *Geschichte der Republik Österreich*, p. 81.
47. Ibid., p. 82.

48. *DBFP*, 1st ser. xii 344.
49. Ibid., p. 356.
50. Ibid., p. 355.
51. Ibid., p. 356.
52. Ibid., p. 361.

Chapter 7

53. Renner, *Österreich von der Ersten zur Zweiten Republik*, pp. 42, 54.
54. Josef Klaus, *Macht und Ohnmacht in Österreich* (Vienna: Verlag Fritz Molden, 1971) p. 23.
55. Renner, *Österreich von der Ersten zur Zweiten Republik*, p. 42.
56. Ibid., p. 42.
57. Bauer, *The Austrian Revolution*, p. 283.
58. Renner, *Österreich von der Ersten zur Zweiten Republik*, p. 80.
59. Macartney, *The Social Revolution in Austria*, p. 161.
60. *DBFP*, 1st ser. xii 88.
61. Ibid., p. 134.
62. Ibid., pp. 222–3.
63. Helmut Andics, *50 Jahre Unseres Lebens* (Vienna: Verlag Fritz Molden, 1968) p. 83.
64. C. A. Macartney, *Journal of the Royal Institute for International Affairs*, November 1929.
65. Ibid.
66. Goldinger, *Geschichte der Republik Österreich*, p. 131.
67. Macartney, *Journal of the Royal Institute for International Affairs*, November 1929.
68. Ibid.
69. Ibid.
70. Renner, *Österreich von der Ersten zur Zweiten Republik*, p. 74.

Chapter 8

71. *Le Monde*, 29 July 1972.
72. *DBFP*, 2nd ser. ii 46–7.
73. Ibid., p. 1.
74. Ibid., p. 11.
75. Ibid., p. 5.
76. Ibid., p. 12.

77. Ibid., pp. 13, 14, 22.
78. Ibid., pp. 17, 19, 20.
79. Ibid., pp. 18–23.
80. Ibid., p. 25.
81. Ibid., p. 30.
82. Ibid., p. 39.
83. Goldinger, *Geschichte der Republik Österreich*, p. 159.
84. Ibid., p. 161.
85. Renner, *Österreich von der Ersten zur Zweiten Republik*, p. 115.

Chapter 9

86. Ibid., pp. 117–19.
87. Otto Bauer, *Der Aufstand der österreichschen Arbeiter* (pamphlet, Prague, 1934) p. 25.
88. *DBFP*, 2nd ser. vi 147.
89. *Dolfuss an Österreich* (speeches) (Vienna: Reinhold Verlag, 1935) pp. 65–7, 77.
90. *DBFP*, 2nd ser. vi 147.
91. Ibid., p. 355.
92. Ibid., p. 395.
93. State Archives Vienna, Liasse Italien, Fasz. 477; quoted in Julius Braunthal, *The Tragedy of Austria* (Gollancz, 1948) pp. 160, 185.
94. Ibid., pp. 167, 188.
95. *DBFP*, 2nd ser. vi 438–9.
96. Ibid., p. 476.
97. Ibid., p. 558.
98. Ibid., p. 584.
99. State Archives, Vienna, quoted in Braunthal, *The Tragedy of Austria*; see also Kurt von Schuschnigg, *The Brutal Takeover* (Weidenfeld & Nicolson, 1961) pp. 99 ff.
100. *DBFP*, 2nd ser. vi 538, 540.
101. Ibid., p. 639.
102. Ibid., pp. 281 ff.
103. Ibid., p. 313.
104. Bauer, *Der Aufstand der Österreichischen Arbeiter*, p. 13.

Chapter 10

105. *International Labour Office Year Book*, quoted in F.O./371/26538.

106. Bauer, *Der Aufstand der Österreichischen Arbeiter*, p. 2.
107. Emil Franzel, *Der Burgerkrieg in Österreich* (pamphlet, Bodenbach, 1934) p. 19.
108. Bauer, *Der Aufstand der Österreichischen Arbeiter*, pp. 14, 19–22.
109. Julius Deutsch, *Putsch oder Revolution?* (pamphlet, Karlsbad, 1934).
110. *Proceedings of the Allied Commission:* Annex ɪ to ALCO/P(46)35.
111. Klaus, *Macht und Ohnmacht in Österreich*, p. 148.

Chapter 11

112. *DBFP*, 2nd ser. vɪ 433.
113. Ibid., p. 411.
114. Ibid., p. 430.
115. Ibid., p. 409.
116. Ibid., p. 743.
117. Dollfuss an Österreich, p. 238.
118. Goldinger, *Geschichte der Republik Österreich*, p. 199.
119. *DBFP*, 2nd ser. vɪ 762.
120. Ibid., p. 996.
121. Ibid., p. 992.
122. Ibid.
123. Ibid., p. 877.
124. Renner, *Österreich von der Ersten zur Zweiten Republik*, p. 142.

Chapter 12

125. Ernst Rüdiger, Prince Starhemberg, *Between Hitler and Mussolini* (Hodder & Stoughton, 1942) p. 235.
126. Ibid., p. 176.
127. Elizabeth Wiskemann, *The Rome–Berlin Axis* (Collins, 1966) p. 115.
128. Starhemberg, *Hitler and Mussolini*, p. 169.
129. Kurt von Schuschnigg, *The Brutal Take-over* (Weidenfeld & Nicolson, 1971) pp. 128–9.
130. Ibid.
131. Starhemberg, *Hitler and Mussolini*, p. 257.
132. Ibid., pp. 237–8.
133. Schuschnigg, *Take-over*, p. 138.
134. Ibid., p. 140.

135. Ibid.
136. Ibid., p. 145.
137. Ibid., p. 141.
138. Ciano's Minute of April 1937; quoted by Wiskemann, *Rome–Berlin Axis*, pp. 100–1.
139. Neurath's circular telegram, quoted by Schuschnigg, *Take-over*, p. 129; *Documents of German Foreign Policy*, Series D (Washington, D.C.: U.S. Government Printing Office) vol. I, no. 1.
140. Wiskemann, *Rome–Berlin Axis*, p. 112.
141. Andics, *50 Jahre Unseres Lebens*, p. 284.
142. Ibid., p. 283 (quoting the Nuremberg trials).
143. Ibid., pp. 283–4 (quoting the Nuremberg trials).
144. Sir Anthony Eden, *Facing the Dictators* (Cassell, 1962) p. 504.
145. Ibid., p. 503.
146. John Evelyn Wrench, *Geoffrey Dawson and Our Times* (Hutchinson, 1955) p. 362.
147. Oliver Harvey, *The Diplomatic Diaries of Oliver Harvey 1937–1940*, ed. John Harvey (Collins, 1970) p. 59.
148. Eden, *Facing the Dictators*, pp. 513 ff.
149. Ibid., p. 519.
150. Ibid., pp. 577 ff.
151. Ibid., p. 587.
152. Kurt von Schuschnigg, *Austrian Requiem* (Gollancz, 1947) pp. 20 ff.
153. Schuschnigg, *Take-over*, p. 226.
154. Ibid., p. 240.
155. *DBFP*, 3rd ser. vol. I, p. 11.
156. Ibid., p. 8.
157. Klaus Berchtold, *Österreichische Parteiprogramme 1868–1966* (Vienna: Verlag für Geschichte und Politik, 1967) p. 42.
158. Josef Buttinger, *In the Twilight of Socialism* (Weidenfeld & Nicolson, 1954) p. 440.
159. Ibid., pp. 441–2.
160. Ibid., p. 471.
161. Harvey, *Diplomatic Diaries*, p. 113.
162. *DBFP*, 3rd ser. vol. I.
163. Schuschnigg, *Take-over*, p. 281.
164. Goldinger, *Geschichte der Republik Österreich*, p. 252.
165. Starhemberg, *Hitler and Mussolini*, p. 289.

166. Harvey, *Diplomatic Diaries*, p. 110.
167. Ibid., p. 90.
168. Ibid., p. 108.
169. Ibid., p. 115.
170. Quoted by Wrench in *Dawson and Our Times*, p. 369.
171. Harvey, *Diplomatic Diaries*, p. 91.
172. Sir Anthony Eden, *The Reckoning* (Cassell, 1965) p. 7.
173. Lord Butler, *The Art of the Possible* (Hamish Hamilton, 1971) pp. 64–5.

PART II

Chapter 13

174. Renner, *Österreich von der Ersten zur Zweiten Republik*, pp. 207–8.
175. See Karl R. Stadler, *Austria* (Benn, 1971). His analysis of Gestapo and S.D. reports and law court records gives a very valuable view of the changing Austrian mood and the various forms of Austrian resistance between 1938 and 1945.
176. Ibid., pp. 167–71.
177. Ibid., p. 212.
178. *Der Freiheitskampf des Österreichischen Volkes 1938–1945* (pamphlet, London, 'Young Austria' (undated)) p. 18.
179. Stadler, *Austria*, pp. 178, 212.
180. Ibid., p. 179.
181. F.O./371/46595.
182. Ludwig Jedlicka, *Der 20 Juli in Österreich* (Vienna: Herold for Dr Theodor-Korner-Stiftung and Bundesministerium für Unterricht, 1965) pp. 68–9.
183. Andics, *50 Jahre unseres Lebens*, pp. 441–4.
184. F.O./371/46593.
185. Ibid.
186. Stadler, *Austria*, p. 221.
187. Adolf Schärf, *Österreichs Erneuerung* (Vienna: Wiener Volksbuchhandlung, 1955) p. 187.
188. Stadler, *Austria*, p. 193.
189. Ibid., p. 225.
190. Schärf, *Österreichs Erneuerung*, pp. 20–1.
191. Ludwig Jedlicka, *Der 20 Juli 1944 in Österreich*, p. 28, quoting Lois Weinberger, *Tatsachen, Begegnungen und Gespräche* (Vienna: Österreichischer Verlag, 1948) p. 135.

192. Stadler, *Austria*, p. 234.

Chapter 14
193. F.O.371/30911.
194. Ibid.
195. F.O.371/26538.
196. F.O.371/30911.
197. F.O.371/34464.

Chapter 15
198. Winston S. Churchill, *The World Crisis: The Aftermath* (Macmillan, 1941) pp. 228–9.
199. F.O.371/26537.
200. F.O.371/26538.
201. Ibid.
202. Eden, *The Reckoning*, p. 289.
203. F.O.371/30910.
204. F.O.371/36992.
205. F.O.371/30910.
206. F.O.371/36992.
207. F.O.371/30910.
208. F.O.371/34464.
209. F.O.371/30911.
210. Ibid.
211. F.O.371/34464.
212. Ibid.
213. Ibid.
214. F.O.371/36991.
215. F.O.371/36992.
216. F.O.371/34465.
217. F.O.371/30910.
218. F.O.371/34466.
219. Ibid.
220. F.O.371/37029.
221. F.O.371/37031.
222. Winston S. Churchill, *The Second World War* (Cassell, 1954) vi 210.

Chapter 16
223. Eden, *The Reckoning*, p. 389.
224. Churchill, *The Second World War*, vi 57.

225. Ibid.
226. Ibid., p. 90.
227. Ibid., p. 137.
228. Ibid., p. 304.
229. Ibid., p. 407.

PART III

Chapter 17

230. Schärf, *Österreichs Erneuerung*, p. 29.
231. Ibid., p. 37.
232. Churchill, *The Second World War*, VI 446.
233. Ibid., p. 452.
234. Ibid., pp. 451–2.
235. Ibid., p. 452.
236. F.O.371/39181.
237. Ibid.
258. Churchill, *The Second World War*, VI 652.
239. Karl Gruber, *Between Liberation and Liberty* (André Deutsch, 1955) p. 28.
240. Allied Council Memorandum to Renner Government, 20/10/1945.
241. F.O.371/36593 (pamphlet giving text).

Chapter 18

242. Gruber, *Liberation and Liberty*, p. 34.
243. Dean Acheson, *Present at the Creation* (Hamish Hamilton, 1969) p. 636.
244. Schärf, *Österreichs Erneuerung*, pp. 381–2.
245. Harry S. Truman, *Year of Decisions 1945* (Hodder & Stoughton, 1955) p. 407.
246. Schärf, *Österreichs Erneuerung*, pp. 64–7.
247. EXCO/P(45)73; ALCO/P(45)35.
248. EXCO/M/4521.
249. F.O.371/46637.
250. James F. Byrnes, *Speaking Frankly* (Heinemann, 1947) p. 163.
251. ALCO/P(46)2.
252. ALCO/P(46)17.
253. ALCO/P(46)44.

Chapter 19

254. F.O.371/46637.
255. Schärf, *Österreichs Erneuerung*, p. 104.
256. Ibid., pp. 110–11.
257. ALCO/P(46)76.
258. ALCO/M(46)23; Cmd. 6958.
259. EXCO/M(46)43.
260. ALCO/M(46)28.
261. ALCO/M(46)29.
262. ALCO/M(46)30.
263. ALCO/M(46)34.
264. William B. Bader, *Austria between East and West 1945–1955* (Palo Alto, Calif.: Stanford University Press, 1966) p. 75; quoting *Dulles Papers*, C.F.M. Minutes, vol. i, USDEL(49)(P).
265. ALCO/M(48)77.
266. ALCO/P(48)124.

Chapter 20

267. VIAC Extraordinary Conference (Protocol No. 85).
268. Schärf, *Österreichs Erneuerung*, p. 162.
269. Ibid., p. 149.
270. ALCO/M(47)51.
271. Gruber, *Liberation and Liberty*, pp. 129–36; Schärf, *Österreichs Erneuerung*, pp. 163–9.
272. ALCO/M(47)54–5.
273. ALCO/M(48)77.
274. ALCO/M(48)80.
275. Karl Gutkas et al., *Österreich 1945–1970* (Vienna: Österreichischer Bundesverlag, 1970) p. 224.
276. ALCO/M(50)131.
277. ALCO/M(50)132.
278. ALCO/M(50)134.
279. ALCO/M(51)136.
280. Gruber, *Liberation and Liberty*, p. 185.

Chapter 21

281. Gruber, *Liberation and Liberty*, pp. 102 ff.; Bader, *Austria between East and West*, pp. 120 ff.
282. Kurt Waldheim, *Der Österreichische Weg* (Vienna: Verlag Fritz Molden, 1971) p. 66.

283. Sven Allard, *Diplomat in Wien* (Cologne: Verlag Wissenschaft und Politik, 1965) p. 90.
284. Waldheim, *Der Österreichische Weg*, p. 68; quoting Bruno Kreisky, 'Österreichs Stellung als neutraler Staat', in *Österreich in Geschichte und Literatur*, No. 3 (1957).
285. Allard, *Diplomat in Wien*, pp. 42–3.
286. Waldheim, *Der Österreichische Weg*, p. 71.
287. Eden, *The Reckoning*, p. 74.
288. ALCO/M(54)233.
289. Allard, *Diplomat in Wien*, p. 134.
290. Walter Kindermann, *Flug nach Moskau* (Vienna: Vienna Ullstein, 1955) pp. 34–6.
291. Waldheim, *Der Österreichische Weg*, p. 87.
292. Kindermann, *Flug nach Moskau*, p. 30.
293. Bader, *Austria between East and West*, p. 205.
294. Harold Macmillan, *The Tides of Fortune 1945–1955* (Macmillan, 1969) pp. 594–5.
295. *International Herald Tribune* 6 September 1971.
296. Macmillan, *Tides of Fortune*, p. 602.
297. Dwight D. Eisenhower, *Mandate for Change* (Heinemann, 1963) pp. 505 ff.
298. Quoted by Bader, *Austria between East and West*, p. 216.
299. Gutkas et al., *Österreich 1945–1970*, p. 67.

PART IV

Chapter 22

300. ALCO/M(46)28.
301. ALCO/P(46)122.
302. ALCO/P(46)140.
303. Richard Hiscocks, *The Rebirth of Austria* (Oxford University Press, 1933) p. 115.
304. Schärf, *Österreichs Erneuerung*, p. 291.
305. Josef Klaus, *Macht und Ohnmacht in Österreich* (Vienna: Verlag Fritz Molden, 1971) p. 66.
306. Schärf, *Österreichs Erneuerung*, p. 337.
307. Klaus, *Macht und Ohnmacht*, p. 100.
308. Klaus W. Mayer, *Die Sozialstruktur Österreichs* (Vienna: Österreichischer Bundesverlag, 1970) p. 82.
309. Ibid., p. 72.
310. Gutkas et al., *Österreich 1945–1970*, p. 255.
311. Mayer, *Die Sozialstruktur Österreichs*, p. 49.

312. Schärf, *Österreichs Erneuerung*, pp. 180–2.
313. Mayer, *Die Sozialstruktur Österreichs*, p. 121.
314. Klaus, *Macht und Ohnmacht*, p. 143.
315. Ibid., p. 144.
316. Ibid., p. 148.
317. Ibid., p. 154.

Chapter 23

318. *The Economic Chambers in Austria* (Vienna: Federal Economic Chamber) p. 4.
319. *The Economic Chambers in Austria*, pp. 12–13; *Financial Times*, August 1972.
320. Trend, *Der Österreichische Wirtschaftsmagazin*, April 1971.
321. Schärf, *Österreichs Erneuerung*, p. 387.
322. Fritz Klenner, *Die Österreichische Gewerkschaftsbewegung* (Vienna: Verlag des Österreichischen Gewerkschaftsbundes) p. 138.
323. *Solidarität*, September 1971.
324. Mayer, *Die Sozialstruktur Österreichs*, p. 48.
325. *Die Presse*, 13 December 1971.
326. Prof. Manfried Welan, article in *Wirtschafts-politische Blätter*, 17 Jahrgang, No. 1/2, p. 33.
327. Klaus, *Macht und Ohnmacht*, p. 389.
328. Ibid., pp. 88–9.
329. O.E.C.D., *The Austrian Economy in the Year 1970* (German edition) pp. 44–5.
330. *Financial Times*, 6 February 1972.
331. Welan, *Wirtschafts-politische*, 17 Jahrgang, No. 1/2, p. 35.
332. Ibid.
333. *Financial Times*, 30 December 1971.

Chapter 24

334. Schärf, *Österreichs Erneuerung*, p. 66.
335. EXCO/P(45)73.
336. Mayer, *Die Sozialstruktur Österreichs*, p. 75.
337. Gutkas et al., *Österreich 1945–1970*, pp. 270–1.
338. Bruno Kreisky, *Österreich und Europa* (Vienna: Verlag des Österreichischen Gewerkschaftsbundes, 1963) p. 10.
339. Ibid.
340. Ibid., p. 16.

341. Charles de Gaulle, *Mémoires D'Espoir: Le Renouveau* (Paris: Librairie Plon, 1970) p. 280.
342. Kreisky, *Österreich und Europa*, p. 10.
343. Mayer, *Die Sozialstruktur Österreichs*, p. 75.
344. Klaus, *Macht und Ohnmacht*, p. 318.
345. Ibid., p. 322.
346. Ibid., p. 247.
347. Ibid., pp. 324–5.
348. Ibid., p. 252.
349. Fritz Bock, *Integrationspolitik von Österreich* (Vienna: Jupiter Verlag, 1970) pp. 77 ff.
350. *Le Monde*, 20–1 June 1971.
351. Rupert Schumacher, *West–Ost Journal*, No. 4, Jahrgang 1971, p. 21.
352. *Le Monde*, 11 July 1972.
353. *Financial Times*, 22 February 1972.
354. Ibid., 22 May 1972.
355. *Le Monde*, 28 July 1972.
356. Ibid., 29 February 1972.

Chapter 25

357. Schärf, *Österreichs Erneuerung*, p. 340.
358. ALCO/M(46)16.
359. For text see Waldheim, *Der Österreichische Weg*, pp. 283–4.
360. Gruber, *Liberation and Liberty*, p. 70.
361. Ibid., p. 71.
362. Ibid., p. 79.
363. Klaus, *Macht und Ohnmacht*, p. 292.
364. For texts see Waldheim, *Der Österreichische Weg*, pp. 291–324.
365. Klaus, *Macht und Ohnmacht*, p. 302.

Chapter 26

366. Ibid., p. 483.
367. *Neue Zürcher Zeitung*, 1 January 1970.
368. Klaus, *Macht und Ohnmacht*, p. 48.
369. Ibid., pp. 149–50.
370. Ibid., pp. 156–8.
371. Gutkas et al., *Österreich 1945–1970*, pp. 148–9.
372. Klaus, *Macht und Ohnmacht*, p. 121.

373. *Neue Zürcher Zeitung,* 28 June 1971.
374. *Le Monde,* 16 July 1971.
375. *Süd-Deutsche Zeitung,* 8 July 1971.
376. *Le Monde,* 9 October 1971.
377. Ibid., 12 October 1971.

Chapter 27

378. *Die Presse,* 23 December 1971.
379. O.E.C.D., *The Industrial Policy of Austria,* pp. 43–4.
380. O.E.C.D., *The Austrian Economy in 1970.*
381. O.E.C.D., *The Industrial Policy of Austria,* p. 135.
382. *Die Presse,* 30 December 1971.
383. Ibid., 11 November 1971.
384. Österreichisches Statistische Zentralamt, *Statistische Nachrichten,* May 1972.
385. Ibid., April 1972.
386. *Die Presse,* 6/7 November 1971.
387. Mayer, *Die Sozialstruktur Österreichs,* p. 23.
388. *Die Presse,* 19 October 1971.
389. O.E.C.D., *The Industrial Policy of Austria,* p. 15.
390. *Statistische Nachrichten,* February 1972.
391. O.E.C.D., *The Industrial Policy of Austria,* p. 156.
392. Mayer, *Sozialstruktur Österreichs,* p. 114.
393. *Die Presse,* 24 November 1971.
394. Ibid., 24–6 December 1971.
395. *Financial Times,* 23 April 1971.
396. *Die Presse,* 11/12 December 1971.
397. *Financial Times,* 24 June 1972.
398. *Die Presse,* 23 December 1971.
399. *West-Ost Journal,* No. 3 Jahrgang 1971.
400. *Le Monde,* 28 July 1972.
401. *Financial Times,* 23 April 1971.

Select Bibliography

Part I (1918–1938)

C. A. Macartney, *The Habsburg Empire 1790–1918* (Weidenfeld & Nicolson, 1969).

A. J. P. Taylor, *The Habsburg Monarchy* (Hamish Hamilton, 1948; Peregrine Books, 1970).

Gordon Brook-Shepherd, *The Last Habsburg* (Weidenfeld & Nicolson, 1968).

C. A. Macartney and A. W. Palmer, *Independent Eastern Europe* (Macmillan, 1962).

Otto Bauer, *The Austrian Revolution* (Leonard Parsons, 1925).

C. A. Macartney, *The Social Revolution in Austria* (Cambridge University Press, 1926).

F. L. Carsten, *Revolution in Central Europe 1918–1919* (Temple Smith, 1972).

G. R. Gedye, *Fallen Bastions* (Gollancz, 1939).

Gordon Brook-Shepherd, *Dollfuss* (Macmillan, 1968).

Ernst Rüdiger, Prince Starhemberg, *Between Hitler and Mussolini* (Hodder & Stoughton, 1942).

Elizabeth Wiskemann, *The Rome–Berlin Axis* (Collins, 1966).

Elizabeth Wiskemann, *Europe of the Dictators 1919–1945* (Collins (Fontana), 1966).

Kurt von Schuschnigg, *Austrian Requiem* (Gollancz, 1947).

Kurt von Schuschnigg, *The Brutal Take-over* (Weidenfeld & Nicolson, 1971).

Julius Braunthal, *The Tragedy of Austria* (Gollancz, 1946).

Josef Buttinger, *In the Twilight of Socialism* (Weidenfeld & Nicolson, 1954).

Gordon Brook-Shepherd, *Anschluss* (Macmillan, 1968).

Sir Anthony Eden, *Facing the Dictators* (Cassell, 1962).

Oliver Harvey, *The Diplomatic Diaries of Oliver Harvey 1937–1940*, ed. John Harvey (Collins, 1970).

Karl R. Stadler, *Austria* (Benn, 1971).

Documents on British Foreign Policy, H.M.S.O., First Series vol. i, vol. xii; Second Series vol. ii, vol. v, vol. vi; Third Series vol. i, vol. ii.

Documents of German Foreign Policy (Washington, D.C.: U.S. Government Printing Office, 1949), Series D, vol. I.

Part II (1938–1945)

Karl R. Stadler, ibid.

Sir Anthony Eden, *The Reckoning* (Cassell, 1965).

Winston S. Churchill, *The Second World War*, esp. vol. VI (Cassell, 1954).

Foreign Office documents 1939–1945, available in Public Record Office. (In notes giving sources, references start 'F.O.371/ . . . followed by number of relevant file.)

Part III (1945–1955)

Richard Hiscocks, *The Rebirth of Austria* (Oxford University Press, 1953).

William B. Bader, *Austria between East and West 1945–1955* (Pato Alto, Calif.: Stanford University Press, 1966).

Karl Gruber, *Between Liberation and Liberty* (André Deutsch, 1955).

Records of Allied Commission in Austria (Foreign Office Library). (In notes giving sources, references start 'ALCO/ . . .' or 'EXCO/ . . .'.)

Sir Anthony Eden, *Full Circle* (Cassell, 1960).

Harold Macmillan, *Tides of Fortune 1945–1955* (Macmillan, 1969).

Part IV (1955–1972)

Reports of Organisation for Economic Co-operation and Development.

Heinrich Siegler, *Austria – Problems and Achievement since 1945* (Bonn–Vienna–Zürich: Siegler & Co., 1969).

The Economic Chambers in Austria (pamphlet) published by the Federal Economic Chamber, Vienna (undated).

The Chambers of Labour in Austria (pamphlet) published by the Federation of Austrian Chambers of Labour, Vienna (1967).

WORKS IN GERMAN

Parts I and II (1918–1945)

Walter Goldinger, *Geschichte der Republik Österreich* (Vienna: Verlag für Geschichte und Politik, 1962).

Karl Renner, *Österreich von der Ersten zur Zweiten Republik* (Vienna: Verlag der Wiener Volksbuchhandlung, 1953).

Otto Bauer, *Bolschewismus oder Sozialdemokratie* (Verlag der Wiener Volksbuchhandlung, 1920).

Klaus Berchtold, *Österreichische Parteiprogramme 1868–1966* (Vienna: Verlag für Geschichte und Politik, 1967).

Hellmut Andics, *50 Jahre Unseres Lebens* (Vienna: Verlag Fritz Molden, 1968).

Ludwig Jedlicka, *Der 20 Juli in Österreich* (Herold for Dr Theodor-Körner-Stiftung and Bundesministerium für Unterricht, 1965).

Dokumente der Deutschen Politik und Geschichte, vol. IV, 1933–38 (Berlin and Munich: Giersch & Co., 1953).

Parts III and IV (1945–1972)

Walter Goldinger, ibid.

Karl Renner, ibid.

Hellmutt Andics, ibid.

Karl Gutkas, Alois Brusatti, Erika Weinzierl, *Österreich 1945–1970* (Vienna: Österreichischer Bundesverlag, 1970).

Kurt Waldheim, *Der Österreichische Weg* (Vienna: Verlag Fritz Molden, 1968).

Adolf Schärf, *Österreichs Erneuerung 1945–1955* (Vienna: Wiener Volksbuchhandlung, 1955).

Josef Klaus, *Macht und Ohnmacht in Österreich* (Vienna: Verlag Fritz Molden, 1971).

Walter Kindermann, *Flug nach Moskau* (Vienna: Ullstein, 1955).

Sven Allard, *Diplomat in Wien* (Cologne: Verlag Wissenschaft und Politik, Cologne, 1965).

Fritz Bock, *Integrationspolitik von Österreich* (Vienna: Jupiter Verlag, 1970).

Bruno Kreisky, *Österreich und Europa* (Vienna: Verlag des Österreichischen Gewerkschaftsbundes, 1963).

Klaus W. Mayer, *Die Sozialstruktur Österreichs* (Vienna: Österreichischer Bundesverlag, 1970).

Fritz Klenner, *Die Österreichische Gewerkschaftsbewegung* (Vienna: Verlag des Österreichischen Gewerkschaftsbundes, 1955).

Österreichisches Statistische Zentralamt: Statistische Nachrichten.

Index